DELICATE WEAR

TIME
LIFE
BOOKS
®

THE ART OF SEWING

DELICATE WEAR

BY THE EDITORS OF TIME-LIFE BOOKS

TIME-LIFE BOOKS, NEW YORK

TIME-LIFE BOOKS

FOUNDER: Henry R. Luce 1898-1967

Editor-in-Chief: Hedley Donovan
Chairman of the Board: Andrew Heiskell
President: James R. Shepley
Group Vice President: Rhett Austell

Vice Chairman: Roy E. Larsen

MANAGING EDITOR: Jerry Korn
Assistant Managing Editors: Ezra Bowen,
David Maness, Martin Mann, A. B. C. Whipple
Planning Director: Oliver E. Allen
Art Director: Sheldon Cotler
Chief of Research: Beatrice T. Dobie
Director of Photography: Melvin L. Scott
Senior Text Editor: Diana Hirsh
Assistant Art Director: Arnold C. Holeywell
Assistant Chief of Research: Myra Mangan

PUBLISHER: Joan D. Manley
General Manager: John D. McSweeney
Business Manager: Nicholas J. C. Ingleton
Sales Director: Carl G. Jaeger
Promotion Director: Paul R. Stewart
Public Relations Director: Nicholas Benton

THE ART OF SEWING
SERIES EDITOR: Carlotta Kerwin
EDITORIAL STAFF FOR
DELICATE WEAR
Assistant Editor: David L. Harrison
Designer: Virginia Gianakos
Assistant Designer: Robert McKee
Text Editors: Don Earnest, Richard Oulahan,
Gerry Schremp
Picture Editor: Kaye Neil
Chief Researchers: Wendy A. Rieder,
Gabrielle Smith (planning)
Staff Writers: Sondra R. Albert, Dick Friedman,
Marian G. Goldman, Angela D. Goodman,
David Johnson, Marilyn Kendig,
Wendy Murphy, Sandra Streepey,
Reiko Uyeshima
Research Staff: Cinda Siler, Laura James,
Tom Lashnits, Vivian Stephens, Jean Stratton
Art Staff: Sanae Yamazaki and Anne B. Landry
(art coordinators), Angela Alleyne,
Penny Burnham, Patricia Byrne,
Catherine Caufield, Jean Held, Jill Lossen
Editorial Assistant: Kathleen Beakley

EDITORIAL PRODUCTION

Production Editor: Douglas B. Graham
Assistant Production Editors:
Gennaro C. Esposito, Feliciano Madrid
Quality Director: Robert L. Young
Assistant Quality Director: James J. Cox
Copy Staff: Rosalind Stubenberg (chief),
Ricki Tarlow, Florence Keith, Pearl Sverdlin
Picture Department: Dolores A. Littles,
Susan Hearn
Traffic: Carmen McLellan

THE CONSULTANTS:
Gretel Courtney taught for several years at the
French Fashion Academy in New York City. She
has studied patternmaking and design at the Fashion Institute of Technology in New York and haute
couture at the French Fashion Academy.

Annette Feldman is a knitting and crocheting de-
signer, both for clothing and interior decoration.
She is the author of several books, including *Knit,
Purl and Design, Crochet and Creative Design* and
Beginner's Needlecraft.

Tracy Kendall has for many years designed sets
and costumes for commercial films and advertis-
ing. She is currently a fashion stylist.

Julian Tomchin is a textile designer who has been
awarded the Vogue Fabric Award and a Coty
Award of the American Fashion Critics. A gradu-
ate of Syracuse University's Fine Arts College, he
has been chairman of the Textile Design Department at the Shenkar College of Fashion and Textile
Technology in Tel Aviv and now teaches at the Par-
sons School of Design in New York.

Valuable assistance was provided by these
departments and individuals of Time Inc.:
Editorial Production, Norman Airey; Library,
Benjamin Lightman; Picture Collection, Doris
O'Neil; Photographic Laboratory, George Karas;
TIME-LIFE News Service, Murray J. Gart;
Correspondents Maria Vincenza Aloisi and
Josephine du Brusle (Paris), Margot Hapgood and
Dorothy Bacon (London), Ann Natanson (Rome).

CONTENTS

1
AFLOAT IN ELIXIRS OF FEMININITY

Newly emancipated, the woman of the fast-paced double decade between the World Wars was forever doing something women had never done before. Incessantly active, she was the most fascinating and promising personality of the new century, and her luxurious fashion image was made in Paris. High on freedom, the new woman —as she was called—set out to prove that everything men could do she could do too.

ANNALS OF THE KINGDOM OF LUXURY

She smoked cigarettes, drank cocktails, drove cars, swam the English Channel, flew the Atlantic, fought for the vote and won it. In the Roaring Twenties, it was the women who did a fair share of the roaring.

Theirs was a cry from the heart, and the cry was answered by Gabrielle (Coco) Chanel, the Edison of fashion, who invented many of the basic styles of the 20th Century. A tiny woman with big dark eyes, Chanel hardly knew one end of a needle from another, but she knew what the current feminine generation needed. Her central idea was simple: if modern woman's place was in the workaday world, she should be dressed as a working girl—in other words, as much as possible like a man.

Accordingly, Chanel offered her clients skirts with pockets, mannish suits, starkly simple dresses, tailored slacks. To stress the boyish silhouette, Chanel lowered waistlines to hide the hips, flattened the breasts, revealed the skull with a boyish bob and topped the bob with a cloche. Coco Chanel caught on as no couturier ever had.

But if Chanel's flattened, boyish look was an emancipation proclamation, it covered up a manifesto of quite a different sort. Liberated underwear was the subject of this declaration—first stated by Paul Poiret in his sensational collection of 1909, in which he had freed women from the ghastly corsets and bindings of the Victorian era. By 1925—the year skirts reached the knees—lingerie was frilly, fragile, sexy and utterly feminine. Made of sheer, flesh-colored silk and rayon, it was decorated with the finest lace and embroidery, and was a harbinger of the delicate fashions that would soon storm the world of haute couture—which Jean Patou, one of the princes of design, called "the kingdom of luxury."

That realm thrives on change, however. In 1929, a few weeks before the stock market collapsed and the long night of the Great Depression began, the boyish look was abruptly banished. Hemlines were lowered, and a dainty, frankly feminine silhouette reappeared in women's wear. Patou led the parade to the new, delicate look. Each of the 350 models in his 1929 collection was long skirted and unmistakably girlish. For a great designer it was an enormous gamble, but it paid off. By 1931 the House of Chanel had sunk to 10th in a listing of the most popular couturiers, based on American sales. Heading the list was a name to conjure with: Madeleine Vionnet.

Born in 1875, Vionnet was the daughter of a Monte Carlo cocotte and a tax collector. She got her start in the fashion trade as a 12-year-old girl picking pins off the floor of a Paris dressmaker's shop. She rapidly became an incomparable seamstress and, in 1912, she opened her own house to produce some of the most beautiful works of art ever committed to cloth.

Vionnet's frocks were architectonic miracles. Fabric cut on the bias, she discovered, has both a pull and a fall; it clings as it flows, one moment moving smoothly over the body, the next swirling off into a sculptural life of its own. As often as not, a Vionnet dress looked like a flimsy little chiffon handkerchief. But Vionnet's confections were as strong as chain mail and just as intricately put together. Subtle mosaics of interdependent and beautifully mitered bias triangles and rectangles, they could be slipped over the head and would magically take on the form of the body as the skin does.

Nothing like these dresses had ever been seen before; the instant they appeared, every dressmaker in Paris had to learn her craft all over again. But none ever really caught up to Vionnet. "No one ever copied her," a fashion historian notes, "because nobody ever could." Like a true creator of masterworks, Vionnet "signed" the label on every one of her gowns with her thumbprint. She was the couturier's couturier.

She made unlined dresses of the sheerest fabrics possible by the artistry of her cutting. She wheedled the great fabrics manufacturers into supplying her with 54-inch widths of silk—twice the standard measure. Her skillful cutting and use of such novel materials as crepe de Chine —previously used only as lining—in dress materials marked Vionnet as a pioneer among designers.

Though 30 years younger than Vionnet, Alix Grès became her only serious challenger in the fine art of fashion design. Grès was a short, slim woman of Italian-German descent, and she was never seen without a formidable turban on her head. A sculptor by training, Grès thought in terms of noble simplicity. Like Vionnet, she was inspired by the lines and masses of the female body and seldom allowed color to dominate detail or flow. She was impressed by Vionnet's adventures with the bias but, wanting to explore a wider range of forms, she often cut with the weave of the cloth and let the folds fall free, like drapery on a Greek statue.

Like Vionnet, Grès was a master technician. Working at home, she composed her gowns on a mannequin. Sometimes in the frenzy of creation, she kept her model standing in the same attitude for hours. If the girl complained, Grès flew into an icy fury and accused the mannequin of lacking the required passion. To Grès, fashion was a religion; she worked as if God were looking over her shoulder.

A Grès, like a Vionnet, was much too fine to be imitated. Grès designed for a small, exclusive clientele, but her influence was steady and profound. Designers studied her creations. After Vionnet retired in 1939, Grès kept the spirit of the art alive.

Grès and Vionnet notwithstanding, fashion of the '20s and '30s was less interested in the search for beauty than in the pursuit of the dollar. Millions were spent on promotion. Twice a year lavish showings of the new couturier collections attracted hundreds of buyers and fashion editors from all over the Western Hemisphere and Europe for a champagne-splashed review of parades of the newest modes. Hundreds of costly ads were placed in the sleek fashion magazines, showing famous, beautiful or stylish women wearing what the trade called "money dresses."

These women were—and are—an important and pampered part of the French fashion scene, for they could be counted on to introduce "what is being worn" to smart society. In the Depression, such celebrated clothes horses were given cut rates—or, in some instances, free wardrobes by grateful couturiers. There have never been more than 50 of these very special, naturally chic ladies at one time, but they have always been the darlings of the "kingdom of luxury": whenever one of these women entered the designers' salons, the most despotic couturiers became cooing courtiers.

Royalty and titled women have always been at the forefront of this mannequin parade. Mainbocher created the Duchess of Windsor's trousseau. Vionnet dressed the Queens of Spain, Belgium and Rumania.

The press went gaga over the wardrobe of the very rich, very chic Lady Edwina Mountbatten, who once arrived in Mexico with 56 trunks bulging with the confections of the greatest houses of Paris. Stars of the theater like Gertrude Lawrence and Ina Claire were popular fashion plates too, and whenever they appeared onstage or off, the copyists got out their sketchbooks.

In the 1930s the soufflé collapsed. The Depression almost destroyed the fashion business. But the greatest designers managed, somehow, to stick to their knitting. Paris continued to produce annual collections of romantic fashions, even though the "kingdom of luxury" had shrunk to the proportions of a principality. Hemlines were lowered, but the standards of haute couture never were. In the depths of the Depression, Vionnet lavished five yards of chiffon on a gown where two would have sufficed.

The guns of September, 1939, finally ended the golden age of the great Paris houses and their exquisite products. Alix Grès continued to stitch away grimly, right under the noses of the German Occupation army, but only in fabrics of patriotic red, white and blue—until she produced a gown in all three colors, and the Nazis closed her workshop. The curtain had gone down on the champagne decades of fashion, and their like would never be seen again.

Three classic formal gowns created by Madeleine Vionnet during the 1930s illustrate why the legendary French designer was called the couturier's couturier: a romantic silk summer evening dress *(left)* with scalloped bands of inset fringe; a net gown for summer dances *(center)* with flared skirt and shoulder cape; an ethereal chiffon design *(right)* with intricate beading on the sleeves and across the shoulders.

12

Subtle styles
for daydreams

Fragile-looking fabrics in subtle pastel colors, molded by meticulous sewing methods, add up to the stuff of delicate dreams in clothing design. Shown here are three dreamy ways to greet the morning. At left is a satin de lys gown shaped with a bias cut and topped off by a fitted bosom of lace. At center is a chiffon pajama set that comes with a jacket but pares down to bra and pants. And at right is a peignoir and gown of nylon tricot, luxuriantly draped from a décolleté bodice. Other delicacies for day and evening appear on the following pages.

Designed for daytime wear, these interpretations of the delicate look play with openwork details to achieve their appeal. From left: rows of fagoting on a sheer wool crepe; lace inserts on a pin-tucked batiste blouse; and appliqué and pin tucks on a chiffon blouse with roll tie.

15

Special evenings may call for any of these three romantic creations: a billowing satin gown paired with a coat of marabou feathers *(far left)*; a lace overblouse *(center)* worn with pants and a ribbon sash; and a nylon matte jersey gown with a draped and beaded bodice *(above)*.

2

A SWIRL OF
ETHEREAL
FABRICS

Silk was invented so that women could go naked in clothes," the prophet Muhammad noted some 13 centuries ago. Were Muhammad on earth to view the current state of fashion, he would find women no more modest than they were in his day —but a good deal more versatile in what they wear to go naked: soft jerseys, floating chiffons, supple crepes, airy laces and gauzy hint-of-glint metallics. These are just

THE SEARCH FOR EXQUISITE TEXTURES

some of today's delicate, figure-enhancing, figure-revealing fabrics made from both natural and synthetic materials. They do not look or feel alike, or function interchangeably. But they share a common premise —that some things in fashion are all the more precious for being vulnerable, fragile and even a little troublesome to take care of.

The basic natural fibers from which delicate fabrics can be made—silk, cotton, linen and wool—all answer these luxurious descriptions, and they continue to be the fibers most celebrated in couture garments. They take colors more subtly than synthetics, behave more predictably when sewed and feel grand—to a degree unmatched by any machine-made fiber.

For all the prestige of natural fibers, however, less expensive, more durable synthetics are increasingly turning up in delicate-looking fabrics. Thanks to Qiana, Nyesta, Jupiter chiffon and a host of other fresh new synthetics, more and more women are wearing a lace blouse in the daytime, or a beaded dress to dinner or glamorous at-home pajamas to entertain on Saturday night. The trend to this soft, pretty look can be expected to continue, as yet uninvented fibers, blends and weaves come ever closer to the qualities of the naturals.

Like so many alchemists trying to turn base metals into gold, chemists investigating synthetics have been working diligently for more than a century. In 1855, a Swiss named George Audemars patented a technique for making "artificial silk." Extracting cellulose from the bark of the mulberry tree, whose leaves form the productive diet of cultured silkworms, Audemars reduced the substance to a honey-like fluid. By dipping needles into the liquid and withdrawing them slowly and laboriously, he was able to extrude an artificial filament.

Thirty years passed before the first commercial rayon could be manufactured in a manner that approximated the way in which the silkworm's secretions solidify in flexible filaments when exposed to the air. In this process, a cellulose solution was forced through a device like a shower head, and continuous silken threads were produced mechanically. Because it could be spun very fine, by 1925 rayon had taken over the cotton- and silk-stocking trade and the lion's share of the lingerie business—though as fancy dress material, rayon was suspect in those early years, for there was little quality control. Modern industrial methods have since filled that gap, however; today's premium rayon textiles include matte jerseys, velvets, linens, crepes and crepe satins.

Nylon followed rayon at a considerable distance, making its first commercial appearance in 1938. Nylon was the first fiber to be entirely man made, a chemical synthetic composed of such apparently gross materials as coal tar and petroleum. But what came out of the nylon extruding machines was even more versatile than rayon, offering greater resilience, greater elasticity and superior washability. The nylons had another distinct advantage—they provided inexpensive simulations of natural fibers. Nylon chiffon, for example, is almost indistinguishable from silk chiffon, yet costs half as much. Polyesters and acrylics, with many of the same characteristics, are more recent sources of delicate synthetics.

But nature is still a source of airy cloths: milk by-products now are spun into such lustrous fabrics as Chinon jerseys and satins. And at least one designer-dreamer, struck by the timeless beauty of spider webs, hopes someday to set the spider to spinning gossamer for the fashion industry—and create still another fabric to clothe the nakedness of tomorrow's women.

A lovely liquefaction of clothing

Whenas in silks my Julia goes,
Then, then, methinks how sweetly
* flows*
That liquefaction of her clothes.

In three brief lines the 17th Century
English poet Robert Herrick cap
tured the essence of all the fabrics
—sheer, delicate-surfaced, knitted
—shown here and on the following
pages. Floating, flowing sheers, for
example, are as soft to the touch as
to the eye. The gowns at left and
right are solid-colored and printed
silk chiffons. Behind them, clock
wise from the upper left, are dotted
silk chiffon, cotton organdy, rayon
georgette, printed silk chiffon and
silk organza. Such sheers—like oth
er delicate fabrics—must be gently
handled, as shown on pages 28-30

Sleek lustrous surfaces, like those on satins, make opaque fabrics difficult to sew—but are worth the extra effort. The elegant gown at right is satin-weave silk (called silk satin), the one opposite is China silk. Behind them, from the left, are rayon crepe with satin-weave stripes, silk satin, silk crepe de Chine and silk jacquard.

Soft translucent knits cling to the body's contours with supple grace. The gown at left, for example, owes its sinuous lines to nylon tricot, the one at right to rayon jersey. In the background, from the left, are napped nylon jersey, polyester matte jersey, cotton jersey, texturized polyester jersey and nylon tricot.

Preparing fine fabrics for sewing

Sheer, delicate-surfaced and soft knit fabrics all need plenty of tender care in the crucial stages of laying out, cutting and marking. Handling must be deft and minimal to prevent soiling. A large work surface is essential to all the special procedures required—as shown here and overleaf—to prevent the fabrics from slipping or stretching.

Ideally the cloth should be prepared and sewed at one sitting; bastings, tailor tacks and pins leave marks if they stay in too long. A necessary exception to the rule is the hemming, which must wait 24 hours until the garment has had a chance to settle into its natural hang.

Delicate fabrics should never be folded; instead, make duplicate pattern pieces so that it is possible to cut out garment sections from single layers. Where dressmaker's carbon paper is appropriate (chart, pages 40-41), use white or blue to prevent tracing-wheel marks from showing through to the right side of garment. And for see-through fabrics that must be underlined anyway, the underlining can carry all the marking and serve as the cutting guide, as shown opposite.

Finally, remember to save all the leftovers. They are the makings of bias strips (overleaf), which, in turn, furnish such details as drawstrings, ruffles and straps.

STRAIGHTENING THE EDGES OF FABRIC

1. Spread the fabric wrong side up on a flat surface.

2. To straighten the crosswise edges of the fabric, start by placing an L-shaped square near one crosswise edge. Align one side of the square with a selvage edge.

3. Draw a chalk line along the other side of the square so that the line is at a right angle to the selvage.

4. Cut along the chalk line from one selvage to the other.

5. Repeat at the opposite end of the fabric.

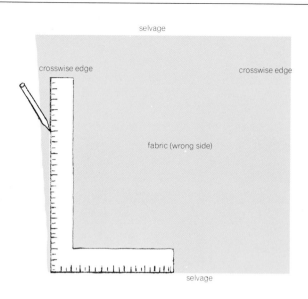

MAKING A DUPLICATE PATTERN PIECE

1. Lay a piece of tracing paper, large enough to accommodate the pattern piece to be copied, on a firm, flat surface. If necessary, tape together sheets of tracing paper.

2. Lay a sheet of dressmaker's carbon paper, carbon side down, over the tracing paper. If the carbon paper is smaller than the pattern piece, place it at one end.

3. Lay the pattern piece, marked side up, over the dressmaker's carbon paper and pin the three pieces together.

4. Using a smooth-edged tracing wheel, outline the entire pattern piece and trace over all notches, seam lines and other markings. Repin the carbon paper to the other end of the pattern piece if necessary; then trace the remaining pattern markings.

5. Remove the original pattern piece and the carbon paper. Cut out the duplicate pattern piece, then mark it with the same number that is printed on the original.

6. If the original pattern was designed to be placed on the fold of the fabric, tape the duplicate to the original along the fold line.

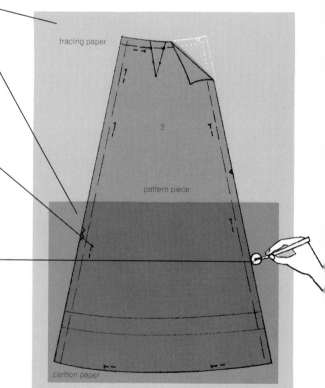

A | CUTTING THE FABRIC

1. Before cutting and marking the garment pieces, cut out the underlining pieces from a fabric suitable for underlining (pages 40-41). Use all the garment pattern pieces except the ones for facings and follow your pattern layout.

2. Using a tracing wheel and light-colored dressmaker's carbon paper (Appendix), mark the underlining pieces.

3. Lay a single layer of garment fabric wrong side up on a flat surface. If the fabric is longer than your work space, fold up the extra fabric so that it will not hang over the edge. This will keep the fabric from slipping as you work.

4. Arrange as many pieces of underlining—marked side up—as can fit on the fabric, allowing at least 2 inches between each piece. Match the grain directions of the underlining and the fabric; refer to the grain-line arrows on the pattern pieces if necessary. Pin at 2-inch intervals within the seam allowances.

5. Cut out the garment pieces 1 inch beyond the edges of the underlining pieces.

6. Repeat Steps 3-5 to cut out any remaining garment pieces.

B | BASTING THE UNDERLINING TO THE GARMENT PIECES

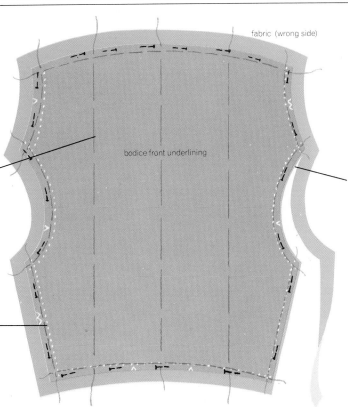

7. Working on one garment piece at a time, remove the pins. Then smooth the fabric, and repin.

8. Starting at the center of the piece, run parallel rows of long basting stitches down the length of the piece. To eliminate puckers and wrinkles, smooth the fabric toward the outside edges as you sew.

9. Baste around the edges of the underlining—just outside any seam lines. As you baste, smooth the layers of fabric outward from the basting made in the previous step. Do not stitch around corners; instead, begin each line at a right angle to the last one basted. Remove the pins.

10. Check to be sure that both the underlining and the garment fabric are smooth. If either layer wrinkles, clip the nearby bastings and rebaste.

11. Trim the garment fabric even with the edge of the underlining.

12. Treat the basted layers as one when you stitch the garment together. Do not remove the bastings until the garment is completed.

MARKING SHEER FABRICS WITH TAILOR TACKS

1. Make rows of tailor tacks (*Appendix*) to mark all seam and fold lines—except dart seam lines, which will be marked with single tailor tacks. Space the stitches at 1/2-inch intervals around curves; on long, straight seam lines, they can be farther apart. Do not sew around corners; instead, after completing one line, start a new line at a right angle to the first one.

2. Mark all pattern dots —including any dart points —circles, notches and any other markings with single tailor tacks (*Appendix*). If the marking is along a seam line, use a different color thread from the one used to mark the seam line.

3. Cut the loops of the tailor tacks and carefully remove the paper pattern.

4. If you are marking folded fabric, gently separate the layers, clipping the tailor tacks between them as you do.

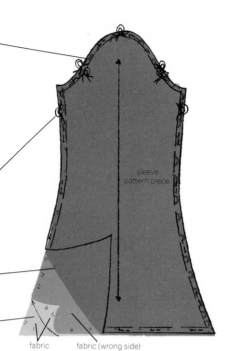

sleeve pattern piece

fabric   fabric (wrong side)

MARKING OPAQUE FABRICS WITH CARBON PAPER

1A. If you are marking two layers of fabric, remove just enough pins from one area at a time so you can slip dressmaker's carbon paper, carbon side down, between the pattern and the upper layer of fabric. Then place another piece of carbon paper, carbon side up, under the bottom layer of fabric. To prevent the markings from showing through the fabric, use a light-colored carbon paper, such as white or pastel blue.

1B. If you are marking only one layer of fabric, simply place a piece of light-colored dressmaker's carbon paper, carbon side up, under the fabric.

2. Run a tracing wheel along all seam and fold lines. Use a straight-edged ruler as a guide for straight lines; trace curves freehand.

3. Using a dull pencil, trace the notches, and draw an "X" through the center of all dots and circles.

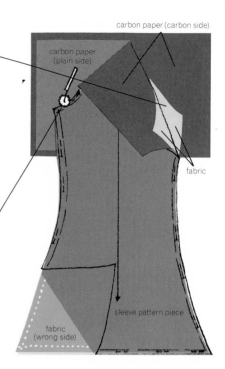

carbon paper (carbon side)

carbon paper (plain side)

fabric

sleeve pattern piece

fabric (wrong side)

MAKING A BIAS STRIP

A MARKING AND CUTTING

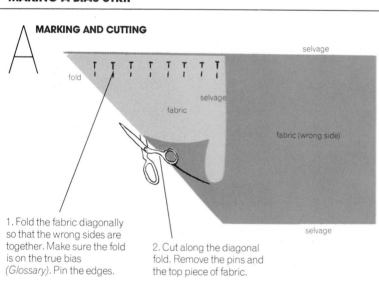

selvage

fold

selvage

fabric

fabric (wrong side)

selvage

selvage

1. Fold the fabric diagonally so that the wrong sides are together. Make sure the fold is on the true bias (*Glossary*). Pin the edges.

2. Cut along the diagonal fold. Remove the pins and the top piece of fabric.

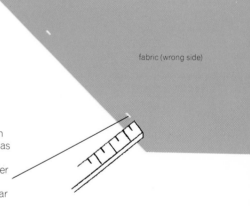

fabric (wrong side)

3. Near one end of the diagonal edge, measure in the desired width of the bias strip, and make a mark. Make sure to place the ruler at a right angle to the diagonal edge. Repeat near the other end.

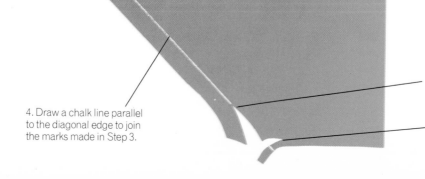

4. Draw a chalk line parallel to the diagonal edge to join the marks made in Step 3.

5. Cut out the bias strip along the chalk line.

6. Trim off both selvages. If you need only one bias strip, skip to Step 13.

7. If the length requires more than one strip of fabric, repeat Steps 3-6 to cut as many strips as you need.

8. Mark 1/4-inch seam allowances with chalk on both ends of each strip.

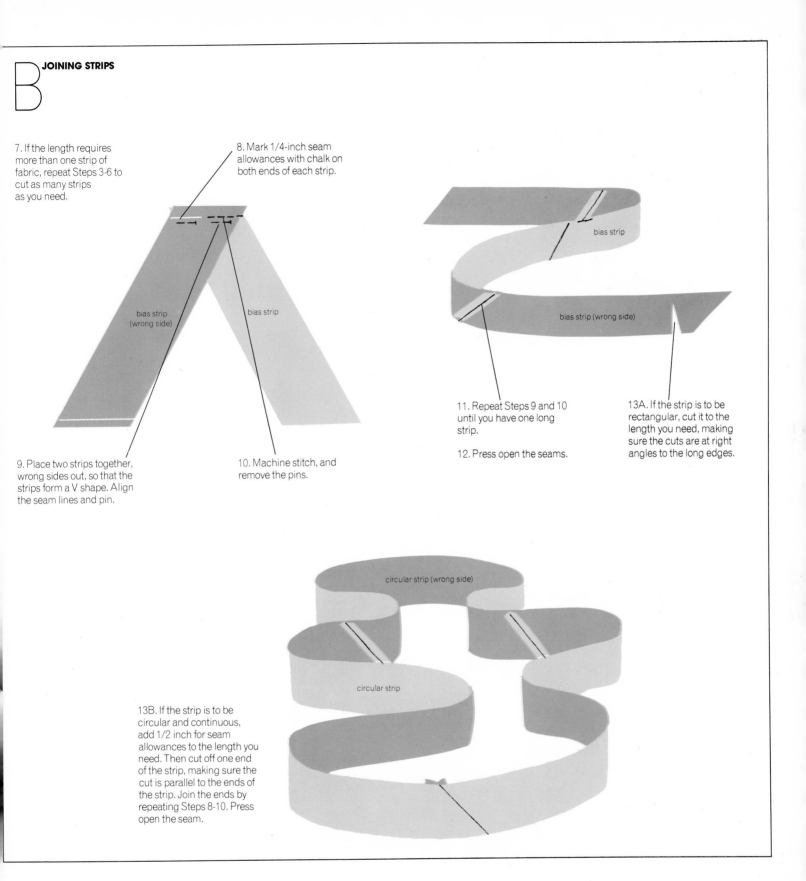

bias strip (wrong side)

bias strip

bias strip

bias strip (wrong side)

9. Place two strips together, wrong sides out, so that the strips form a V shape. Align the seam lines and pin.

10. Machine stitch, and remove the pins.

11. Repeat Steps 9 and 10 until you have one long strip.

12. Press open the seams.

13A. If the strip is to be rectangular, cut it to the length you need, making sure the cuts are at right angles to the long edges.

circular strip (wrong side)

circular strip

13B. If the strip is to be circular and continuous, add 1/2 inch for seam allowances to the length you need. Then cut off one end of the strip, making sure the cut is parallel to the ends of the strip. Join the ends by repeating Steps 8-10. Press open the seam.

Cascades of metallics and sequins

Fragile fabrics laced by metallic threads or spangled with metal or plastic sequins shimmer glamorously and flow as languidly as quicksilver. The cotton and polyester lace dress at left, for example, flashes with highlights of silver thread. The silk chiffon dress *(opposite)* glitters with metal sequins. Swatches, from the left, show metal-sequined polyester chiffon, silver-dotted polyester organza, iridescent plastic-sequined polyester chiffon, gold-striped rayon chiffon and rayon knit with golden threads. Each cloth has its own basic sewing methods, but the ornaments dictate the special procedures described overleaf.

Dealing with shimmery disks and threads

On a finished dress, metallic and sequined fabrics may give off the ethereal shimmer of moonbeams, but in the sewing room they can prove amazingly tough and resistant—to the point of dulling scissors and breaking needles. Furthermore, on sequined cloth, seams cannot be ripped out, no matter how carefully, without leaving a telltale spoor of broken metallic disks, or a permanent line of unsightly stitching holes.

For all these reasons, the best results can be had by choosing patterns devoid of gathers, pleats or buttonholes that require fancy cutting or sewing. The material, after all, looks striking enough without fussy details—and unseen snaps can hold as tightly as buttons.

With all metallic and sequined cloth, however, even the simplest patterns require careful preparation for sewing. The special methods used for modifying patterns, laying them out for cutting and transferring pattern markings are explained at right. Furthermore, these fabrics call for linings; metal threads and disks scratch. But because many of these fabrics are also partially transparent, such linings can often be made from contrasting or complementary colors to play a decorative role as well as a functional one.

A **MODIFYING THE PATTERN**

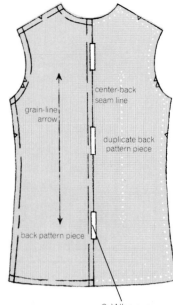

1. Make duplicates *(page 28)* of all pattern pieces designed to be cut from folded fabric.

2. Wherever possible, eliminate the center-front or the center-back seam by joining the original and duplicate pattern pieces along the seam lines.

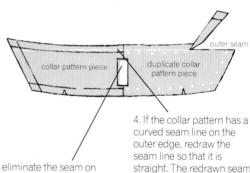

3. To eliminate the seam on the outer edge of the collar, start by making sure that you have duplicated the collar pattern piece, as shown, if it was designed to be placed on the fold of the fabric.

4. If the collar pattern has a curved seam line on the outer edge, redraw the seam line so that it is straight. The redrawn seam line should run midway between the extremes of the curve on the original.

5. Trim the collar pattern piece along the outer seam line.

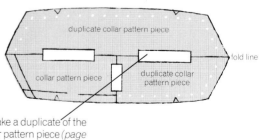

6. Make a duplicate of the collar pattern piece *(page 28),* and tape it to the original along the outer seam line, which will now be a fold line.

B LAYING OUT THE PATTERN PIECES

7. Spread out the sequined or metallic-surfaced fabric wrong side down on a firm flat surface.

8. Arrange the pattern pieces on the fabric with the grain-line arrows parallel to the selvages. Leave at least 2 inches between the pattern pieces and 1 inch between the pattern pieces and the edge of the fabric. Make sure that the top-to-bottom direction on all of the pieces is the same.

9. If the fabric has a design, make sure that seam lines that will be joined fall in the same position on the design. Also, make sure that each notch is at the same point on the design as its numbered counterpart.

10. Pin the patterns in place inside the seam lines. On sequined fabric, make sure to insert the pins under the sequins, not through them.

11. Cut out the garment pieces 1 inch outside the seam lines. Do not trim off this excess seam allowance until after the seam is sewed.

12. Mark the garment pieces with thread tracings, following the instructions in the box below.

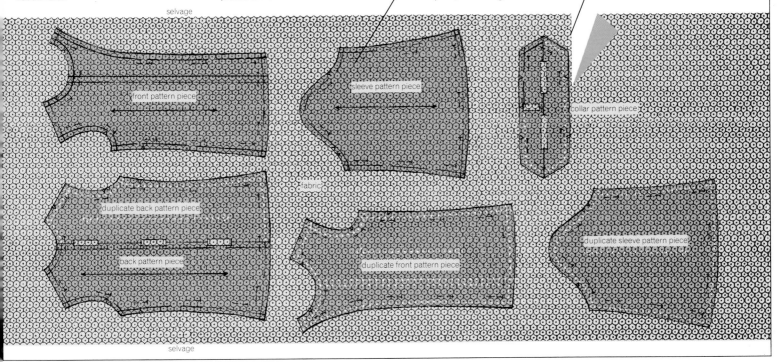

MARKING WITH THREAD TRACINGS

1. Remove any pins in the seam allowances, and reinsert them just inside the seam lines.

2. To mark straight seam lines, fold back the seam allowances of the pattern along the seam line. Then, using unknotted thread, make a row of basting stitches along the folded edge of the pattern. Do not sew around corners. Instead, cut the thread and start a new line of basting at a right angle to the first line.

3. To mark curved seam lines, make a row of tailor tacks (Appendix) along the seam line.

4. Mark each pattern dot and notch with a single tailor tack (Appendix). Use thread of a different color to distinguish these tailor tacks from the ones marking seam lines.

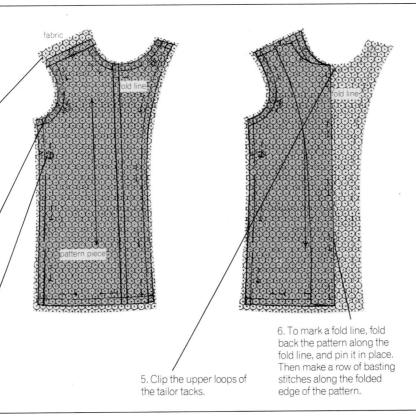

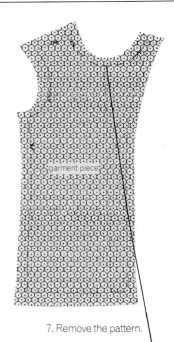

5. Clip the upper loops of the tailor tacks.

6. To mark a fold line, fold back the pattern along the fold line, and pin it in place. Then make a row of basting stitches along the folded edge of the pattern.

7. Remove the pattern.

8. On curved seam lines, make a row of bastings along the tailor tacks. Then remove the tailor tacks.

Intricacies of lace and embroidery

Laces and sheer cloth with embroidered designs form the most feminine—and fragile—of all delicate fabrics. Their designs, intricately worked in fine threads, make them as ethereal as sunbeams: gowns sewed from such fabrics are gossamer fancies—as the silk organza with silk embroidery at right and the cotton lace opposite demonstrate. Behind the gowns, clockwise from the lower left, are swatches of rayon lace, rayon organdy with cotton embroidery, cotton eyelet and nylon organza with cotton embroidery. Because all of these fragile fabrics have repeated patterns, they require careful preparation, as detailed overleaf.

Layouts for cutting fancywork

The filigrees and florals that give charm to lace and embroidered fabrics also make them challenging to lay out and cut. Invisible seams require some juggling of the fabric design along the edges of the paper pattern. Positioning pattern pieces on a prominent design like that in the lace at right demands extra care —as described here.

Lace fabrics and embroidered fabrics both lend themselves to pattern layouts arranged lengthwise or crosswise. The choice depends on the width of the material, the direction of its design and the nature of its selvages. Laces usually come scalloped on one or both selvage edges; many embroidered fabrics feature similar scallops or finished edges. With planning, these edges can serve as decorative hems.

Whatever direction the pattern arrangement takes, all pattern pieces should be laid out on a single thickness of fabric. To do this, duplicates must be made of those pieces normally placed on a double thickness of fabric. Such duplicates make it possible to position each pattern piece so that the design of the fabric will fall attractively on the garment after it has been sewed together.

A LAYING OUT THE GARMENT PIECES

1. Make duplicates (page 28) of all pattern pieces designed to be cut from folded fabric.

2. Wherever possible, eliminate the center-front or the center-back seam by joining the original and duplicate pattern pieces at the seam lines.

3. Spread out the lace fabric wrong side down.

4. Loosely arrange the pattern pieces lengthwise on the fabric, leaving at least one design motif (a rose in this example) plus 1 inch between the edges of the pattern pieces that are side by side. On the main garment section, make sure the center line falls in the middle of a motif.

5. Make sure that the edges of the pattern pieces are at least 2 inches inside the scalloped edge, so that the edge can be used to border the hems and openings.

6. On vertical seams that will be finished by making an invisible lace seam (page 53), make sure seam lines that will be joined fall in the same position on the lace motif. Also make sure that each notch falls at the same point in the motif as its numbered counterpart on the adjacent pattern piece.

7. Pin the pattern pieces in place.

bodice front pattern piece · *duplicate bodice front pattern piece* · *lace fabric* · *center line* · *scalloped edge* · *bodice back pattern piece* · *duplicate bodice back pattern piece*

8. On the side seams of the garment front pattern pieces, cut out the lace following the outline of the design that extends beyond the edges of the pattern pieces. If any other vertical seam is to be finished with an invisible lace seam, cut outside one of the seam lines following the design outline.

9. On all other seam lines, cut out the lace 1 inch outside the seam line.

10. Cutting along the design nearest the edge, trim off the scalloped edge.

B MARKING THE LACE PIECES

11. Mark straight hemlines and other straight pattern markings with thread tracing (page 35).

12. Mark all other pattern markings with tailor tacks (page 30).

13. Mark curved hemlines with tailor tacks, then baste along the marked hemline.

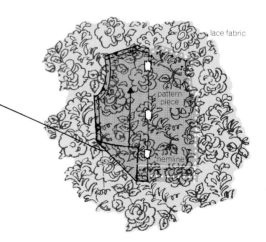

lace fabric · *pattern piece* · *hemline*

CUTTING LACE GARMENTS ON THE CROSSWISE GRAIN

A LAYING OUT THE GARMENT PIECES

1. For each garment piece that will have the scalloped or finished edge of the lace along the hem, determine the desired finished hem length. Then mark a new hemline on the pattern piece parallel to the original hemline.

2. Make duplicates (page 28) of all pattern pieces designed to be cut from folded fabric.

3. Wherever possible, eliminate the center-front or the center-back seam by joining the original and duplicate pattern pieces along the seam lines.

4. Spread out the lace fabric wrong side down on a firm flat surface.

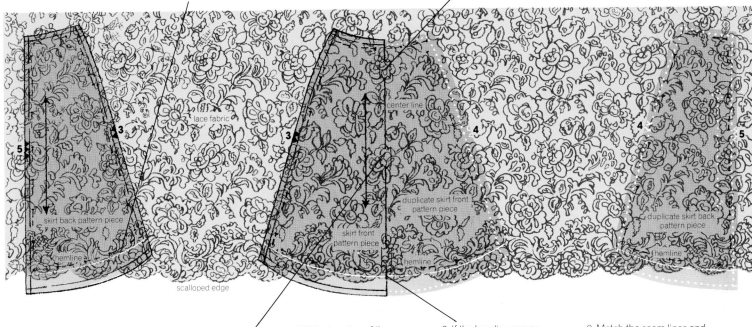

5. Loosely arrange the pattern pieces on the fabric so that there is at least one repeat of the lace motif plus 1 inch between the edges of the pattern pieces that are side by side.

6. On the main garment section, make sure the center line is in the middle of a lace motif.

7. If the hemline of the pattern piece is straight, align the hemline with a scalloped or finished edge. If the hem curves less than 3/4 inch, the pattern can be laid out the same way.

8. If the hemline curves more than 3/4 inch, align only the center part of the hemline with a scalloped or finished edge.

9. Match the seam lines and the notches; then pin the pattern pieces in place and cut them out, following the directions in Box A (left, Steps 6-9).

B FINISHING THE LACE PIECES

10. On each pattern piece with a curved hemline, remove the pins from the bottom part of the pattern piece so that you can use it as a guide while you are adjusting the hem edge.

11. Cutting along the design motif nearest the scalloped edge of the lace, cut from the side seams across to the point where the hemline on the pattern piece curves away from the scalloped edge.

12. Raise the cut edge so that it overlaps the garment section and is aligned with the hemline on the pattern piece. If necessary, make 1/8-inch clips along the cut edge so that the section will lie flat. Pin.

13. Baste the hem in place, and remove the pins on the scalloped edge.

14. Repin the bottom of the pattern piece to the fabric.

15. Mark the straight seam lines on the garment pieces, following the directions for marking with thread tracing (page 35). Mark all other pattern markings with tailor tacks (Appendix). Remove the pattern pieces.

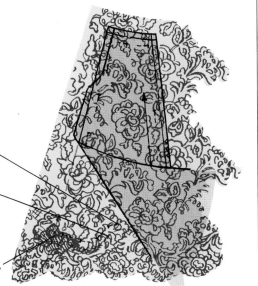

16. On each garment piece with a curved basted hem, sew the hem to the garment by making an invisible lace seam (page 53, Steps 4-6). The lace design will not match perfectly.

Guidelines to delicate materials

Like many other beautiful things, delicate fabrics such as chiffon and crepe de Chine can cause problems. The solutions lie in understanding the various idiosyncracies of these materials and dealing with each one properly. As the chart at right shows, every variety of delicate fabric requires a distinctive method of shopping, cutting, sewing and cleaning. Fine knits, for example, stretch, and they need seams made with a zigzag stitch. Delicate-surfaced fabrics, on the other hand, tend to pucker, and they must be sewed with your machine's even-feed foot attachment.

From bolt to finished garment, these materials demand other kinds of special attention. Scissors should be sharp—even the old pair of shears recommended for sequined surfaces or metallics. Needles and threads must be selected carefully, then tested on a swatch to be sure that the stitching they produce looks fine and inconspicuous.

Only one suggested procedure works with all delicate fabrics: buy more yardage than the pattern envelope suggests. Paradoxically, even this generality applies to each different material for a different reason, as the chart explains.

FABRIC TYPE	SHOPPING SUGGESTIONS
SHEERS AND EMBROIDERED SHEERS **Batiste, chiffon, gauze, georgette, handkerchief linen, marquisette, organdy, organza, voile**	These lightweight transparent fabrics come in natural fibers such as cotton, silk or linen, as well as in synthetics like nylon, rayon or polyester. Chiffon or georgette prove especially slippery to handle, buy a little extra yardage to provide for wider seam allowances and possible cutting errors. Select China or synthetic silk for smooth linings and underlinings; substitute a binding of garment fabric for conventional facings.
DELICATE SURFACES **Charmeuse, China silk, silk broadcloth, crepe de Chine, moire, peau de soie, pongee, satin, satin crepe, taffeta**	These lightweight, translucent or opaque fabrics come in silk, cotton and a wide range of synthetics. With slippery China silk, crepe de Chine and satin crepe, provide for wider seam allowances and possible cutting errors by buying a little extra yardage. With satins, moires, taffetas and other shiny fabrics, check to see if the sheen follows a distinct direction; if so, buy the yardage recommended for fabrics with nap.
FINE KNITS **Jersey, lightweight double knits, lightweight matte jersey, tricot**	These lightweight translucent or opaque fabrics come in cotton, silk and wool as well as in such synthetics as rayon, polyester or nylon. When a knit has a napped surface, buy the yardage recommended for fabrics with nap. For washable finished garments, cotton knits must be preshrunk by being immersed in cool water and then thoroughly dried.
METALLICS AND SEQUINED SURFACES	Metal or metalized-plastic threads and metal or plastic sequins may be woven through or applied to all kinds of natural and synthetic sheers, delicately surfaced fabrics, fine knits and laces. On both metallic and sequined surfaces, the sheen of the threads and sequins follows a distinct direction; purchase the extra amount of yardage recommended for fabrics with nap in order to be able to lay out all the garment pieces in the sheen direction. Choose a matching plain fabric for lining. Satin cording can be substituted for facings to finish off edges at the neckline and armholes.
LACE YARDAGE AND TRIMMING	Lightweight laces may be made from cotton, linen, fine wool, silk or synthetics such as rayon, nylon or acetate. Lace trimmings are sometimes also embellished with beads, sequins, metallic threads or ribbons. Lace yardage usually comes in conventional 36- to 45-inch fabric widths, lace trimmings in widths ranging from 1/4 inch to several inches. Purchase at least an extra half yard of lace to allow for matching the designs. To determine yardage requirements for lace trimming, pin seam tape around the area to be trimmed and measure its length. Select China or synthetic silk for underlinings.

CUTTING, MARKING, BASTING	SEWING	CLEANING AND PRESSING
Prepare duplicates of pattern pieces designed to be cut from folded fabric, then lay out and cut the sheer in a single layer. When attaching pattern pieces to the fabric, insert silk pins in the seam allowances at frequent intervals. Provide extra-wide 1-inch seam allowances. Indicate stitching lines and other pattern markings with tailor tacks. Use silk thread for the tailor tacks and bastings and remove both as quickly as possible to avoid marking the fabric permanently.	Machine stitch at 12 to 15 stitches to the inch, using a Size 9 or 11 needle and choosing silk thread for silk, dual-duty or cotton thread for other fibers. Place tissue paper beneath the fabric to prevent it from shifting or snagging in the machine; gently tear away the paper after finishing each seam. Allow chiffon, which stretches, to hang into its final shape for 24 hours before hemming the garment.	Check the fabric label to determine the recommended pressing and cleaning methods. Most sheers must be dry-cleaned, but some cottons and synthetics may be hand washed. All can be pressed safely; before pressing, test a fabric swatch. Set embroidered sheers face down on a terry towel for pressing to protect them from flattening.
For fabrics with sheen direction, follow the layout recommended for napped fabrics. Insert silk pins in the seam allowances to attach pattern pieces to the fabric. Provide extra-wide 1-inch seam allowances on slippery China silk, crepe de Chine and satin crepe. Indicate stitching lines and other pattern markings with tailor tacks. Use silk thread for marking and basting. If the garment is underlined, make all markings on the underlining fabric.	Machine stitch at 12 to 15 stitches to the inch, using a Size 9 or 11 needle and choosing silk thread for silk, dual-duty or cotton thread for other fibers. Use an even-feed foot attachment to prevent puckering, or stretch the fabric taut while stitching it.	Check the fabric label to determine the recommended pressing and cleaning methods. Most delicately surfaced materials must be dry-cleaned. Nearly all of them can be pressed safely with a cool, dry iron and light pressure; before pressing, test a fabric swatch. Place a pressing cloth over the fabric and use brown paper under seams to avoid marking the garment.
For knits with napped surfaces, follow the layout recommended for nap fabrics. Insert ballpoint pins in the seam allowances to attach pattern pieces to the fabric. Transfer pattern markings with a smooth-edged tracing wheel and dressmaker's carbon paper. Cut with sharp knit scissors, leaving extra-wide 1-inch seam allowances wherever possible.	Machine stitch at 12 to 15 stitches to the inch, using a Size 11 or 14 ballpoint needle, dual-duty thread and a very fine zigzag stitch. Stretch the fabric taut while stitching. Sew straight seam binding across the shoulders and around the waistline of the garment to prevent stretching in these areas.	Check the fabric label to determine the recommended pressing and cleaning methods. Most fine knit fabrics must be dry-cleaned, but can be pressed safely. Before pressing, test a swatch of fabric.
Make duplicates of all pattern pieces designed to be cut from folded fabric, then lay out and cut the metallic or sequined fabric in a single layer. Follow the layout recommended for nap fabrics. Insert ballpoint or silk pins—depending on the basic fabric—to attach pattern pieces to the fabric; pin under the sequins and not through them. Mark straight seam lines with thread tracing (page 35); indicate other pattern markings with tailor tacks. Cut with a well-sharpened pair of old shears—metallic threads and sequins will dull blades, and may eventually ruin shears.	Use the pins, needles and thread that are recommended for sewing the base fabric under the chart entries for sheers, delicate surfaces and fine knits (above). Metallic threads and sequins may dull needles; change them as they become dull. If sequins break in the seams, pull them off and attach new sequins.	Check the fabric label to determine the recommended pressing and cleaning methods. Most metallic or sequin-surfaced fabrics must be dry-cleaned, but can be pressed safely wrong side up with a cool, dry iron and pressing cloth. Before pressing, test a fabric swatch. Steam may discolor and even melt some metallics.
On richly ornamented lace, pattern pieces can be laid out lengthwise or crosswise; on other laces, follow the conventional lengthwise layout recommended in the pattern. Use silk pins with colored heads—which will stand out against the lace designs—to attach pattern pieces to the fabric or to fasten the trimming in place. Mark straight seam lines with basting stitches; use tailor tacks for other pattern markings. Make tacks and bastings with dual-duty or cotton thread.	Fragile laces require hand sewing with a fine needle and silk thread. Others may be machine stitched. Set the machine at 15 to 20 stitches to the inch and use a Size 11 or 14 needle with silk, dual-duty or cotton thread—depending on the weight of the lace. For invisible seaming, use a fine zigzag stitch.	Check the label to determine the recommended pressing and cleaning methods. Most lace and lace-trimmed garments must be dry-cleaned, but can be pressed with a cool iron and light pressure. Before pressing, test a swatch. Place laces with raised designs face down on a terry towel for pressing to protect them from flattening.

3
SWINGING INTO AIRY FASHIONS

ashion designer George Stavropoulos, like any true artist, has high regard for the raw materials he works with. In Stavropoulos' case, fabrics are the medium and silk chiffon one of his favorite fabrics: "I have enormous respect for fabric, total respect." Chiffon, he adds, in an observation that may not appeal to all of his clients, is "like a woman; you must be gentle but strong." Stavropoulos uses more silk chiffon than any other ma-

MASTERFUL SCULPTURES IN CHIFFON

terial for his evening gowns. And a gown by Stavropoulos, as any connoisseur can tell at a glance, has a hallmark of its own: long, elegant and diaphanous.

Although the designer occasionally creates gowns for specific customers, he usually makes anywhere from three to 50 copies of a dress, each of which sells for $600 to $2,500 in the country's most fashionable stores. If a design is a particularly difficult one, Stavropoulos drapes each copy himself. But usually his staff produces the dresses from his original design, cutting and sewing under his direct supervision.

Working alone in his studio, Stavropoulos takes about five minutes to drape one of his dresses. He does not make preliminary designs with muslin in the ordinary way, because it is too heavy and bulky. Instead, he pulls clouds of chiffon from the bolts that surround him and, with masterly deftness, drapes the fabric onto a size 8 dressmaker's dummy. (He never uses a live model.) Most of the dresses are simply lengths of fabric draped from the neck.

As he works, Stavropoulos adds layer upon layer of the gossamer fabric, sometimes using different shades of a basic color, sometimes contrasting colors. Nothing guides him but his eye, the natural folds of the material and the curves of the feminine torso. Stavropoulos says of his work: "My dresses must fit many, many personalities, many heights, many weights. My inspirations come from all over. I may watch a woman walking in the street. I see her legs, how she walks, and I imagine how the fabric will follow that walk. I try to make a customer more elegant, more beautiful and more sophisticated."

With some of his gowns, Stavropoulos uses as much as 25 yards of material—and yet, because it is so light, the chiffon moves in zephyrs created by the slightest movement. The fabric seems alive. As a woman walks, gossamer layers waft and ripple around her, in constantly changing colors and forms. At one moment, the chiffon floats grandly behind like a royal train. At another, it clings to the body in graceful curves.

Under the master designer's skilled fingers, the fabric seems to respond to his touch. Indeed, Stavropoulos' gowns often look as if they had never been touched by a needle. Nevertheless, his gowns are not held together by talent alone: they have seams that are all but invisible, graceful halter necklines that support as well as point up the flattering flow of the fabric, artfully draped sleeves that camouflage their stitches and extra narrow hems that do nothing to disrupt the lines of the skirts. Stavropoulos never uses lining on chiffon, because he believes it would destroy the natural folds of his designs. The multiple layers of silk chiffon he uses in a gown eliminate the need for a slip or lining.

Stavropoulos, like many of the classic dressmakers since Madeleine Vionnet, makes frequent use of the bias cut—draping the fabric to fall diagonally across the body. This adds to the sensuality of his gowns by allowing the fabric to cling and yet to move freely with the body. The bias cut is practical, too. Because of its flexibility, one size will fit many shapes: a single dress cut on the bias can be as flattering to a size 16 as it is to a size 8.

George Stavropoulos started designing clothes as a teenager in Athens, when he put together a gown for his sister to wear to a dance. As a promising young designer after World War II, he refused an invitation by Christian Dior to join his corps of couturiers in Paris; instead, he stayed in his own atelier, in Athens' fashionable Constitution

Square, and rapidly established himself as one of the foremost Athenian designers. In 1957 he met an American girl, Nancy Angelakos, who was working in the U.S. Embassy in Athens, and fell in love with her. Nancy succeeded where the House of Dior had failed: when she refused to stay in Greece, Stavropoulos closed his salon, married the girl, left his native land and came to America with his bride.

Within a few years he was one of New York's leading designers. The show windows of Bonwit Teller and Henri Bendel were dedicated to his collections. Lady Bird Johnson turned up in a stunning Stavropoulos chiffon gown at the gala opening of the new Metropolitan Opera at New York's Lincoln Center, and a week later the First Lady attended the opening of the San Francisco Opera wearing yet another of his gowns. After that, many other celebrities clamored for Stavropoulos' elegant, totally feminine look, and the smartest stores from coast to coast sought the privilege of selling his confections.

Besides his evening gowns, the designer creates coats, capes, daytime dresses and evening pants. In addition to his favorite fabric, he uses wool, velvet, satin and lace. Yet even in casual wear, Stavropoulos has respect for airy elegance (he scorned the mini skirt when it appeared). Whether he is making an afternoon dress or an evening gown, his key to success is a delicate, luxurious fabric, handled with discernment and disarming simplicity.

1. In his studio, master designer George Stavropoulos begins to create a gown by selecting subtle shades of coral chiffon from several bolts of fabric.

2. He considers which tone of the fabric he wants to use for the bottom layer of the gown before pinning the material on the dressmaker's dummy.

4. Stavropoulos begins to shape the gown —pinning the layers together, first at one side of the waist and then on the other side.

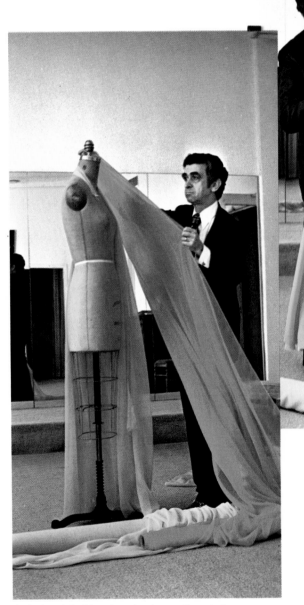

3. As he picks his colors, he drapes them in layers on the dummy, pinning each layer at the neck.

47

5. The design completed, Stavropoulos elevates the dummy to make sure the chiffon drapes properly.

7. Raising the dummy once more, he cuts the hemline. The gown is then whisked away to his seamstresses, who will sew in the hems and buttons.

8. Stavropoulos swirls the finished garment, testing his design to see that the gown retains the fluidity c the fabric. In the background is a photomural of the Parthenon—a reminder of his native Greece

6. Lowering the dummy, the designer checks the neckline and makes some minor adjustments.

Seams suited to soft stuff

Sheers, satins, knits and laces, although alike in fragility, vary enough in other ways to require different seams. Double-layered sheers, for example, can be well finished with enclosed French seams like those that form elegant binding around the collar, lapels and cuffs of the overblouse shown here. Single-layer sheers and satiny fabrics can also be stitched with plain French seams, whipped French seams and self-bound seams. When they are sewed in widths as narrow as an eighth of an inch, French and self-bound seams become nearly invisible and almost weightless to help preserve the flow of the fabric they join.

Knits are best seamed with machine zigzag stitches that can give somewhat with the stretch of the fabric. The seam should be reinforced with a second row of zigzag stitches to prevent fabric edges from rolling or fraying.

Laces employ the most ingenious seam of all. The pieces are overlapped and sewed along the lace design so that, when excess fabric has been trimmed away, not even the sharpest eye can detect the stitching. Instructions for all of these seams begin on the opposite page.

THE FRENCH SEAM

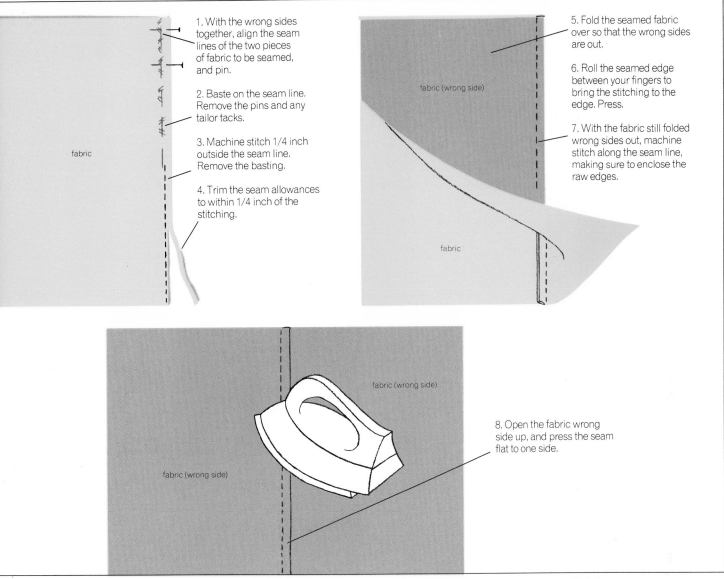

1. With the wrong sides together, align the seam lines of the two pieces of fabric to be seamed, and pin.

2. Baste on the seam line. Remove the pins and any tailor tacks.

3. Machine stitch 1/4 inch outside the seam line. Remove the basting.

4. Trim the seam allowances to within 1/4 inch of the stitching.

5. Fold the seamed fabric over so that the wrong sides are out.

6. Roll the seamed edge between your fingers to bring the stitching to the edge. Press.

7. With the fabric still folded wrong sides out, machine stitch along the seam line, making sure to enclose the raw edges.

8. Open the fabric wrong side up, and press the seam flat to one side.

THE ENCLOSED FRENCH SEAM

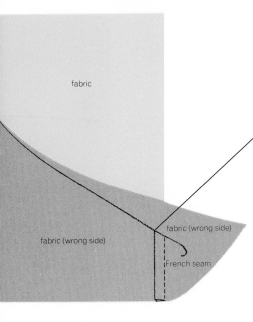

1. To make a French seam on an outside edge between two layers of sheer fabric that are not interfaced, as on the collar and cuffs on the overblouse at left, start by following Steps 1-7 for making a French seam.

2. Then refold the seamed fabric so that the wrong sides are together and the French seam is between two layers of fabric.

3. Roll the seamed edge between your fingers to bring the stitching to the edge.

4. Using a pressing cloth, press the seam.

5. Finish the garment, following your pattern instructions.

THE WHIPPED FRENCH SEAM

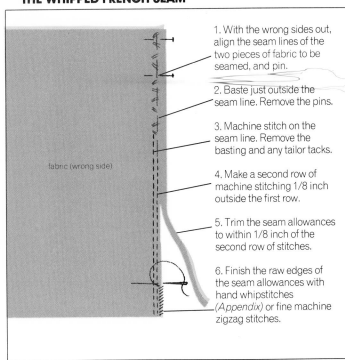

1. With the wrong sides out, align the seam lines of the two pieces of fabric to be seamed, and pin.

2. Baste just outside the seam line. Remove the pins.

3. Machine stitch on the seam line. Remove the basting and any tailor tacks.

4. Make a second row of machine stitching 1/8 inch outside the first row.

5. Trim the seam allowances to within 1/8 inch of the second row of stitches.

6. Finish the raw edges of the seam allowances with hand whipstitches (Appendix) or fine machine zigzag stitches.

THE SELF-BOUND SEAM

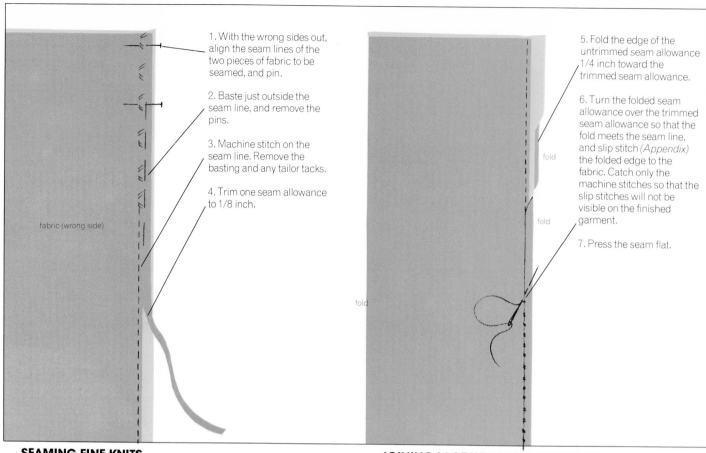

1. With the wrong sides out, align the seam lines of the two pieces of fabric to be seamed, and pin.

2. Baste just outside the seam line, and remove the pins.

3. Machine stitch on the seam line. Remove the basting and any tailor tacks.

4. Trim one seam allowance to 1/8 inch.

fabric (wrong side)

fold

fold

fold

5. Fold the edge of the untrimmed seam allowance 1/4 inch toward the trimmed seam allowance.

6. Turn the folded seam allowance over the trimmed seam allowance so that the fold meets the seam line, and slip stitch (Appendix) the folded edge to the fabric. Catch only the machine stitches so that the slip stitches will not be visible on the finished garment.

7. Press the seam flat.

SEAMING FINE KNITS

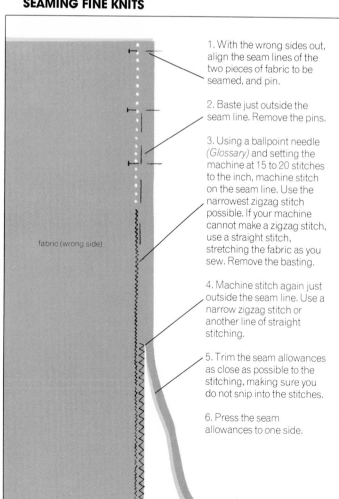

fabric (wrong side)

1. With the wrong sides out, align the seam lines of the two pieces of fabric to be seamed, and pin.

2. Baste just outside the seam line. Remove the pins.

3. Using a ballpoint needle (Glossary) and setting the machine at 15 to 20 stitches to the inch, machine stitch on the seam line. Use the narrowest zigzag stitch possible. If your machine cannot make a zigzag stitch, use a straight stitch, stretching the fabric as you sew. Remove the basting.

4. Machine stitch again just outside the seam line. Use a narrow zigzag stitch or another line of straight stitching.

5. Trim the seam allowances as close as possible to the stitching, making sure you do not snip into the stitches.

6. Press the seam allowances to one side.

JOINING LACE WITH STRAIGHT EDGES

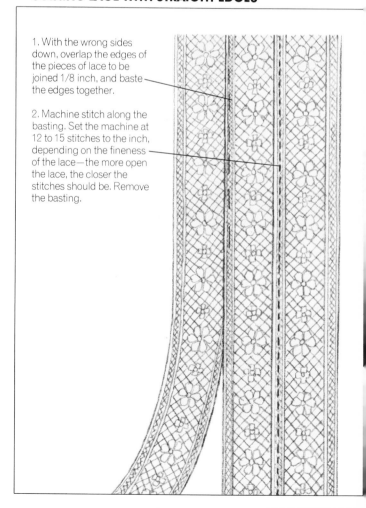

1. With the wrong sides down, overlap the edges of the pieces of lace to be joined 1/8 inch, and baste the edges together.

2. Machine stitch along the basting. Set the machine at 12 to 15 stitches to the inch, depending on the fineness of the lace—the more open the lace, the closer the stitches should be. Remove the basting.

JOINING LACE WITH ONE DECORATIVE BORDER

1. With the wrong sides down, lay the scalloped edge of one piece of lace over the straight edge of the piece to which it will be joined. Make sure the inner edge of the border on the scallops overlaps the lace piece beneath it by at least 1/8 inch. Pin.

2. Baste the pieces together. Remove the pins.

3. Machine stitch along the inner edge of the border on the scallops. Set the machine at 12 to 15 stitches to the inch—the finer the lace, the fewer stitches are needed. Remove the basting.

THE INVISIBLE LACE SEAM

1. To cut and mark the lace pieces, follow the instructions on page 38.

2. With the wrong sides down, overlap the edges of the lace pieces to be joined so that the thread-traced seam lines and the designs closest to them are perfectly aligned. Pin along the thread-traced seam lines.

3. Baste the pieces together along the seam line, and remove the pins.

4. Baste the pieces of lace together again. This time sew just to one side of the pattern in the design that is closest to the seam line. The basting may cross the seam line.

5. Following the basted edge of the pattern in the design, sew the lace pieces together. To hand sew, use a whipstitch (Appendix). To sew by machine, use narrow zigzag stitches and set the machine at 15 to 20 stitches to the inch, depending on the fineness of the lace —the finer the lace, the fewer stitches are needed. Remove the bastings.

6. Cut away both the top and bottom layers of lace close to the stitching, making sure you do not snip the stitches.

53

Layers that billow, linings that hide

Both layering and lining involve putting one thickness of cloth on top of another. But while layering composes sheers purely for decoration, lining employs opaque fabrics for reasons that are primarily functional.

In layering, two, three or more thicknesses of cloth are stitched together to intensify a single color, to blend several hues into a rainbow or perhaps to set off a print with a solid color. Individual layers might be shaped identically, or graduated in size or length to form tiers like those on the chiffon sleeve shown here.

Lining, on the other hand, effaces itself because its purpose is not to look dramatic, but to provide modest cover beneath transparent fabrics and to form smooth finishes for the inside seams and surfaces of a garment. Cut from opaque silks or synthetics, linings are sewed separately and slip stitched into place under the garment. Instructions for lining and layering bodices, sleeves and skirts appear on the following pages.

A LAYERED BODICE

A CUTTING THE FABRIC

1. Make duplicates of the bodice pattern pieces that were designed to be laid out on folded fabric, following the instructions on page 28.

2. To cut out the pieces for the first layer, start by laying a single thickness of fabric wrong side down on a flat surface. If the fabric is longer than your work space, fold up the extra fabric so that it will not hang over the edge. This will keep the fabric from slipping as you work.

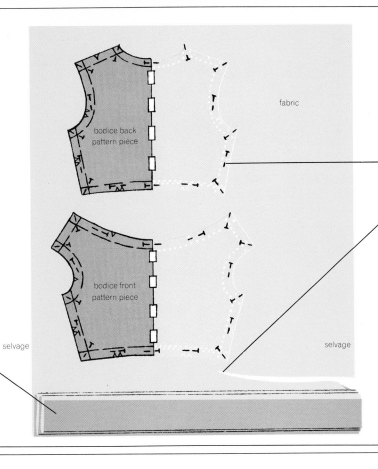

3. Arrange the pattern pieces on the fabric, allowing at least 2 inches between each piece. Pin within the seam allowance at 2-inch intervals.

4. Cut out the pieces for the first layer 1 inch beyond the edges of the pattern pieces. Then remove the pattern pieces.

5. Using the same pattern pieces, repeat Steps 2-4 to cut out each of the remaining layers.

B BASTING THE LAYERS

6. Working on one section of the bodice at a time, stack the layers wrong sides down in the order you want them to appear in the finished garment. Smooth the layers and pin in the center and then at 2-inch intervals along the edges.

7. Starting at the center of the piece, run parallel rows of basting stitches about 2 inches apart down the length of the piece. Remove the pins as you go. To eliminate puckers, smooth the fabric toward the outside edges as you baste.

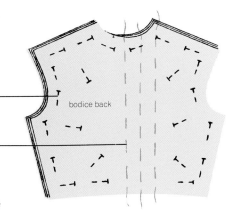

8. Lay the pattern piece on the quilted garment layers, and pin it in place within the seam allowance at 2-inch intervals.

9. Mark the fabric with tailor tacks, following instructions on page 30.

10. Trim the layered fabric even with the edges of the pattern piece. Remove the pins and set the pattern piece aside.

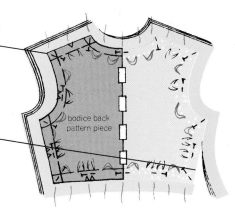

11. Baste just outside all seam lines. As you do, smooth the layers of fabric outward from the bastings made in Step 7 so that all layers lie as flat as possible. Do not stitch around corners, but after making one line, begin the next at a right angle to the last line stitched.

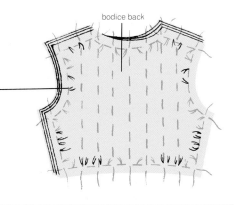

12. Check to be sure that all layers are smooth. If any layer wrinkles, clip the nearby bastings, smooth, then rebaste.

13. Treating the quilted layers as one, stitch the garment together following your pattern instructions. Do not remove the bastings until the garment is completed.

CUTTING THE LAYERS

1. Make duplicates of the skirt pattern pieces that were designed to be laid out on folded fabric, following the instructions on page 28.

2. Lay a single layer of the fabric you want to use for the innermost layer wrong side down on a flat surface. If the fabric is longer than your work space, fold up the extra fabric so that it will not hang over the edge. This will keep the fabric from slipping as you work.

3. Arrange the pattern pieces on the fabric, allowing at least 2 inches between each piece. Pin within the seam allowances at 2-inch intervals.

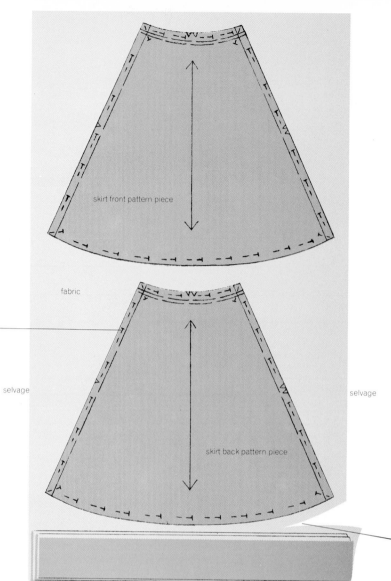

fabric

selvage   selvage

4. Cut out the pieces for the inner layer 1 inch beyond the edges of the pattern pieces.

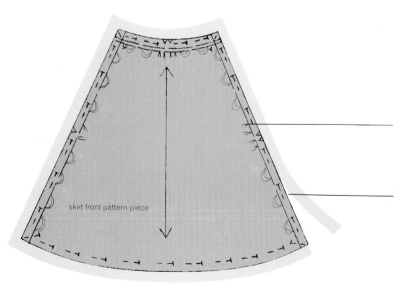

5. Mark the fabric with tailor tacks, following the instructions on page 30.

6. Trim the fabric even with the edges of the pattern piece. Then remove the pattern piece.

7. Using the same pattern pieces, repeat Steps 2-6 to cut out the pieces for the remaining layers. On these pieces, however, do not trim the waist edge even with the pattern.

B PREPARING THE LAYERS

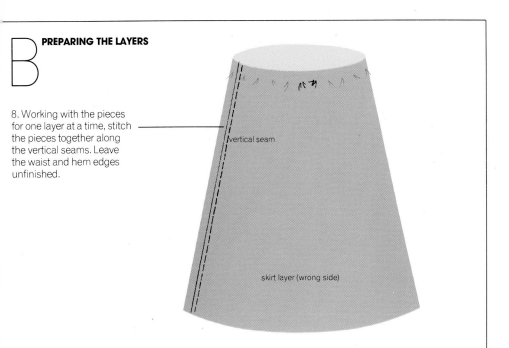

8. Working with the pieces for one layer at a time, stitch the pieces together along the vertical seams. Leave the waist and hem edges unfinished.

vertical seam

skirt layer (wrong side)

C JOINING THE LAYERS

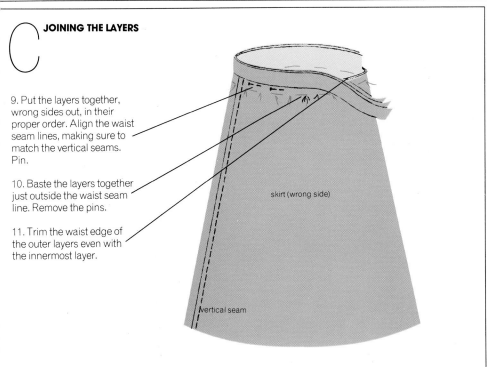

9. Put the layers together, wrong sides out, in their proper order. Align the waist seam lines, making sure to match the vertical seams. Pin.

10. Baste the layers together just outside the waist seam line. Remove the pins.

11. Trim the waist edge of the outer layers even with the innermost layer.

skirt (wrong side)

vertical seam

D ATTACHING THE SKIRT TO THE BODICE

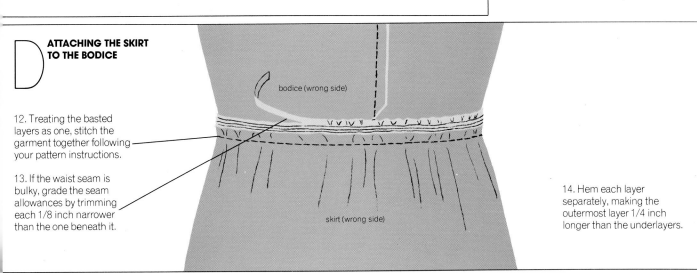

12. Treating the basted layers as one, stitch the garment together following your pattern instructions.

13. If the waist seam is bulky, grade the seam allowances by trimming each 1/8 inch narrower than the one beneath it.

bodice (wrong side)

skirt (wrong side)

14. Hem each layer separately, making the outermost layer 1/4 inch longer than the underlayers.

A SLEEVE LAYERED IN TIERS

A ADAPTING THE PATTERN

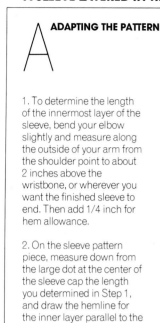

1. To determine the length of the innermost layer of the sleeve, bend your elbow slightly and measure along the outside of your arm from the shoulder point to about 2 inches above the wristbone, or wherever you want the finished sleeve to end. Then add 1/4 inch for hem allowance.

2. On the sleeve pattern piece, measure down from the large dot at the center of the sleeve cap the length you determined in Step 1, and draw the hemline for the inner layer parallel to the original hemline.

3. Trim the pattern piece along the new hemline.

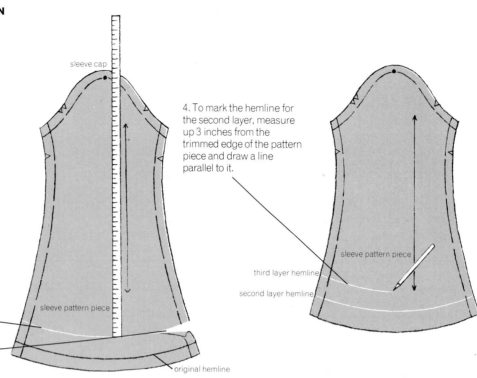

sleeve cap

sleeve pattern piece

original hemline

4. To mark the hemline for the second layer, measure up 3 inches from the trimmed edge of the pattern piece and draw a line parallel to it.

5. To mark the hemline for the third layer, draw another parallel line 3 inches above the one drawn in the preceding step.

6. Repeat Step 5 to mark the hemline for the fourth layer.

7. Make a duplicate of the pattern piece following the instructions on page 28. Make sure to transfer the new hemlines. Then set aside the duplicate pattern piece.

sleeve pattern piece

third layer hemline

second layer hemline

B CUTTING OUT THE LAYERS

8. Using the original pattern piece, cut and mark the innermost layer for one of the sleeves. Follow the directions in Steps 2-6 for a layered skirt (page 56).

9. Trim off the hem edge of the pattern along the hemline for the second layer. Then, using the trimmed pattern, cut and mark the second layer in the same manner. This time, however, do not trim the armhole edge of the layer even with the pattern.

10. Trimming the pattern along the hemlines each time, cut and mark the third and fourth layers in the same manner. Again, do not trim the armhole edge of the layer.

11. Using the duplicate pattern, repeat Steps 8-10 to cut and mark the layers for the other sleeve.

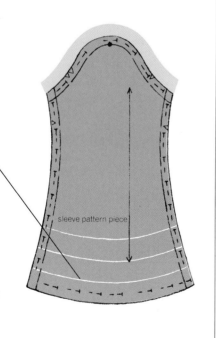

sleeve pattern piece

C ASSEMBLING THE LAYERS

12. Close the underarm seam on each layer.

underarm seam

sleeve layer (wrong side)

13. Hem each layer.

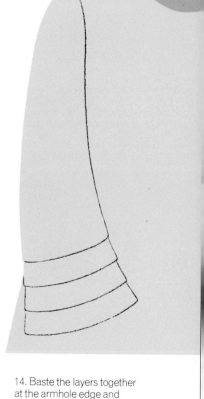

14. Baste the layers together at the armhole edge and attach them to the garment, following the instructions in Steps 10-14 for a layered skirt (page 57).

15. Repeat Steps 12-14 on the other sleeve.

LINING A DRESS

A LINING THE SKIRT

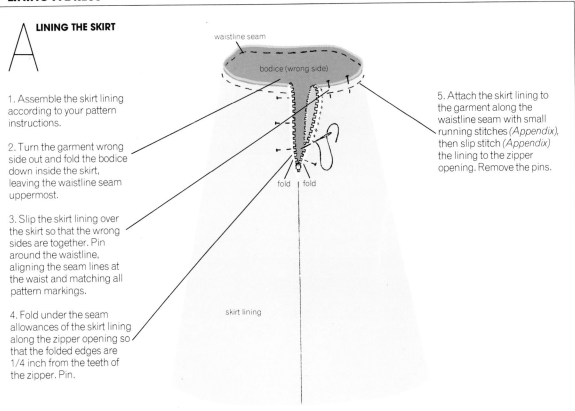

1. Assemble the skirt lining according to your pattern instructions.

2. Turn the garment wrong side out and fold the bodice down inside the skirt, leaving the waistline seam uppermost.

3. Slip the skirt lining over the skirt so that the wrong sides are together. Pin around the waistline, aligning the seam lines at the waist and matching all pattern markings.

4. Fold under the seam allowances of the skirt lining along the zipper opening so that the folded edges are 1/4 inch from the teeth of the zipper. Pin.

5. Attach the skirt lining to the garment along the waistline seam with small running stitches (Appendix), then slip stitch (Appendix) the lining to the zipper opening. Remove the pins.

waistline seam

bodice (wrong side)

fold   fold

skirt lining

B LINING THE BODICE

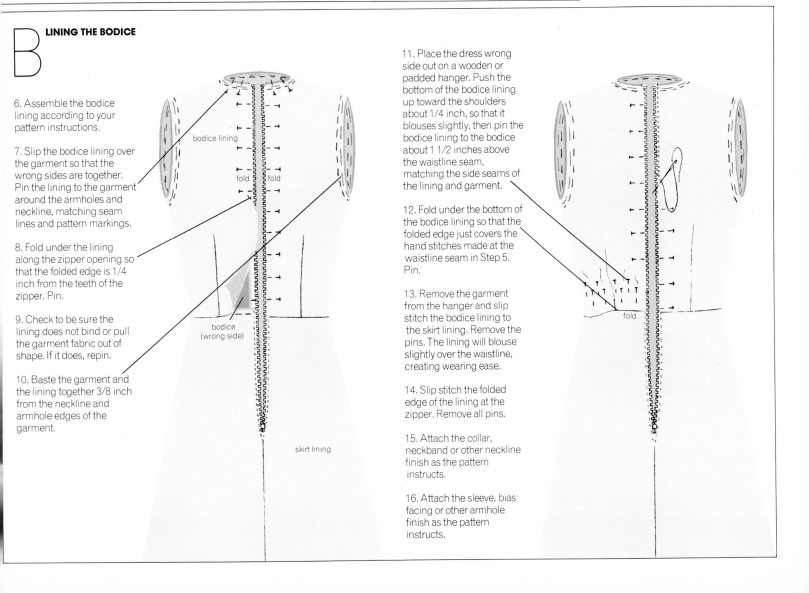

6. Assemble the bodice lining according to your pattern instructions.

7. Slip the bodice lining over the garment so that the wrong sides are together. Pin the lining to the garment around the armholes and neckline, matching seam lines and pattern markings.

8. Fold under the lining along the zipper opening so that the folded edge is 1/4 inch from the teeth of the zipper. Pin.

9. Check to be sure the lining does not bind or pull the garment fabric out of shape. If it does, repin.

10. Baste the garment and the lining together 3/8 inch from the neckline and armhole edges of the garment.

11. Place the dress wrong side out on a wooden or padded hanger. Push the bottom of the bodice lining up toward the shoulders about 1/4 inch, so that it blouses slightly, then pin the bodice lining to the bodice about 1 1/2 inches above the waistline seam, matching the side seams of the lining and garment.

12. Fold under the bottom of the bodice lining so that the folded edge just covers the hand stitches made at the waistline seam in Step 5. Pin.

13. Remove the garment from the hanger and slip stitch the bodice lining to the skirt lining. Remove the pins. The lining will blouse slightly over the waistline, creating wearing ease.

14. Slip stitch the folded edge of the lining at the zipper. Remove all pins.

15. Attach the collar, neckband or other neckline finish as the pattern instructs.

16. Attach the sleeve, bias facing or other armhole finish as the pattern instructs.

bodice lining

fold   fold

bodice (wrong side)

skirt lining

fold

Drapes and tucks for fit and trim

With natural folds and undulations, delicate fabrics invite pleating. Silky satins, soft knits and gauzy sheers are ideal for drapes—unpressed pleats stitched shut at one or both ends, but left curvaceously open in between. And all these materials are enhanced by tucks—pressed pleats that are stitched from end to end; knits, which do not hold a crease, look best with narrow tucks.

. Drapes can be used for decoration alone or—like those in the bodice and sash of the sheer wool dress shown here—can be sophisticated substitutes for darts and other fitting seams. Tucks, on the other hand, are purely ornamental; they can be added to most designs by sewing them into the cloth before the pattern pieces are cut. How much extra material to allow for tucks depends on their width—which may range from a mere 1/8 inch for pin tucks, up to several inches for wide tucks. Directions for both drapes and tucks begin on the opposite page.

STABILIZING DRAPES

A DETERMINING THE ANCHORING POINTS

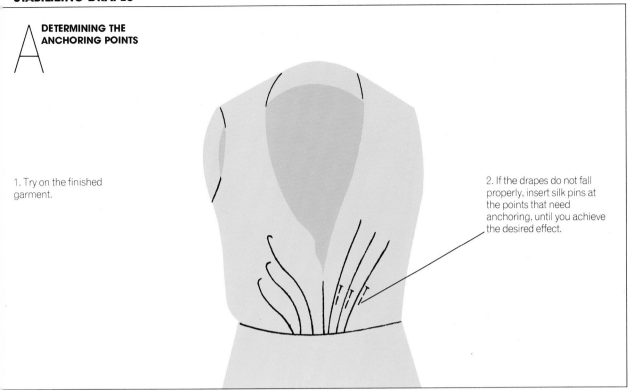

1. Try on the finished garment.

2. If the drapes do not fall properly, insert silk pins at the points that need anchoring, until you achieve the desired effect.

B SECURING THE DRAPES

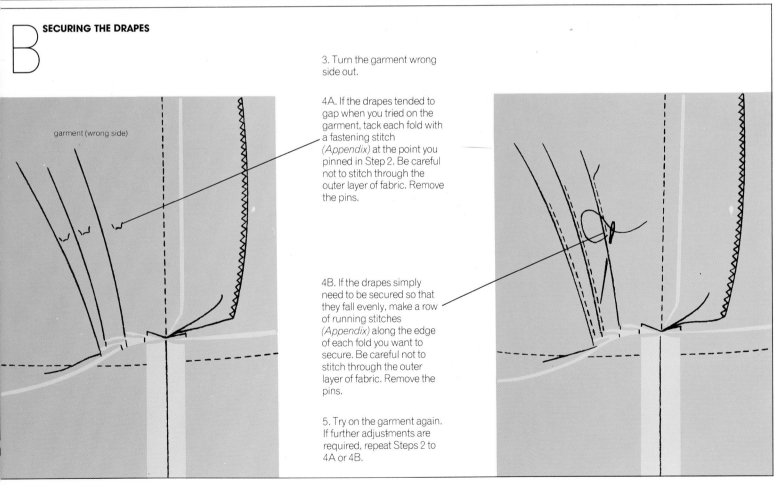

garment (wrong side)

3. Turn the garment wrong side out.

4A. If the drapes tended to gap when you tried on the garment, tack each fold with a fastening stitch (*Appendix*) at the point you pinned in Step 2. Be careful not to stitch through the outer layer of fabric. Remove the pins.

4B. If the drapes simply need to be secured so that they fall evenly, make a row of running stitches (*Appendix*) along the edge of each fold you want to secure. Be careful not to stitch through the outer layer of fabric. Remove the pins.

5. Try on the garment again. If further adjustments are required, repeat Steps 2 to 4A or 4B.

MAKING A TUCKED SAMPLE

A MAKING THE TUCKING GUIDE

1. To determine the marking interval for tucks, first decide how wide you want each tuck to be and how wide you want the space between the stitching lines of the tucks to be. Then double the tuck width and add the width of the space to it.

2. On a piece of stiff paper, such as an index card, measure in from one corner the amount you determined in the preceding step, and make a pencil mark.

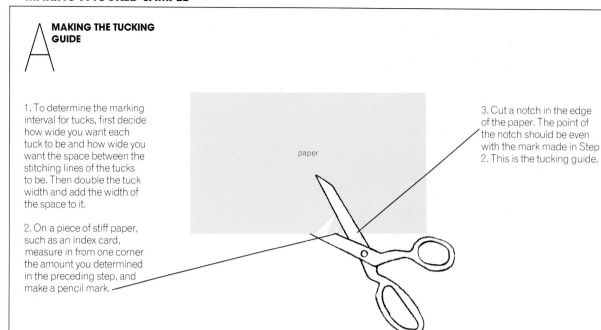

paper

3. Cut a notch in the edge of the paper. The point of the notch should be even with the mark made in Step 2. This is the tucking guide.

B CUTTING AND MARKING THE FABRIC

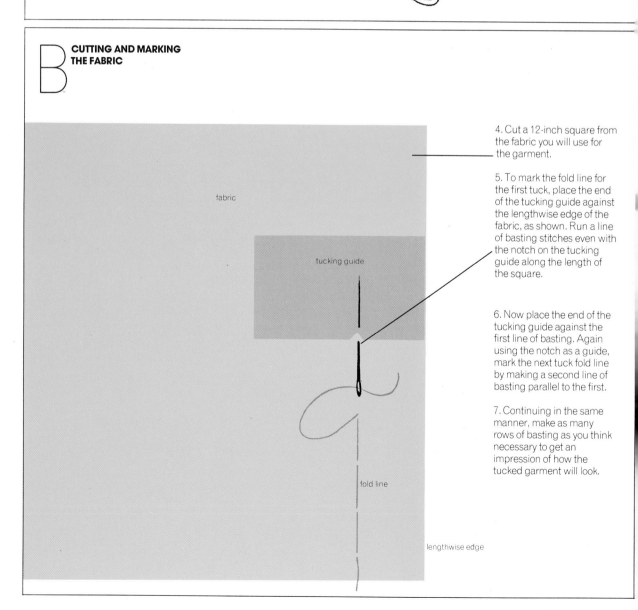

fabric

tucking guide

fold line

lengthwise edge

4. Cut a 12-inch square from the fabric you will use for the garment.

5. To mark the fold line for the first tuck, place the end of the tucking guide against the lengthwise edge of the fabric, as shown. Run a line of basting stitches even with the notch on the tucking guide along the length of the square.

6. Now place the end of the tucking guide against the first line of basting. Again using the notch as a guide, mark the next tuck fold line by making a second line of basting parallel to the first.

7. Continuing in the same manner, make as many rows of basting as you think necessary to get an impression of how the tucked garment will look.

STITCHING THE TUCKS

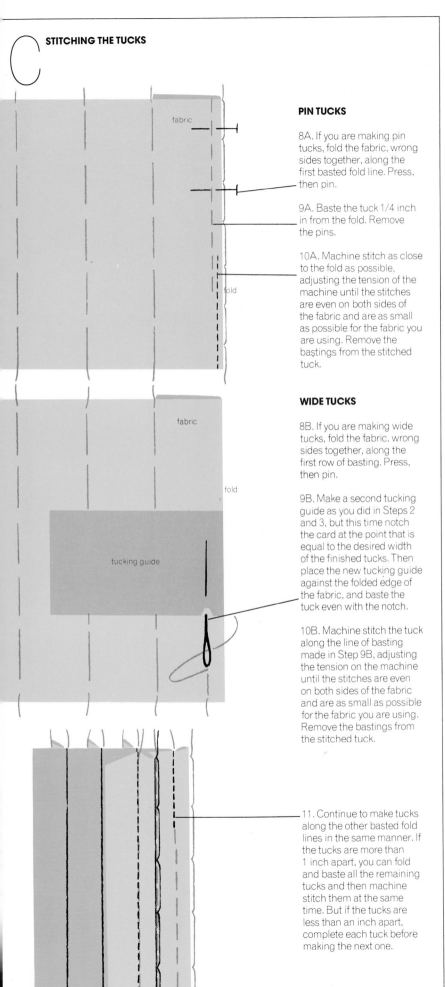

fabric

fold

fabric

fold

tucking guide

PIN TUCKS

8A. If you are making pin tucks, fold the fabric, wrong sides together, along the first basted fold line. Press, then pin.

9A. Baste the tuck 1/4 inch in from the fold. Remove the pins.

10A. Machine stitch as close to the fold as possible, adjusting the tension of the machine until the stitches are even on both sides of the fabric and are as small as possible for the fabric you are using. Remove the bastings from the stitched tuck.

WIDE TUCKS

8B. If you are making wide tucks, fold the fabric, wrong sides together, along the first row of basting. Press, then pin.

9B. Make a second tucking guide as you did in Steps 2 and 3, but this time notch the card at the point that is equal to the desired width of the finished tucks. Then place the new tucking guide against the folded edge of the fabric, and baste the tuck even with the notch.

10B. Machine stitch the tuck along the line of basting made in Step 9B, adjusting the tension on the machine until the stitches are even on both sides of the fabric and are as small as possible for the fabric you are using. Remove the bastings from the stitched tuck.

11. Continue to make tucks along the other basted fold lines in the same manner. If the tucks are more than 1 inch apart, you can fold and baste all the remaining tucks and then machine stitch them at the same time. But if the tucks are less than an inch apart, complete each tuck before making the next one.

PRESSING THE TUCKS

12. When you have finished stitching the tucks, lay the fabric wrong side down and press all of the tucks in one direction. To make a perfect crease along the tuck stitching lines, pull the edge of the fabric away from the iron as you press.

13. Turn the fabric wrong side up. Using a pressing cloth, press the tucks, again all in one direction.

14. Examine the tucks on the sample. If they are not spaced as you want them, make another sample with a different marking interval.

sample
(wrong side)

TUCKING FABRIC BEFORE CUTTING OUT THE GARMENT

A MARKING THE PATTERN

1. To determine the number of tucks you will need and the best size and spacing for them, make a sample, following the instructions on page 62.

2. Decide where on the garment you want the tucks to be.

3. If the area of the pattern piece where the tucks will be was designed to be placed on the fold of the fabric, make a duplicate pattern piece, and tape the two pieces together along the fold line (page 28).

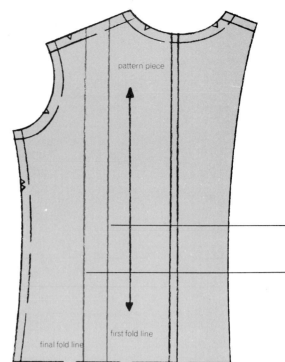

4. Using your tucked sample as a guide, draw a line on the pattern piece where you want the fold of the first tuck to be.

5. Draw a second line where you want the fold of the final tuck to be.

B CUTTING THE FABRIC PIECE

6. Lay a single layer of fabric, wrong side down, on a flat surface. Over it, arrange the pattern piece so that the vertical edge closest to the first tuck fold line is the width of one finished tuck plus 1 inch from the edge of the fabric. Make sure the grain-line arrow is parallel to the selvage. Pin the pattern in place.

7. Mark the fabric with pins 1/2 inch outside the top and bottom edges of the pattern.

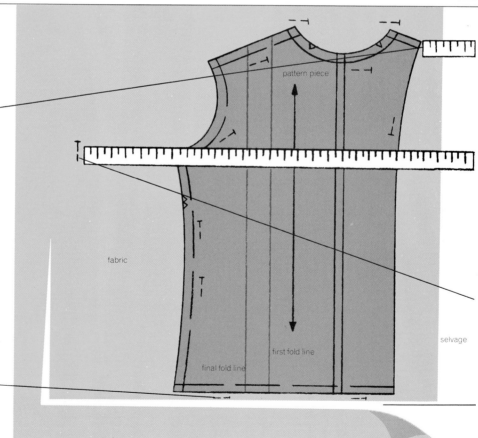

8. To determine how much fabric the tucking will take, first multiply the finished width of a single tuck by two, then multiply this figure by the number of tucks you will be making.

9. At the vertical edge of the pattern nearest the final tuck fold line, measure out from the widest point the distance you determined in Step 8, and mark with pins.

10. Cut the fabric at least 1 inch outside the lines indicated by the pins. Remove the pins along the outer edge of the fabric.

C TUCKING THE FABRIC

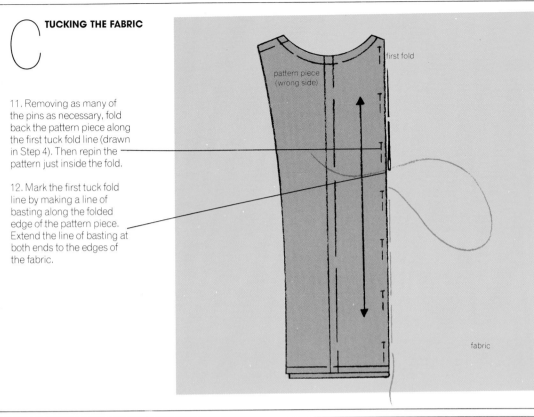

11. Removing as many of the pins as necessary, fold back the pattern piece along the first tuck fold line (drawn in Step 4). Then repin the pattern just inside the fold.

12. Mark the first tuck fold line by making a line of basting along the folded edge of the pattern piece. Extend the line of basting at both ends to the edges of the fabric.

13. Remove the pattern piece from the fabric.

14. Mark the remaining tuck fold lines, and make the tucks in the fabric as you did on the sample.

D CUTTING AND MARKING THE PRETUCKED FABRIC

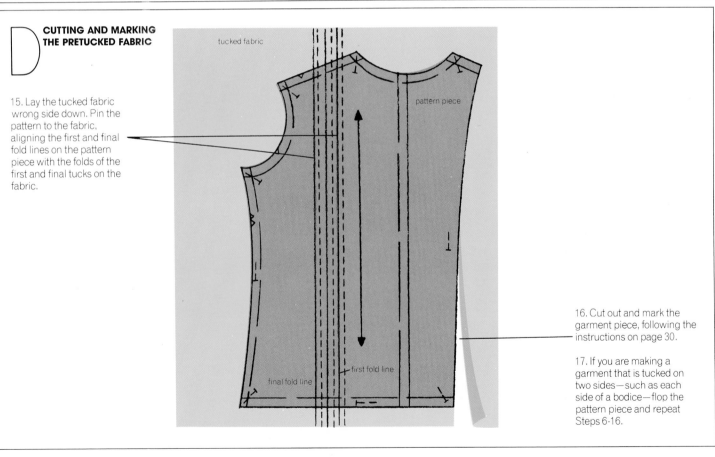

15. Lay the tucked fabric wrong side down. Pin the pattern to the fabric, aligning the first and final fold lines on the pattern piece with the folds of the first and final tucks on the fabric.

16. Cut out and mark the garment piece, following the instructions on page 30.

17. If you are making a garment that is tucked on two sides—such as each side of a bodice—flop the pattern piece and repeat Steps 6-16.

Discreet hems on fine fabrics

An old rule of sewing states that the lighter a fabric, the deeper its hem should be. But this rule breaks down with superdelicate fabrics such as chiffon, crepe de Chine or lace, whose fluid lines would be ruined by deep hems. With these materials, subtler, less obtrusive hemming techniques, like those shown on the following pages, should be used.

A hand-rolled hem, for example, is barely visible on the collar and cuffs of the chiffon jacket shown here. This technique, demonstrated at right, is time consuming, but well worth the effort. A more decorative variation is the hand-overcast shell hem *(page 68)*. More elegant still is the device of finishing edges by adding a lace border—which becomes, in effect, the hem.

A garment with a full skirt does not require such meticulous work, since most of the hem is concealed in the folds of the fabric. Here, a machine-stitched narrow hem *(page 69)* produces satisfactory results.

If the garment has been cut on the bias, hang it up for at least 24 hours before you hem it, so that the fabric will stretch out into its final shape.

THE HAND-ROLLED HEM

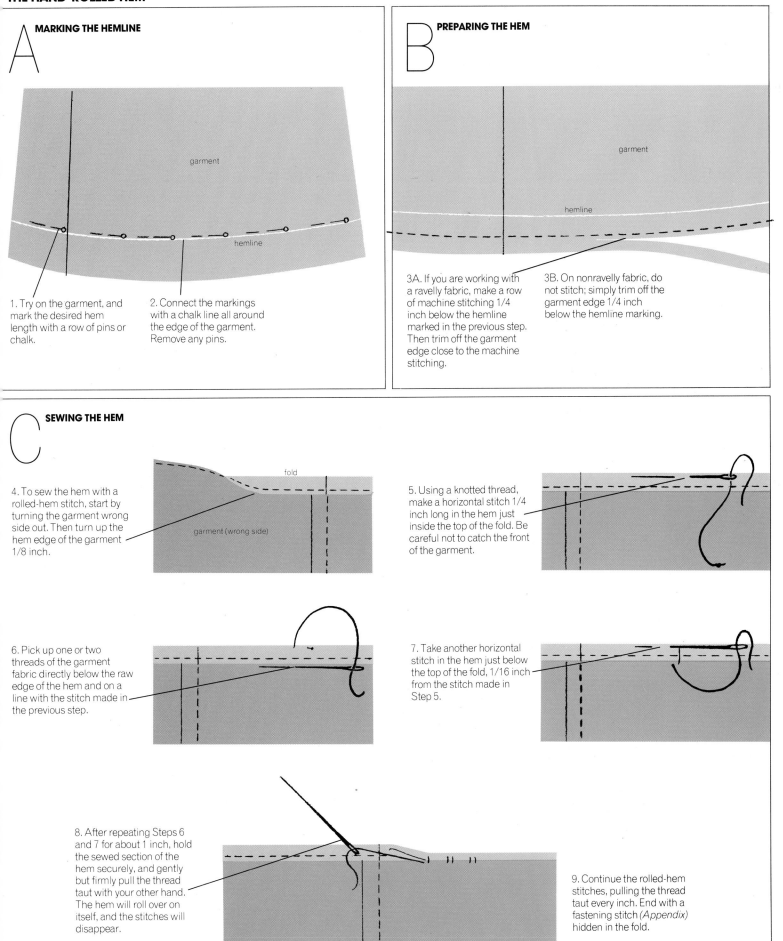

A MARKING THE HEMLINE

garment

hemline

1. Try on the garment, and mark the desired hem length with a row of pins or chalk.

2. Connect the markings with a chalk line all around the edge of the garment. Remove any pins.

B PREPARING THE HEM

garment

hemline

3A. If you are working with a ravelly fabric, make a row of machine stitching 1/4 inch below the hemline marked in the previous step. Then trim off the garment edge close to the machine stitching.

3B. On nonravelly fabric, do not stitch; simply trim off the garment edge 1/4 inch below the hemline marking.

C SEWING THE HEM

fold

garment (wrong side)

4. To sew the hem with a rolled-hem stitch, start by turning the garment wrong side out. Then turn up the hem edge of the garment 1/8 inch.

5. Using a knotted thread, make a horizontal stitch 1/4 inch long in the hem just inside the top of the fold. Be careful not to catch the front of the garment.

6. Pick up one or two threads of the garment fabric directly below the raw edge of the hem and on a line with the stitch made in the previous step.

7. Take another horizontal stitch in the hem just below the top of the fold, 1/16 inch from the stitch made in Step 5.

8. After repeating Steps 6 and 7 for about 1 inch, hold the sewed section of the hem securely, and gently but firmly pull the thread taut with your other hand. The hem will roll over on itself, and the stitches will disappear.

9. Continue the rolled-hem stitches, pulling the thread taut every inch. End with a fastening stitch (Appendix) hidden in the fold.

THE OVERCAST SHELL HEM

A TURNING UP THE HEM

1. Mark the hemline, following the instructions for the hand-rolled hem *(page 67, Boxes A and B).*

2. Turn the garment wrong side out. Turn up the hem edge 1/8 inch, and press it flat.

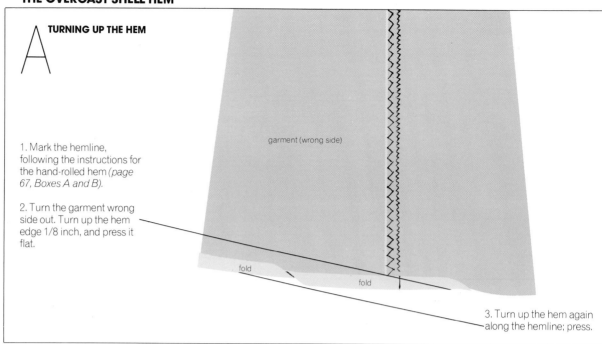

garment (wrong side)

fold

fold

3. Turn up the hem again along the hemline; press.

B SEWING THE HEM

4. Using a knotted double thread, insert the needle in the garment fabric from the wrong side. Make sure to insert it just below the hem so that the knot will be concealed inside the hem. Pull the needle through.

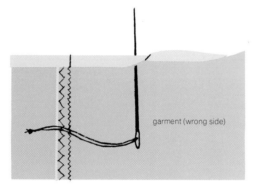

garment (wrong side)

5. Bring the needle over the hem to the wrong side, and insert it at the inside folded hem edge 1/4 inch from the point that it was inserted in Step 4. Go through all thicknesses of fabric, but do not pull the needle through.

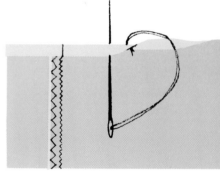

6. Angle the needle and bring the tip over the top of the hem. Then insert it —again at the inside folded hem edge—1/4 inch from the previous stitch. It will pull the fabric down, creating a scalloped effect. Do not pull the needle all the way through the fabric.

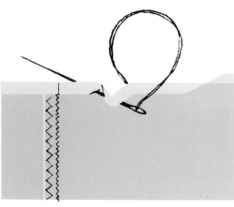

7. Repeat Step 6 one or two times, weaving the needle over and then back into the hem.

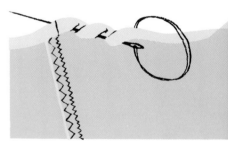

8. Pull the needle through the fabric to complete the first series of stitches. You are now ready to begin the next series of stitches.

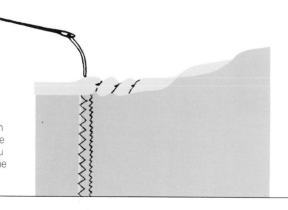

9. Continue to repeat Steps 5-8, pulling the stitches tight after each series of stitches, until you have formed a shell-shaped scallop around the hem edge. End with a fastening stitch *(Appendix)* hidden in the fold.

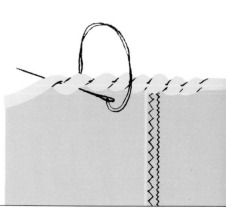

THE MACHINE-STITCHED NARROW HEM ON SHEER FABRICS

A PREPARING THE HEM

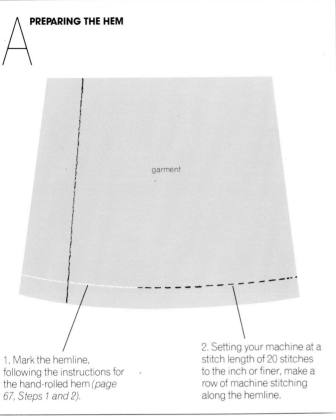

garment

1. Mark the hemline, following the instructions for the hand-rolled hem (page 67, Steps 1 and 2).

2. Setting your machine at a stitch length of 20 stitches to the inch or finer, make a row of machine stitching along the hemline.

B SEWING THE HEM

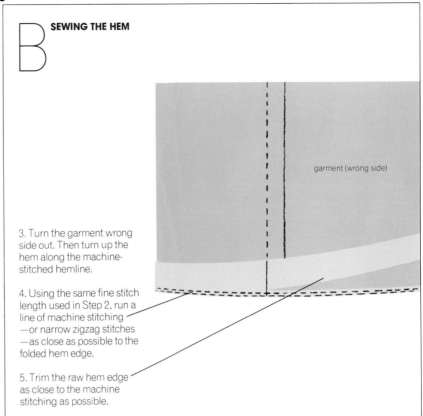

garment (wrong side)

3. Turn the garment wrong side out. Then turn up the hem along the machine-stitched hemline.

4. Using the same fine stitch length used in Step 2, run a line of machine stitching —or narrow zigzag stitches —as close as possible to the folded hem edge.

5. Trim the raw hem edge as close to the machine stitching as possible.

THE MACHINE-STITCHED NARROW HEM ON FINE KNITS

A PREPARING THE HEM

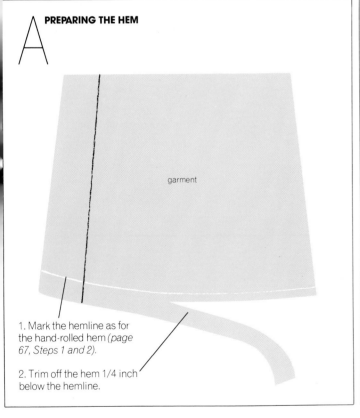

garment

1. Mark the hemline as for the hand-rolled hem (page 67, Steps 1 and 2).

2. Trim off the hem 1/4 inch below the hemline.

B SEWING THE HEM

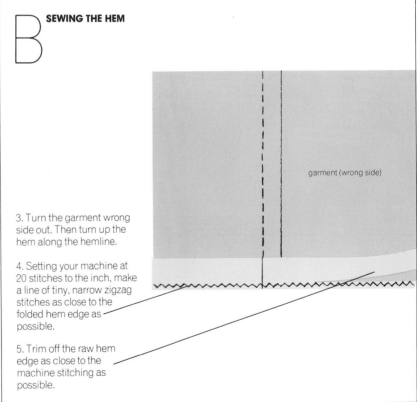

garment (wrong side)

3. Turn the garment wrong side out. Then turn up the hem along the hemline.

4. Setting your machine at 20 stitches to the inch, make a line of tiny, narrow zigzag stitches as close to the folded hem edge as possible.

5. Trim off the raw hem edge as close to the machine stitching as possible.

THE LACE HEM WITH A CURVED UPPER EDGE

A PREPARING THE HEM AND THE LACE

1. Mark the hemline, following the instructions for the hand-rolled hem (page 67, Steps 1 and 2).

2. Trim off the hem 1/4 inch below the hemline.

3. Measure the circumference of the hem along the trimmed edge.

4. Following the instructions for lace seams on page 53, cut a strip of lace and join the ends so that you have one continuous circular strip equal to the circumference of the hem measured in Step 3.

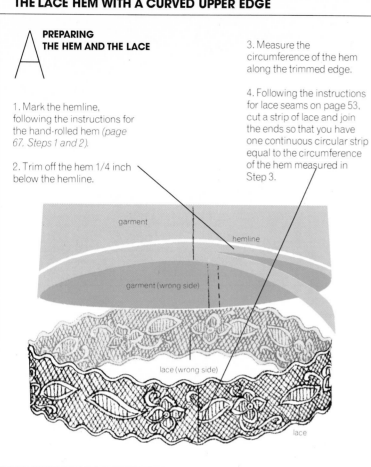

B ATTACHING THE LACE

5. Turn up the hem along the hemline so that the hem is against the outside of the garment. Press the hem flat.

6. Pin the lace over the hem so that the upper edge of the lace just conceals the raw hem edge. Pin at 1-inch intervals, and match the lace seam with a garment seam.

7. Sew along the upper edge of the lace, going through all fabric thicknesses. To machine stitch, use a setting of 15 to 20 stitches to the inch. To hand sew, use a prick stitch (Appendix). Remove the pins as you sew.

THE LACE HEM WITH A STRAIGHT UPPER EDGE

A ATTACHING THE LACE

1. Prepare the hem and the lace strip, following the instructions for the lace hem with a curved upper edge (above, Steps 1-4).

2. Turn the garment wrong side out. Turn the lace strip right side out and slip it over the hem edge of the garment, wrong sides together.

3. Align the straight edge of the lace with the raw edge of the hem; pin at 1-inch intervals. Match the lace seam with a garment seam.

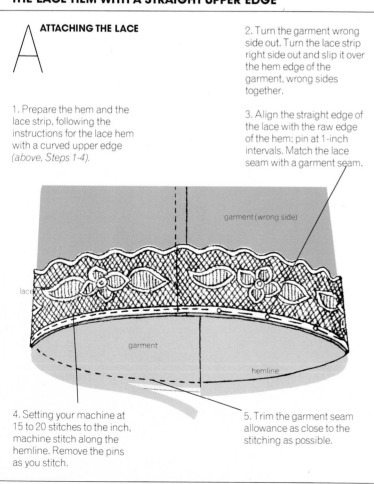

4. Setting your machine at 15 to 20 stitches to the inch, machine stitch along the hemline. Remove the pins as you stitch.

5. Trim the garment seam allowance as close to the stitching as possible.

B FINISHING THE HEM

6. Turn the garment right side out, and fold down the lace so that it is away from the garment.

7. Sew along the straight edge of the lace, going through all fabric thicknesses. To machine stitch, use the same fine setting used in Step 4. To hand sew, use a prick stitch.

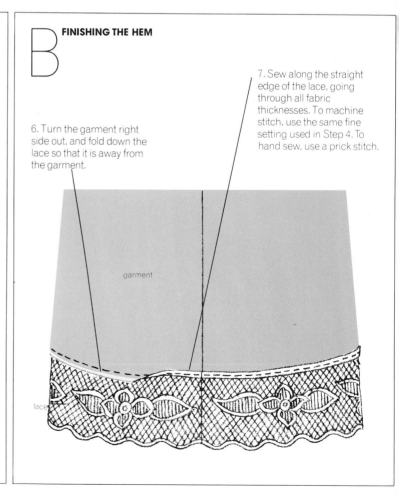

HEMMING A LACE GARMENT WITH A LACE BORDER

A | BASTING THE BORDER IN POSITION

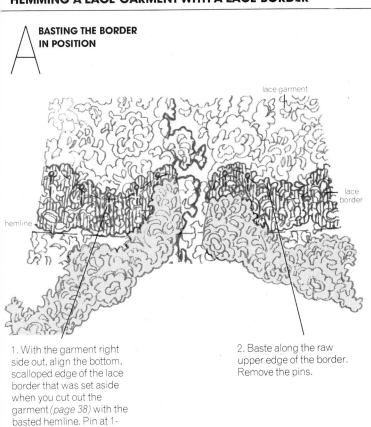

1. With the garment right side out, align the bottom, scalloped edge of the lace border that was set aside when you cut out the garment *(page 38)* with the basted hemline. Pin at 1-inch intervals, leaving the end of the border free.

2. Baste along the raw upper edge of the border. Remove the pins.

B | STITCHING THE BORDER

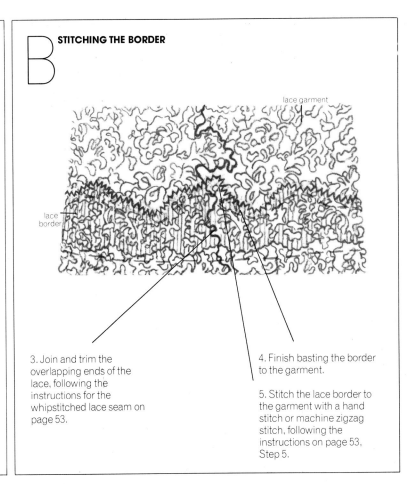

3. Join and trim the overlapping ends of the lace, following the instructions for the whipstitched lace seam on page 53.

4. Finish basting the border to the garment.

5. Stitch the lace border to the garment with a hand stitch or machine zigzag stitch, following the instructions on page 53, Step 5.

HEMMING AN UNDERLINED LACE GARMENT

A | PREPARING THE GARMENT

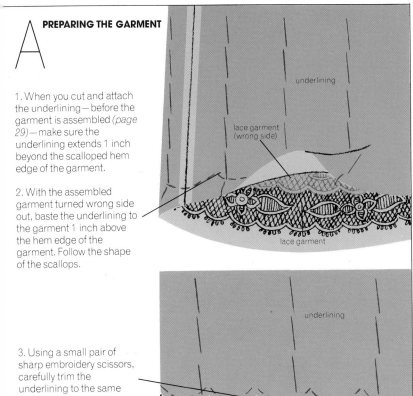

1. When you cut and attach the underlining—before the garment is assembled *(page 29)*—make sure the underlining extends 1 inch beyond the scalloped hem edge of the garment.

2. With the assembled garment turned wrong side out, baste the underlining to the garment 1 inch above the hem edge of the garment. Follow the shape of the scallops.

3. Using a small pair of sharp embroidery scissors, carefully trim the underlining to the same length as the garment. Follow the scalloped shape of the garment edge.

B | SEWING THE HEM

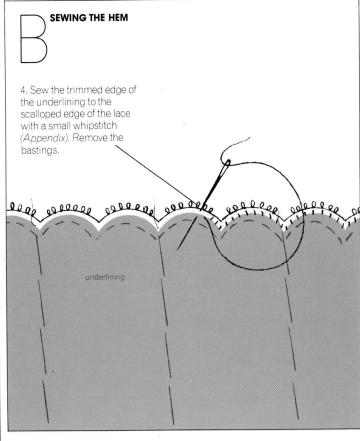

4. Sew the trimmed edge of the underlining to the scalloped edge of the lace with a small whipstitch *(Appendix)*. Remove the bastings.

Halters—decorous and daring

All halters look feminine—and sexy. Whether they conceal or reveal, however, depends on the fabric from which they are made and the way the halters are cut and lined (if at all).

This crossover halter top, for example, might be made of any delicate fabric soft enough to drape fluidly. Simple but sophisticated, the halter is made of a pair of panels that hug the neck on each side, cross demurely in front, then wrap around to the back on opposite sides. Here, the style is shown in two colors of chiffon that alternately complement and merge with one another. Chiffon underlining accentuates the sheer look of the halter, while a heavier silk lining hides the seams and prevents a complete see-through.

By comparison, the equally simple drawstring-gathered halter looks as seductively slinky as lingerie when made of clinging knits like jersey or tricot. Yet the styling is deceptively prim—a triangle of cloth scooped out at the neckline and held up in back by an elastic casing. Instructions for both halters appear on the following pages.

THE CROSSOVER HALTER

A ALTERING THE HALTER FRONT PATTERN

1. Make a duplicate of the halter front pattern piece, following the instructions on page 28. Mark the appropriate halter front pattern pieces "right" and "left."

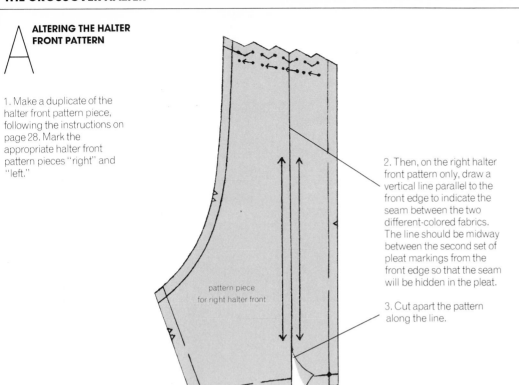

pattern piece for right halter front

2. Then, on the right halter front pattern only, draw a vertical line parallel to the front edge to indicate the seam between the two different-colored fabrics. The line should be midway between the second set of pleat markings from the front edge so that the seam will be hidden in the pleat.

3. Cut apart the pattern along the line.

B CUTTING AND UNDERLINING THE HALTER PIECES

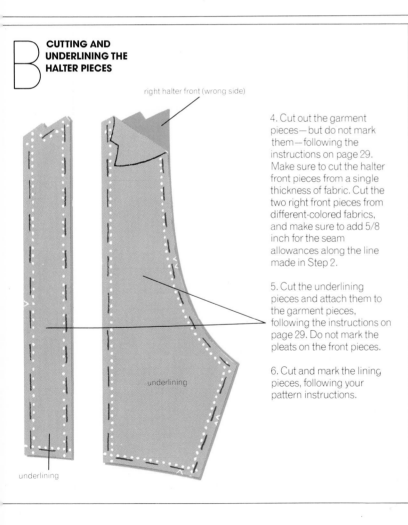

right halter front (wrong side)

underlining

underlining

4. Cut out the garment pieces—but do not mark them—following the instructions on page 29. Make sure to cut the halter front pieces from a single thickness of fabric. Cut the two right front pieces from different-colored fabrics, and make sure to add 5/8 inch for the seam allowances along the line made in Step 2.

5. Cut the underlining pieces and attach them to the garment pieces, following the instructions on page 29. Do not mark the pleats on the front pieces.

6. Cut and mark the lining pieces, following your pattern instructions.

C JOINING THE TWO DIFFERENT-COLORED FABRICS ON THE RIGHT HALTER FRONT

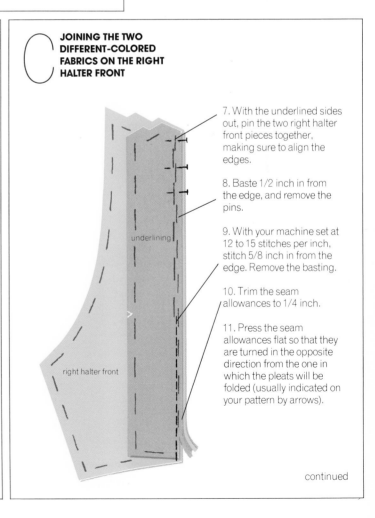

underlining

right halter front

7. With the underlined sides out, pin the two right halter front pieces together, making sure to align the edges.

8. Baste 1/2 inch in from the edge, and remove the pins.

9. With your machine set at 12 to 15 stitches per inch, stitch 5/8 inch in from the edge. Remove the basting.

10. Trim the seam allowances to 1/4 inch.

11. Press the seam allowances flat so that they are turned in the opposite direction from the one in which the pleats will be folded (usually indicated on your pattern by arrows).

continued

73

D ▶ PREPARING THE HALTER FRONT

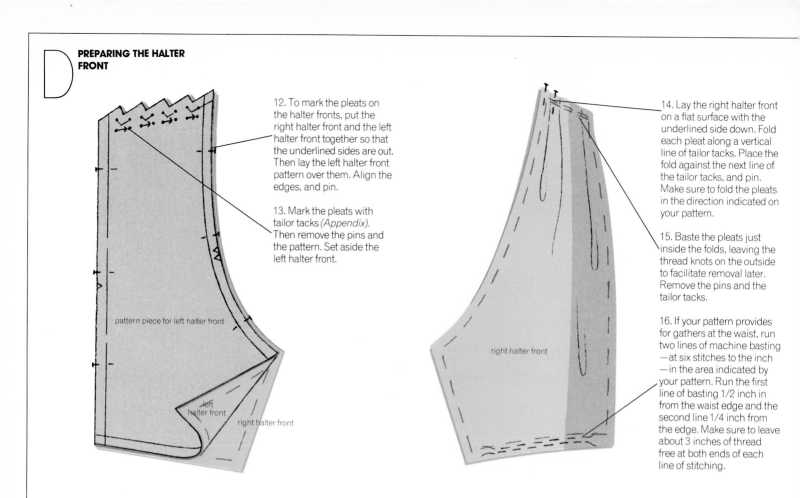

12. To mark the pleats on the halter fronts, put the right halter front and the left halter front together so that the underlined sides are out. Then lay the left halter front pattern over them. Align the edges, and pin.

13. Mark the pleats with tailor tacks (Appendix). Then remove the pins and the pattern. Set aside the left halter front.

pattern piece for left halter front

left halter front

right halter front

14. Lay the right halter front on a flat surface with the underlined side down. Fold each pleat along a vertical line of tailor tacks. Place the fold against the next line of the tailor tacks, and pin. Make sure to fold the pleats in the direction indicated on your pattern.

15. Baste the pleats just inside the folds, leaving the thread knots on the outside to facilitate removal later. Remove the pins and the tailor tacks.

16. If your pattern provides for gathers at the waist, run two lines of machine basting —at six stitches to the inch —in the area indicated by your pattern. Run the first line of basting 1/2 inch in from the waist edge and the second line 1/4 inch from the edge. Make sure to leave about 3 inches of thread free at both ends of each line of stitching.

right halter front

E ▶ JOINING THE HALTER FRONT AND THE HALTER BACK

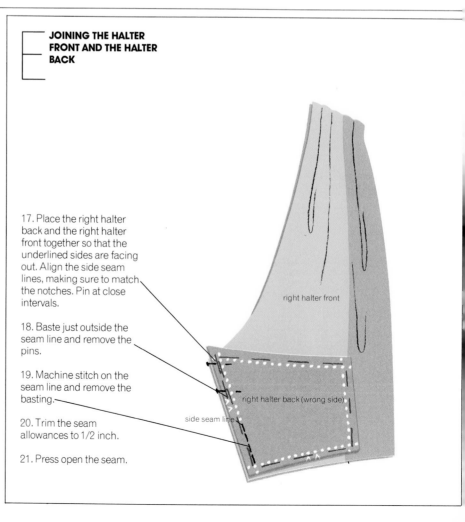

17. Place the right halter back and the right halter front together so that the underlined sides are facing out. Align the side seam lines, making sure to match the notches. Pin at close intervals.

18. Baste just outside the seam line and remove the pins.

19. Machine stitch on the seam line and remove the basting.

20. Trim the seam allowances to 1/2 inch.

21. Press open the seam.

right halter front

right halter back (wrong side)

side seam line

F PREPARING THE LINING

22. Close the dart on the right-front lining piece by folding the dart in half so that the wrong sides are out. Align the dart stitching lines, and pin.

23. Baste just outside the stitching lines and remove the pins.

24. Machine stitch on the dart stitching line. Remove the basting.

25. Trim the dart seam allowances to 1/4 inch. Clip the lower pointed end up to —but not through—the line of stitching.

26. Press open the seam.

27. Attach the right halter front lining and the right halter back lining by repeating Steps 17-21.

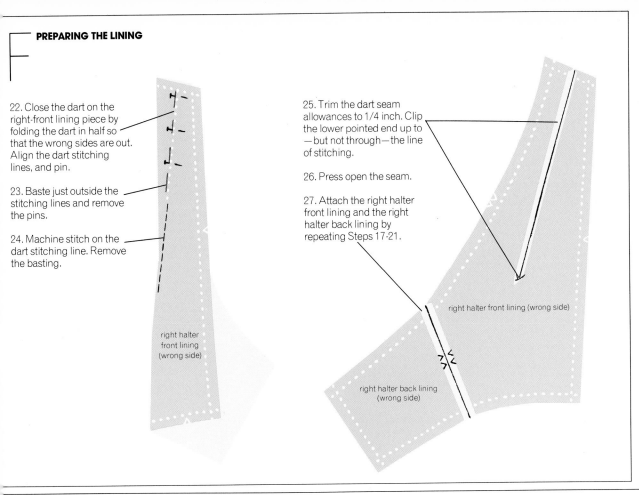

right halter front lining (wrong side)

right halter front lining (wrong side)

right halter back lining (wrong side)

G LINING THE HALTER

28. Lay the assembled right half of the halter wrong side down. Over it, lay the assembled right half of the lining wrong side up. Align the front, top-back and underarm seam lines, matching the side seams and notches. Pin at close intervals along the seam lines.

29. Baste just outside the seam lines, making sure not to catch any excess fullness in the halter fabric. Remove the pins.

30. Machine stitch on the seam lines, pivoting (Appendix) at the corners.

31. Trim the seam allowances to 1/4 inch, and cut the corners diagonally.

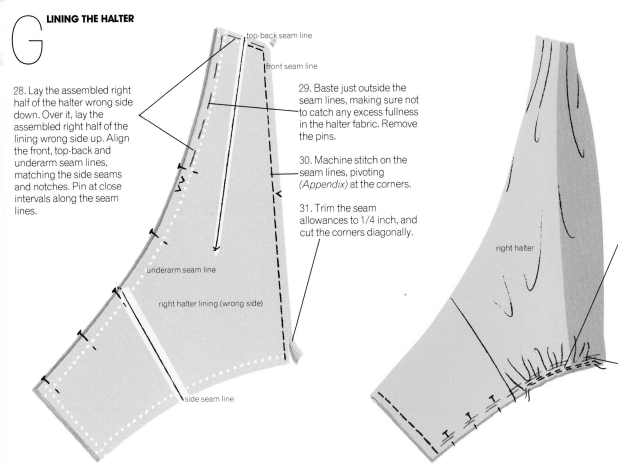

top-back seam line

front seam line

underarm seam line

right halter lining (wrong side)

side seam line

right halter

32. Turn the halter right side out. Pull out the corners with a needle.

33. Remove the bastings on the pleats.

34. Roll the seamed edges between your fingers to bring the stitching out to the edge. Lightly press the edges.

35. If the halter front is to have gathers at the waist edge, pull the loose bobbin threads at both ends of the double row of machine basting made in Step 16. Gather the fullness in the halter front until it is the same width as the lining. Make sure the gathers are evenly distributed.

36. Pin the waist edge to the lining.

37. Baste 1/2 inch from the edge, adjusting the gathers to distribute them evenly. Remove the pins.

38. Make the left half of the halter by repeating Steps 14-37.

continued

H ATTACHING THE HALTER

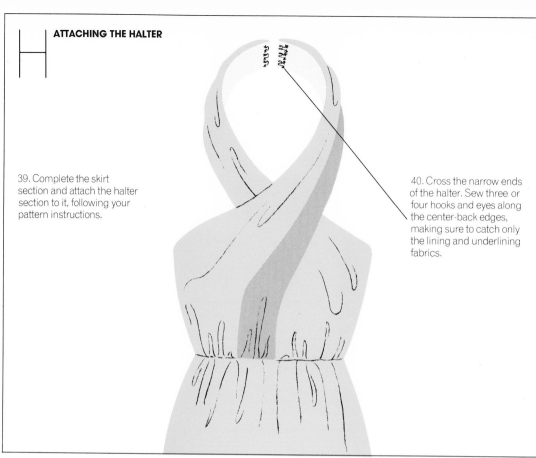

39. Complete the skirt section and attach the halter section to it, following your pattern instructions.

40. Cross the narrow ends of the halter. Sew three or four hooks and eyes along the center-back edges, making sure to catch only the lining and underlining fabrics.

THE DRAWSTRING-GATHERED HALTER

A PREPARING THE GARMENT

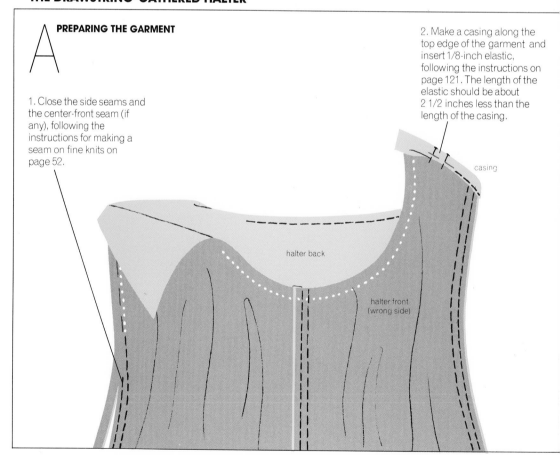

1. Close the side seams and the center-front seam (if any), following the instructions for making a seam on fine knits on page 52.

2. Make a casing along the top edge of the garment and insert 1/8-inch elastic, following the instructions on page 121. The length of the elastic should be about 2 1/2 inches less than the length of the casing.

casing

halter back

halter front (wrong side)

B MAKING THE CASING FOR THE DRAWSTRING

3. To determine the length of the casing, measure along the curved edge of the opening in the garment front, then add 1 1/2 inches.

4. Cut a 1 3/8-inch-wide bias strip *(page 30)* from garment fabric, using the length you determined in Step 3.

5. Turn the garment right side out.

6. Pin the bias strip, wrong side up, along the curved edge of the opening in the garment front. As you pin, ease the strip in along the curve. Make sure the ends of the strip extend 1/2 inch beyond the top garment edges.

7. Baste 1/2 inch in from the curved edge, and remove the pins.

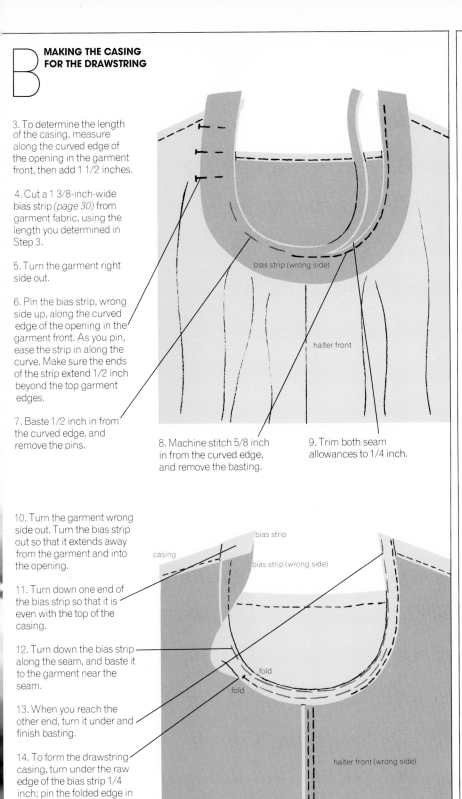

bias strip (wrong side)

halter front

8. Machine stitch 5/8 inch in from the curved edge, and remove the basting.

9. Trim both seam allowances to 1/4 inch.

10. Turn the garment wrong side out. Turn the bias strip out so that it extends away from the garment and into the opening.

11. Turn down one end of the bias strip so that it is even with the top of the casing.

12. Turn down the bias strip along the seam, and baste it to the garment near the seam.

13. When you reach the other end, turn it under and finish basting.

14. To form the drawstring casing, turn under the raw edge of the bias strip 1/4 inch; pin the folded edge in place. Be sure the distance between the two folded edges is 1/2 inch so that the casing will be wide enough to accommodate the drawstring.

15. Baste close to the second folded edge; remove the pins.

casing

bias strip

bias strip (wrong side)

fold

fold

halter front (wrong side)

16. Machine stitch close to the second folded edge. Remove both bastings.

17. Lightly press the casing.

C FINISHING THE HALTER

18. To make the drawstring for the halter, prepare 1/4-inch-wide tubing from your garment fabric, following the instructions for making straps *(page 117, Steps 2-7, 8B-9B)*. The drawstring should be the length your pattern suggests.

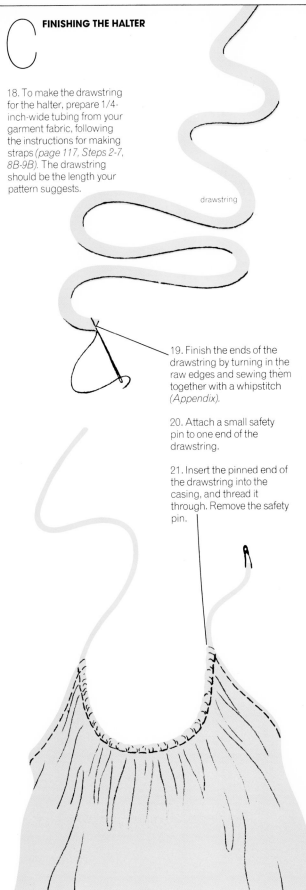

drawstring

19. Finish the ends of the drawstring by turning in the raw edges and sewing them together with a whipstitch *(Appendix)*.

20. Attach a small safety pin to one end of the drawstring.

21. Insert the pinned end of the drawstring into the casing, and thread it through. Remove the safety pin.

A beguiling range of necklines

With flattery but no fuss, collarless necklines underscore the obvious femininity of fragile fabrics. And such styles as cowl, jewel and tie necklines also eliminate facings that would be obtrusive under transparent or translucent materials.

The graceful cowl neck shown here in chiffon, for example, allows a supple fabric to drape itself spontaneously. The fluid folds are supported by underlining and anchored permanently by an unseen interior weight—a dime-sized metal disk sewed beneath the dip in front.

On the other hand, a jewel neckline arranges the fabric with prim formality that emphasizes the texture and finish of crisp and shiny fabrics as well as that of softer cloth. Bias binding makes facing the edge of the neckline unnecessary.

For more swagger, the jewel neckline can be produced with a front slit and a narrow neckband that ties into a bow in front. And on garments with front buttons, the neckline can flaunt a wide tie that makes a crisp bow in organdy, but a softly flowing one in silk or georgette. Instructions for all these necklines appear opposite and on the following pages.

THE COWL NECKLINE

A PREPARING THE GARMENT PIECES

1. Attach the underlinings to the bodice front and both bodice back sections, following the instructions on page 29.

2. On the front and both back bodice sections, mark the neck facing fold line with a row of basting stitches.

3. Lay one of the back pieces on a flat surface with the underlining side facing up.

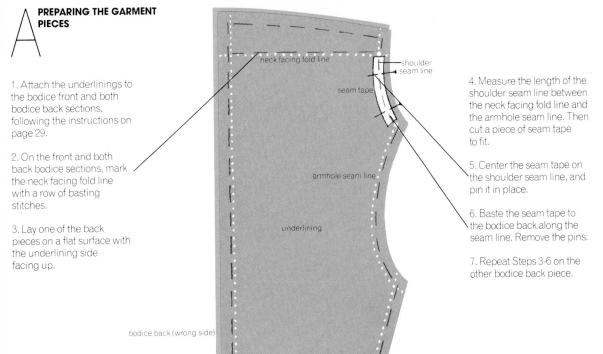

neck facing fold line

shoulder seam line

seam tape

armhole seam line

underlining

bodice back (wrong side)

4. Measure the length of the shoulder seam line between the neck facing fold line and the armhole seam line. Then cut a piece of seam tape to fit.

5. Center the seam tape on the shoulder seam line, and pin it in place.

6. Baste the seam tape to the bodice back along the seam line. Remove the pins.

7. Repeat Steps 3-6 on the other bodice back piece.

B PREPARING THE FACING

8. Assemble the bodice by first closing the shoulder seams and then closing the side seams.

9. Insert a zipper or other closure.

10. To prevent the edges of the neck facing from stretching as you work, run a line of machine stitching 1/4 inch in from the raw edges of the facing.

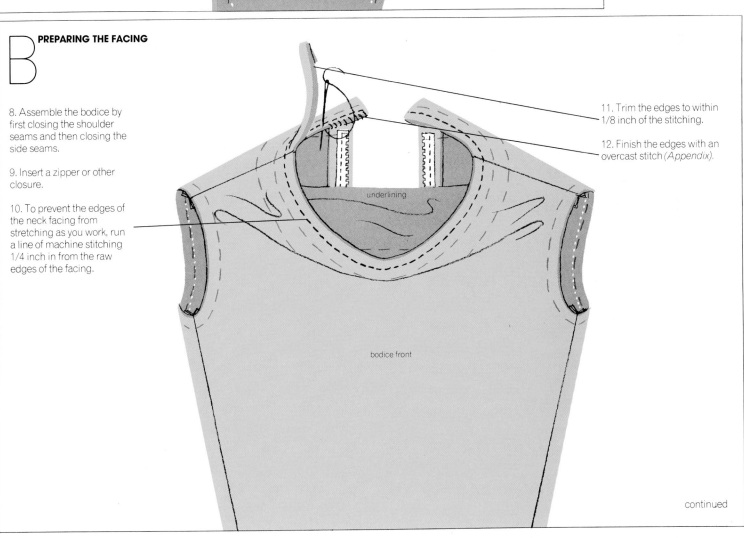

underlining

bodice front

11. Trim the edges to within 1/8 inch of the stitching.

12. Finish the edges with an overcast stitch (Appendix).

continued

C ATTACHING THE FACING

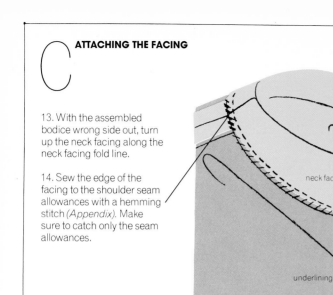

13. With the assembled bodice wrong side out, turn up the neck facing along the neck facing fold line.

14. Sew the edge of the facing to the shoulder seam allowances with a hemming stitch (*Appendix*). Make sure to catch only the seam allowances.

15. Turn under the center-back edges of the facing so that the folds are 1/8 inch from the zipper teeth.

16. Sew the folded edge to the zipper tape only, using slip stitches (*Appendix*).

D FINISHING THE COWL NECKLINE

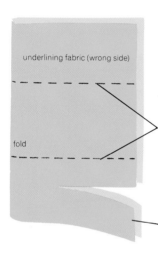

17. Cut a small piece of underlining fabric large enough to cover the weight and to allow for stitching.

18. Fold the fabric piece in half, wrong sides out.

19. Run two parallel lines of machine stitching at right angles to the fold. Make sure the lines of stitching are far enough apart to allow the weight to slip between them.

20. Trim the seam allowances to 1/8 inch.

21. Turn the weight cover right side out, and press.

22. Trim the raw edges of the cover so that it is about 1/4 inch longer than the weight.

23. Slip the weight into the cover.

24. Turn in the raw edges 1/8 inch and sew them together with a slip stitch.

25. Sew the corner of the covered weight to the edge of the neck facing at the center front by making several fastening stitches (*Appendix*).

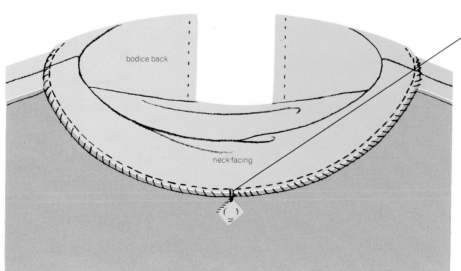

ADDING A HOOK WITH A THREAD EYE

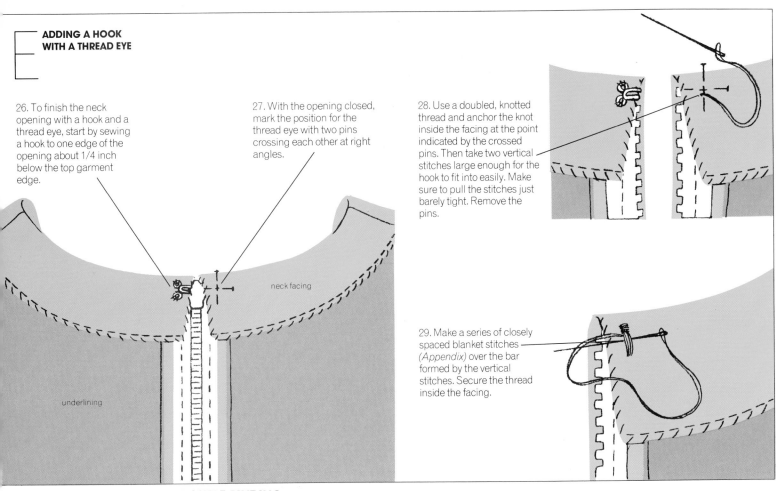

26. To finish the neck opening with a hook and a thread eye, start by sewing a hook to one edge of the opening about 1/4 inch below the top garment edge.

27. With the opening closed, mark the position for the thread eye with two pins crossing each other at right angles.

28. Use a doubled, knotted thread and anchor the knot inside the facing at the point indicated by the crossed pins. Then take two vertical stitches large enough for the hook to fit into easily. Make sure to pull the stitches just barely tight. Remove the pins.

29. Make a series of closely spaced blanket stitches (Appendix) over the bar formed by the vertical stitches. Secure the thread inside the facing.

neck facing

underlining

THE JEWEL NECKLINE WITH DOUBLE BINDING

A PREPARING THE GARMENT BODICE

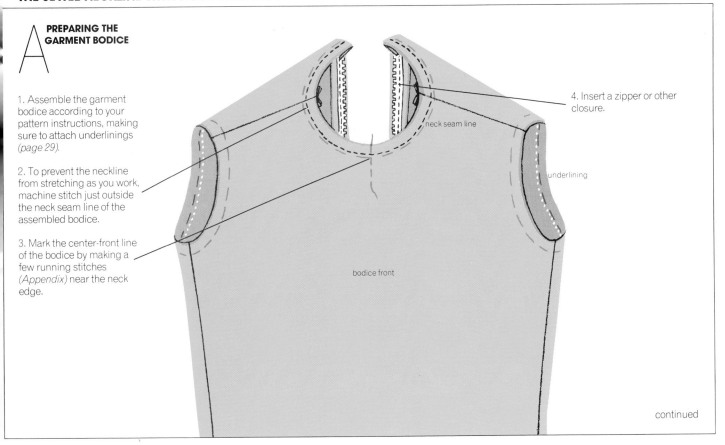

1. Assemble the garment bodice according to your pattern instructions, making sure to attach underlinings (page 29).

2. To prevent the neckline from stretching as you work, machine stitch just outside the neck seam line of the assembled bodice.

3. Mark the center-front line of the bodice by making a few running stitches (Appendix) near the neck edge.

4. Insert a zipper or other closure.

neck seam line

underlining

bodice front

continued

B PREPARING THE BINDING

5. To determine the length of the binding, measure the neck seam line on the bodice, then add 1 inch for finishing the ends.

6. To determine the width of the binding, multiply the desired finished width —usually between 1/4 and 1/2 inch— by six, then add 1/4 inch to allow for stretching and turning.

7. Cut a bias strip *(page 30)*, using the length you determined in Step 5 and the width you determined in Step 6.

8. Fold the strip in half lengthwise so that the wrong sides are together. Press lightly.

9. To aid in positioning the binding on the bodice, measure and mark the middle of the binding on the folded edge with a tailor tack *(Appendix)*.

10. Turn up both long edges of the strip so that they overlap, forming a band of the desired final width. Turn up the raw edges first and then the tailor-tacked edge. Press.

11. Using an iron, press the binding into a circular shape about the size of the garment neckline. Make sure the tailor-tacked edge is on the outside.

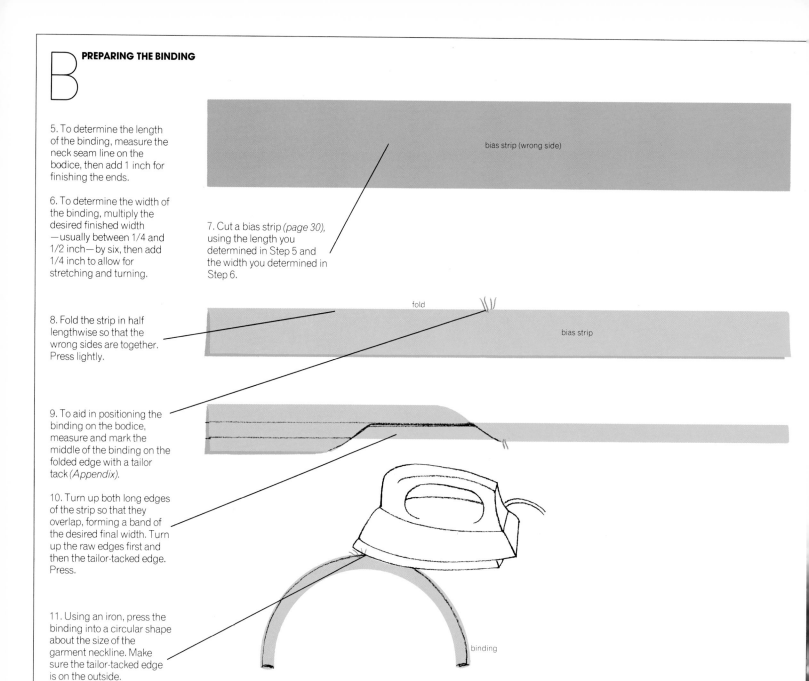

bias strip (wrong side)

fold

bias strip

binding

C ATTACHING THE BINDING

12. Open the binding along the folds made in Step 9.

13. With the bodice turned right side out, pin the binding to the bodice so that the crease nearest the raw edges is aligned with the neck seam line. Make sure to match the center-front markings.

14. Baste along the seam line and remove the pins.

15. Machine stitch along the seam line. Remove the basting.

16. Trim the garment seam allowances even with the edge of the binding.

17. Clip the bodice seam allowances diagonally at the corners.

18. Trim the ends of the binding to within 1/4 inch of the bodice edge at the zipper opening.

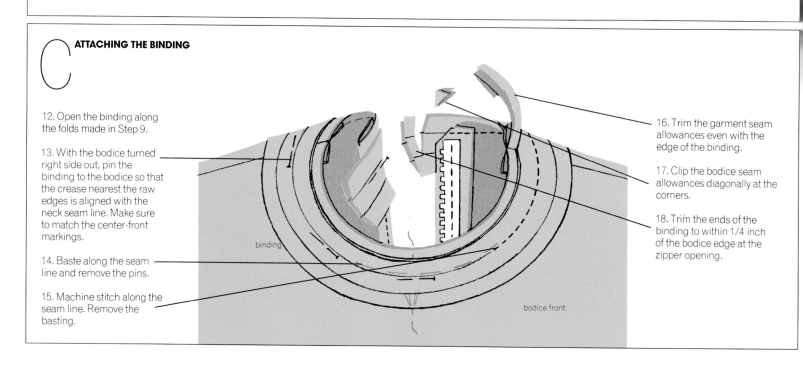

binding

bodice front

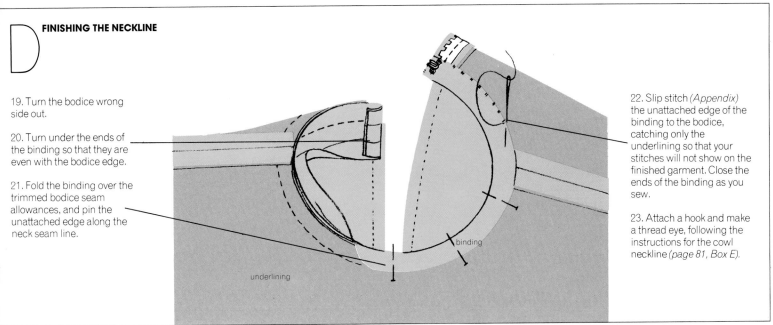

D FINISHING THE NECKLINE

19. Turn the bodice wrong side out.

20. Turn under the ends of the binding so that they are even with the bodice edge.

21. Fold the binding over the trimmed bodice seam allowances, and pin the unattached edge along the neck seam line.

underlining

binding

22. Slip stitch (Appendix) the unattached edge of the binding to the bodice, catching only the underlining so that your stitches will not show on the finished garment. Close the ends of the binding as you sew.

23. Attach a hook and make a thread eye, following the instructions for the cowl neckline (page 81, Box E).

THE SLIT JEWEL NECKLINE WITH A TIE

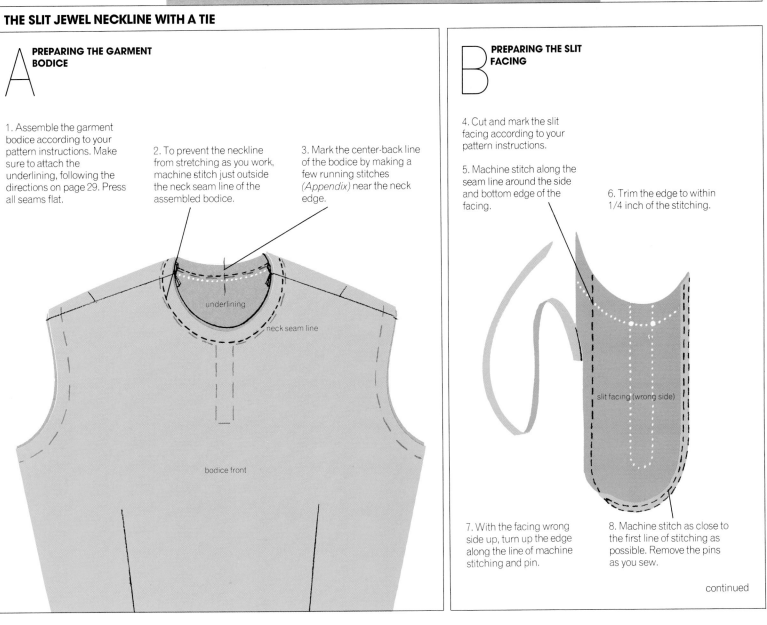

A PREPARING THE GARMENT BODICE

1. Assemble the garment bodice according to your pattern instructions. Make sure to attach the underlining, following the directions on page 29. Press all seams flat.

2. To prevent the neckline from stretching as you work, machine stitch just outside the neck seam line of the assembled bodice.

3. Mark the center-back line of the bodice by making a few running stitches (Appendix) near the neck edge.

underlining

neck seam line

bodice front

B PREPARING THE SLIT FACING

4. Cut and mark the slit facing according to your pattern instructions.

5. Machine stitch along the seam line around the side and bottom edge of the facing.

6. Trim the edge to within 1/4 inch of the stitching.

slit facing (wrong side)

7. With the facing wrong side up, turn up the edge along the line of machine stitching and pin.

8. Machine stitch as close to the first line of stitching as possible. Remove the pins as you sew.

continued

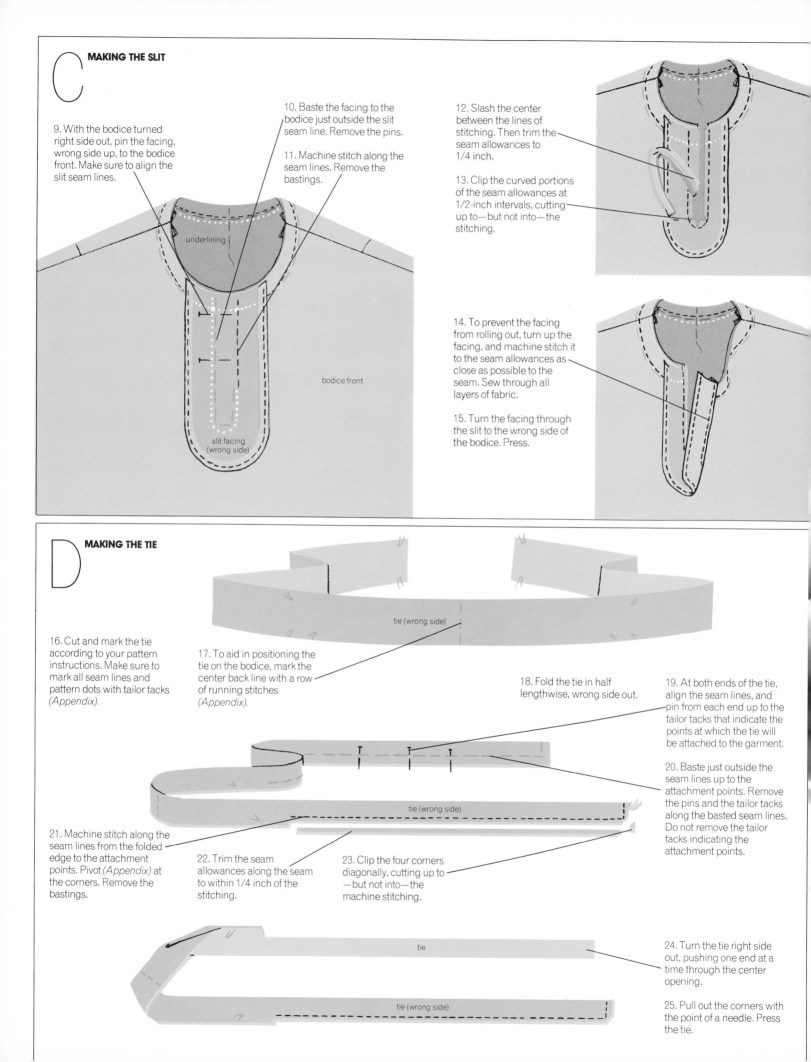

C MAKING THE SLIT

9. With the bodice turned right side out, pin the facing, wrong side up, to the bodice front. Make sure to align the slit seam lines.

10. Baste the facing to the bodice just outside the slit seam line. Remove the pins.

11. Machine stitch along the seam lines. Remove the bastings.

12. Slash the center between the lines of stitching. Then trim the seam allowances to 1/4 inch.

13. Clip the curved portions of the seam allowances at 1/2-inch intervals, cutting up to—but not into—the stitching.

14. To prevent the facing from rolling out, turn up the facing, and machine stitch it to the seam allowances as close as possible to the seam. Sew through all layers of fabric.

15. Turn the facing through the slit to the wrong side of the bodice. Press.

underlining

bodice front

slit facing (wrong side)

D MAKING THE TIE

16. Cut and mark the tie according to your pattern instructions. Make sure to mark all seam lines and pattern dots with tailor tacks (Appendix).

17. To aid in positioning the tie on the bodice, mark the center back line with a row of running stitches (Appendix).

18. Fold the tie in half lengthwise, wrong side out.

19. At both ends of the tie, align the seam lines, and pin from each end up to the tailor tacks that indicate the points at which the tie will be attached to the garment.

20. Baste just outside the seam lines up to the attachment points. Remove the pins and the tailor tacks along the basted seam lines. Do not remove the tailor tacks indicating the attachment points.

21. Machine stitch along the seam lines from the folded edge to the attachment points. Pivot (Appendix) at the corners. Remove the bastings.

22. Trim the seam allowances along the seam to within 1/4 inch of the stitching.

23. Clip the four corners diagonally, cutting up to —but not into—the machine stitching.

24. Turn the tie right side out, pushing one end at a time through the center opening.

25. Pull out the corners with the point of a needle. Press the tie.

tie (wrong side)

tie (wrong side)

tie

tie (wrong side)

E ⌐ ATTACHING THE TIE

26. Turn the bodice right side out. Open the center part of the tie, and align the seam line on the notched edge of the tie with the neck seam line on the bodice. Make sure to match the center markings, notches and attachment points. Pin at 1-inch intervals.

27. Baste just outside the seam line. Remove the pins.

28. Machine stitch along the seam line between the attachment points. Remove the basting and the tailor tacks.

29. Trim the seam allowances to 1/4 inch.

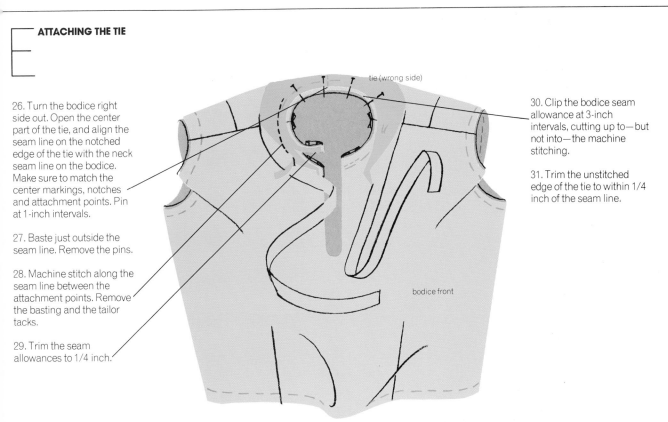

tie (wrong side)

bodice front

30. Clip the bodice seam allowance at 3-inch intervals, cutting up to—but not into—the machine stitching.

31. Trim the unstitched edge of the tie to within 1/4 inch of the seam line.

F ⌐ FINISHING THE NECKLINE

32. Turn the bodice wrong side out. Press the seam allowances flat toward the tie.

33. Turn up the unattached edge of the tie along the seam line, and place it over the seam allowances so that it just covers the machine stitching. Pin.

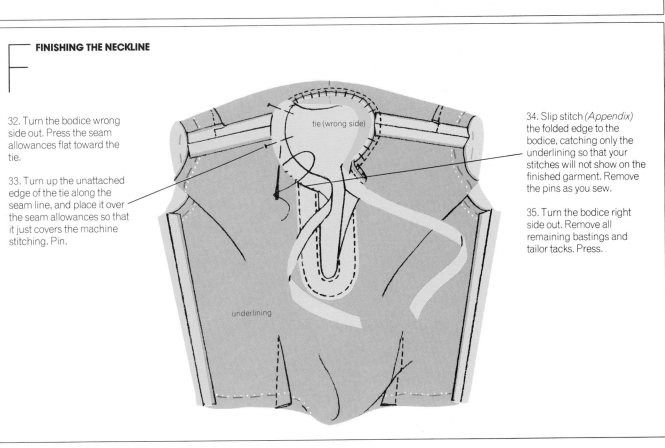

tie (wrong side)

underlining

34. Slip stitch (*Appendix*) the folded edge to the bodice, catching only the underlining so that your stitches will not show on the finished garment. Remove the pins as you sew.

35. Turn the bodice right side out. Remove all remaining bastings and tailor tacks. Press.

THE TIE NECKLINE

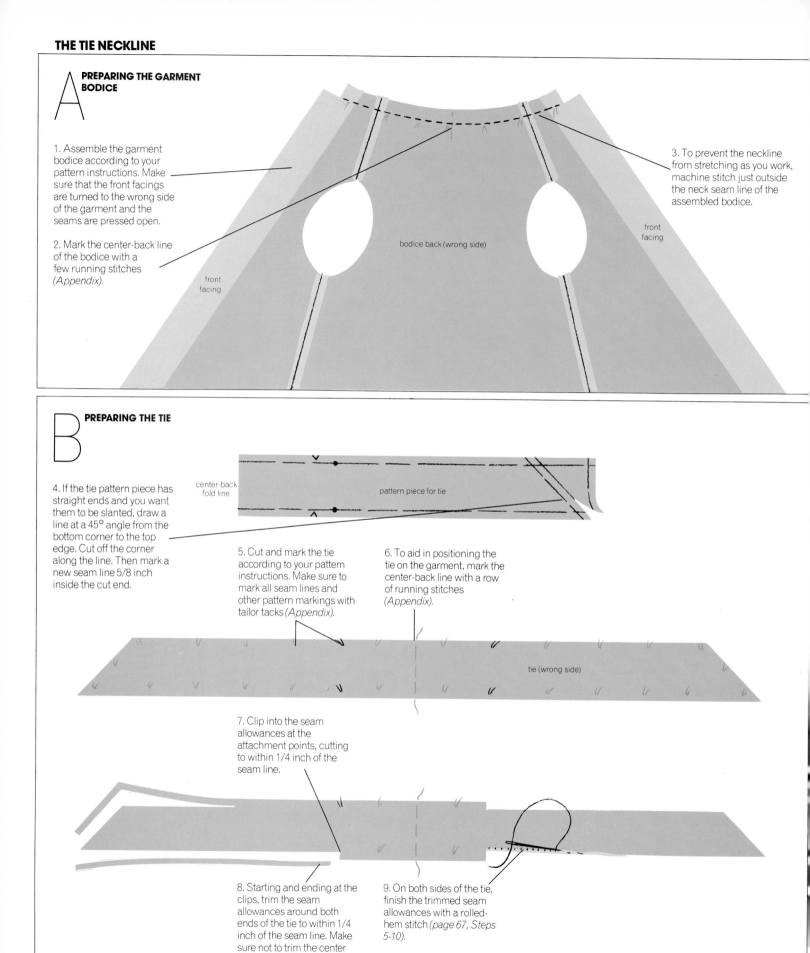

A PREPARING THE GARMENT BODICE

1. Assemble the garment bodice according to your pattern instructions. Make sure that the front facings are turned to the wrong side of the garment and the seams are pressed open.

2. Mark the center-back line of the bodice with a few running stitches (*Appendix*).

3. To prevent the neckline from stretching as you work, machine stitch just outside the neck seam line of the assembled bodice.

front facing

bodice back (wrong side)

front facing

B PREPARING THE TIE

4. If the tie pattern piece has straight ends and you want them to be slanted, draw a line at a 45° angle from the bottom corner to the top edge. Cut off the corner along the line. Then mark a new seam line 5/8 inch inside the cut end.

center-back fold line

pattern piece for tie

5. Cut and mark the tie according to your pattern instructions. Make sure to mark all seam lines and other pattern markings with tailor tacks (*Appendix*).

6. To aid in positioning the tie on the garment, mark the center-back line with a row of running stitches (*Appendix*).

tie (wrong side)

7. Clip into the seam allowances at the attachment points, cutting to within 1/4 inch of the seam line.

8. Starting and ending at the clips, trim the seam allowances around both ends of the tie to within 1/4 inch of the seam line. Make sure not to trim the center seam allowances. Remove the tailor tacks along the trimmed edges.

9. On both sides of the tie, finish the trimmed seam allowances with a rolled-hem stitch (*page 67, Steps 5-10*).

C ATTACHING THE TIE TO THE BODICE

10. With the bodice turned right side out, place the tie, wrong side up, along the neck edge of the bodice. Align the seam lines, making sure to match the center markings and the attachment points. Pin at 1-inch intervals.

11. Baste just outside the seam line. Remove the pins and tailor tacks along the basted seam line.

12. Machine stitch along the seam line. Remove the basting.

13. Trim the seam allowances to 1/4 inch.

14. Clip the seam allowances at 3-inch intervals, cutting up to—but not into—the machine stitching.

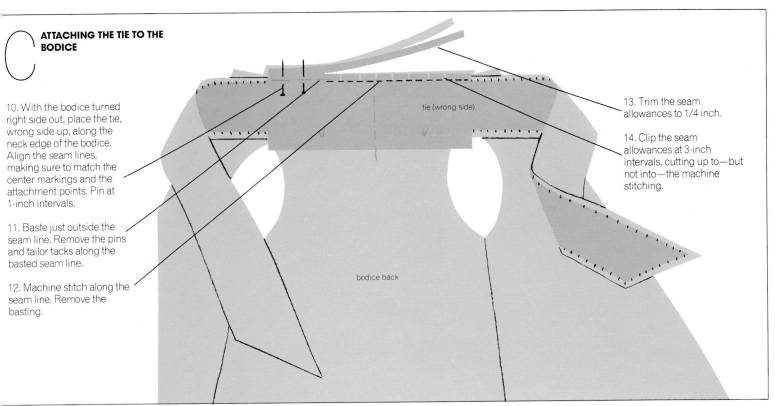

tie (wrong side)

bodice back

D FINISHING THE NECKLINE

15. Turn the bodice wrong side out. With the tie turned away from the garment, press the seam allowances toward the tie.

16. Trim the unstitched edge of the tie to within 1/4 inch of the seam line.

17. Fold the tie in half, wrong sides together. Turn under the trimmed edge along the seam line and pin it over the seam allowances so that it just covers the line of machine stitching. Pin. Remove the tailor tacks.

18. Slip stitch (Appendix) the folded edge to the bodice, catching only the machine stitching so that the stitches will not show on the finished garment. Remove the pins as you sew.

19. Turn the bodice right side out and press.

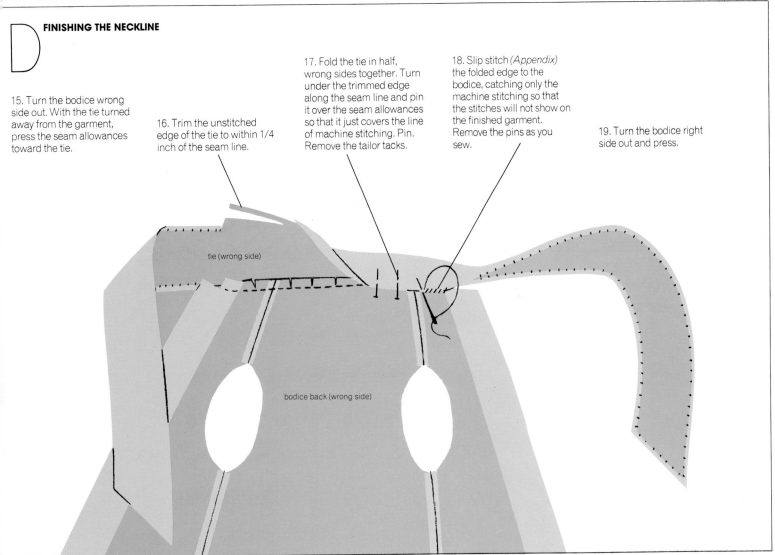

tie (wrong side)

bodice back (wrong side)

Stylishly sleeved or sleeveless

Sleeves for garments made from soft, light fabrics like pongee, chiffon, crepe de Chine and other fine silks and synthetics require special consideration, since most patterns are made for a wide range of fabrics. While patterns that are designed with puff, bishop or cape sleeves are often appropriate, none offers the ultrafullness of the one shown here. This sumptuous sleeve, which perfectly complements the luxurious draping of the chiffon dress, is created by enlarging the pattern for a gathered cape sleeve. Instructions for making the sleeve begin on the opposite page.

At the other extreme of sleeve styling is no sleeve at all. Even here, sheer fabrics require special attention. Standard facings for sleeveless garments are often 2 to 3 inches deep; but, like wide hems, such facings would destroy the soft look of garments made from filmy fabrics. A narrow facing of the same fabric as the garment solves the problem (page 92). Cut on the bias, the facing stretches gracefully around the armhole, finishing the armhole seam without binding or calling attention to itself.

THE GATHERED CAPE SLEEVE

A MAKING THE BASIC SLEEVE PATTERN

1. To determine the sleeve length, bend your elbow slightly, and measure along the outside of the arm from the shoulder point to the place where you want the finished sleeve to end. Then add 1/4 inch for hem allowance.

2. Pin the sleeve pattern piece that came with your purchased pattern to a large sheet of brown wrapping paper.

3. Measure the sleeve pattern piece from the large dot at the center of the sleeve cap to the hem edge.

4. To mark a new hemline, measure down from the pattern hem edge a distance equal to the difference between the measurements taken in Steps 1 and 3. Make a series of dashes all equidistant from the pattern hem edge.

5. Connect the dashes to form the new hemline.

6. Extend the underarm cutting lines so that they join the new hemline.

7. Cut out the new pattern by trimming around the upper edges of the original pattern piece and along the newly drawn underarm cutting lines and hemline.

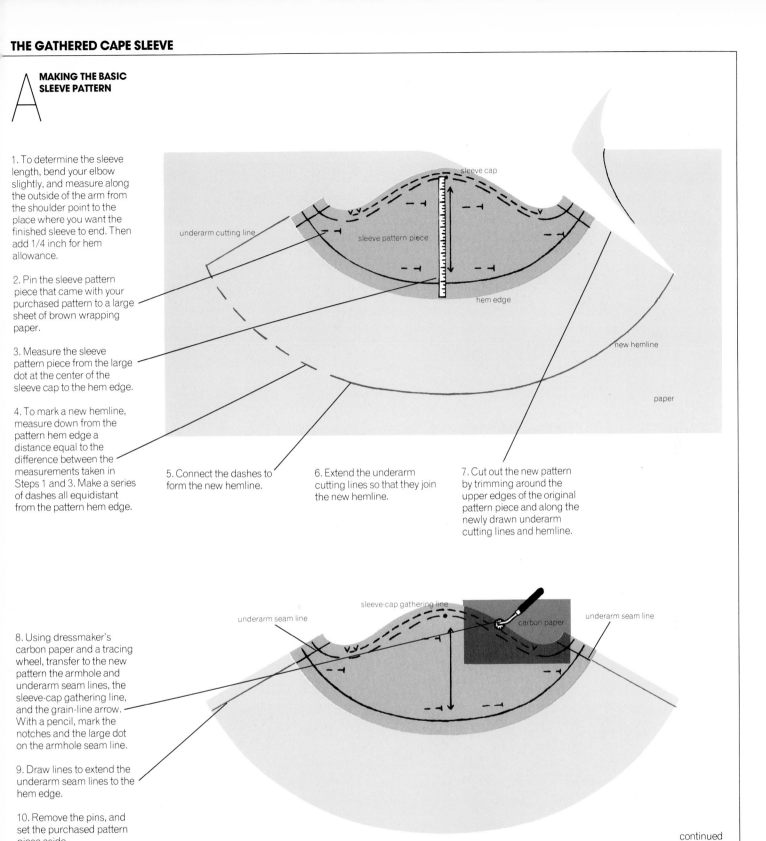

8. Using dressmaker's carbon paper and a tracing wheel, transfer to the new pattern the armhole and underarm seam lines, the sleeve-cap gathering line, and the grain-line arrow. With a pencil, mark the notches and the large dot on the armhole seam line.

9. Draw lines to extend the underarm seam lines to the hem edge.

10. Remove the pins, and set the purchased pattern piece aside.

continued

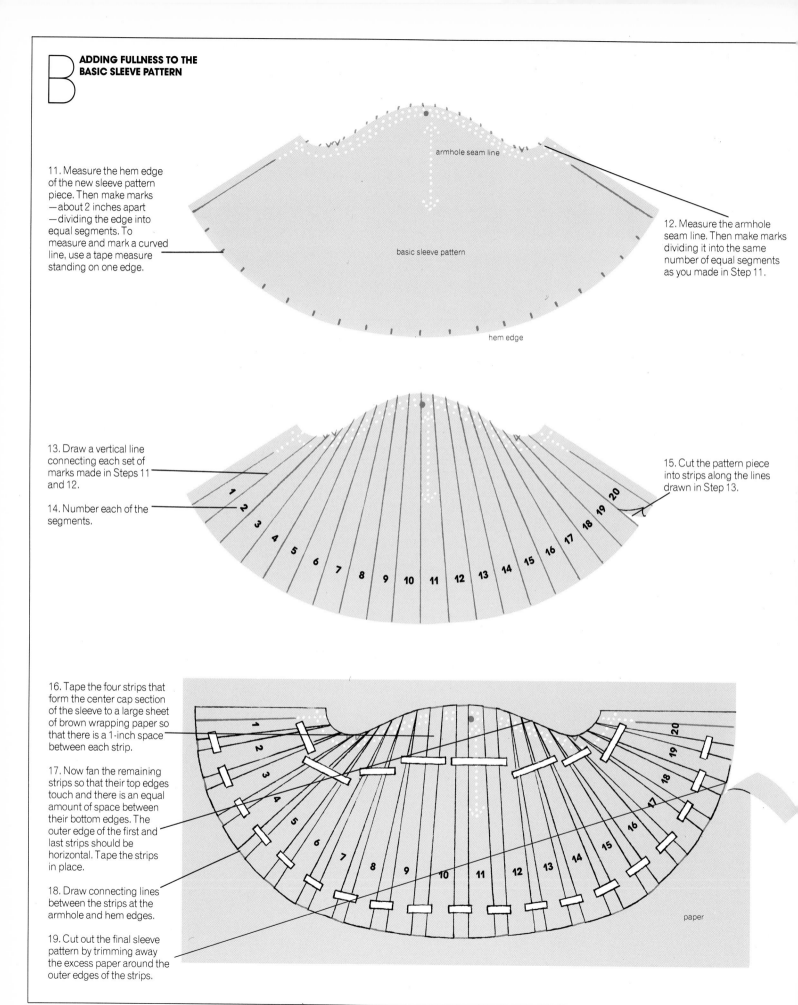

11. Measure the hem edge of the new sleeve pattern piece. Then make marks —about 2 inches apart —dividing the edge into equal segments. To measure and mark a curved line, use a tape measure standing on one edge.

armhole seam line

basic sleeve pattern

hem edge

12. Measure the armhole seam line. Then make marks dividing it into the same number of equal segments as you made in Step 11.

13. Draw a vertical line connecting each set of marks made in Steps 11 and 12.

14. Number each of the segments.

15. Cut the pattern piece into strips along the lines drawn in Step 13.

16. Tape the four strips that form the center cap section of the sleeve to a large sheet of brown wrapping paper so that there is a 1-inch space between each strip.

17. Now fan the remaining strips so that their top edges touch and there is an equal amount of space between their bottom edges. The outer edge of the first and last strips should be horizontal. Tape the strips in place.

18. Draw connecting lines between the strips at the armhole and hem edges.

19. Cut out the final sleeve pattern by trimming away the excess paper around the outer edges of the strips.

paper

C CONSTRUCTING THE SLEEVE

20. Cut the sleeve from a single layer of fabric, and mark it with tailor tacks, following the instructions on page 30.

21. Make a row of machine basting—at six stitches to the inch—1/2 inch from the edge of the fabric between the tailor tacks that designate the ends of the gathering line. Make a second row 1/8 inch outside the first. Leave 3 or 4 inches of thread free at the ends of each row of stitching.

22. Close the underarm seam with a French seam (page 51).

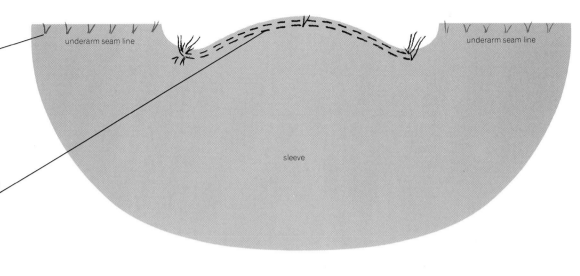

D ATTACHING THE SLEEVE TO THE GARMENT

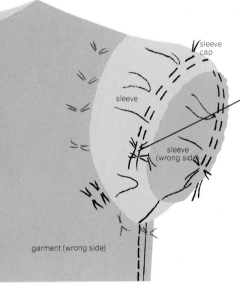

23. Turn the sleeve right side out and gently pull the loose bobbin threads of the basting made in Step 21. Pull first from one end, then the other—gathering the fullness of the sleeve cap until it is approximately the size of the garment armhole.

24. With the assembled garment bodice turned wrong side out, slip the sleeve into the armhole. Align the armhole seam lines.

25. Roll the cap of the sleeve over the armhole of the garment. Match the tailor tack indicating the top center of the sleeve cap to the shoulder seam of the garment. Pin.

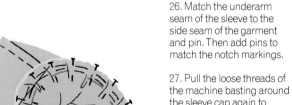

26. Match the underarm seam of the sleeve to the side seam of the garment and pin. Then add pins to match the notch markings.

27. Pull the loose threads of the machine basting around the sleeve cap again to gather the fabric until the sleeve cap fits the armhole exactly.

28. Add pins at 1/2-inch intervals around the sleeve, starting at the top center of the sleeve cap and working around the armhole in both directions.

29. Hand baste the sleeve to the garment just outside the seam line. As you baste, readjust the gathers, if necessary, so that they are evenly distributed. Remove the pins and the tailor tacks.

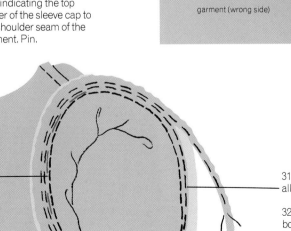

30. Machine stitch the sleeve to the garment along the seam line. Begin and end at the underarm seam. Remove the basting.

31. Trim the sleeve seam allowance only to 1/4 inch.

32. Finish the seam as a self-bound seam, following the instructions on page 52, Steps 5-7.

continued

E FINISHING THE SLEEVE

33. Hem the sleeve, using any of the methods for hemming sheer fabrics described on pages 67-69.

34. Repeat Steps 20-33 to make the other sleeve.

THE BIAS-FACED SLEEVELESS ARMHOLE

A PREPARING THE ARMHOLE

1. To prevent the fabric from stretching as you work, run a row of machine stitching just outside the armhole seam line of the assembled, underlined garment.

2. Trim the armhole seam allowance to 1/8 inch.

3. Remove the basting marking the armhole seam line.

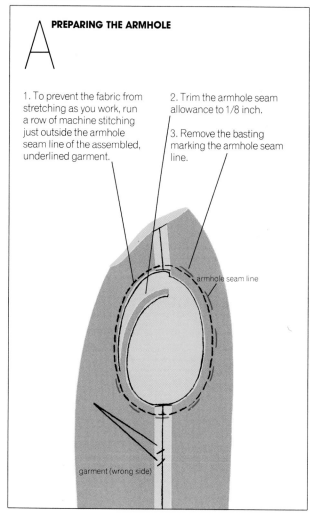

armhole seam line

garment (wrong side)

B PREPARING THE BIAS FACING

4. Cut a bias strip (page 30) 1 3/8 inches wide and at least 3 inches longer than the armhole seam line. This strip is the armhole facing.

bias facing

fold

5. Cut the ends of the facing at right angles to the long edges.

6. Fold the facing in half, wrong sides together.

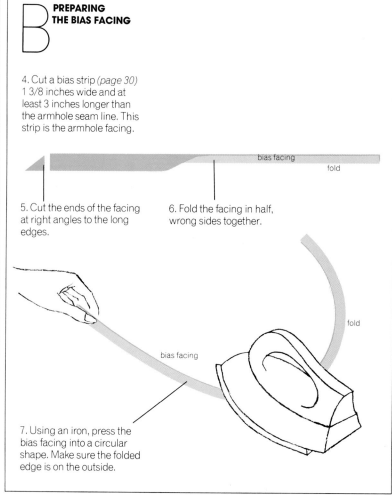

bias facing

fold

7. Using an iron, press the bias facing into a circular shape. Make sure the folded edge is on the outside.

C ATTACHING THE FACING TO THE ARMHOLE

8. With the garment turned right side out, arrange the armhole of the garment over the narrow end of an ironing board, as shown. Make sure the side seam is on top.

9. To pin the bias facing to the garment, start by turning up one end of the facing 1/4 inch. Align the end with the side seam of the garment. Make sure the raw edges of the facing align with the raw edge of the armhole. Pin.

10. Using an iron to further shape the facing, continue to pin around the armhole. Rotate the garment around the ironing board as you work.

11. Finish pinning by overlapping the ends of the facing by 1/4 inch. Trim away any excess facing.

12. Baste the facing in position and remove the pins.

13. Machine stitch 1/8 inch inside the raw edge of the facing. Start and end at the underarm seam. Remove the basting.

14. Clip the facing and armhole seam allowances at 1/2-inch intervals, cutting up to, but not into, the stitching.

D FINISHING THE BIAS FACING

15. Turn the garment wrong side out. Arrange the armhole over the narrow end of the ironing board.

16. Turn the facing to the wrong side of the garment, rolling the facing between your fingers so that the seam is just inside the garment edge. Press, then pin every 4 or 5 inches.

17. Slip stitch (*Appendix*) the folded edge of the facing to the underlining of the garment. Remove the pins.

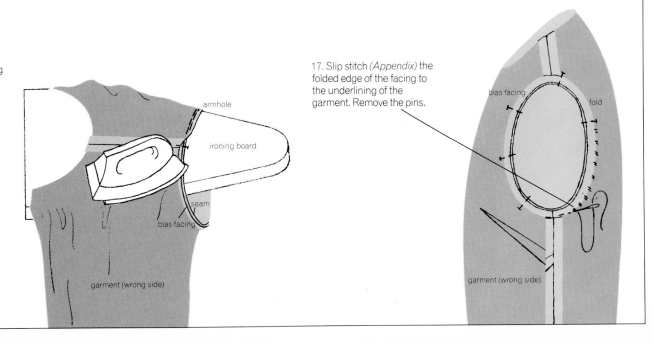

Head-turning adornments

Delicate fabrics deserve equally delicate adornments like beads, or sequins or feathers that are light in weight as well as airy in appearance. Such fripperies can be used lavishly; on the evening wrap at right, for example, ostrich feathers swathe the sleeves. Or they can be applied sparingly to add fluff or glint to a neckline, a hem or a yoke.

Fluttering marabou and ostrich feathers—available at dress trimming shops—come in strips, assembled on invisible central cords. The strips may be stitched permanently in place, or fastened temporarily with thread loops so that the feathers can be easily removed when the garment is cleaned. Both attachment techniques are described on the following pages.

Sequins and beads are available in ready-made strips, too, and in patterns assembled on fabric backing. Sequins and beads that are sold loose to be attached one by one can be arranged in any fashion. To create or copy a special design, draw or trace it on tissue paper, pin the tissue to the fabric, transfer the design to the cloth with basting stitches, then lift off the paper and sew beads or sequins along the lines.

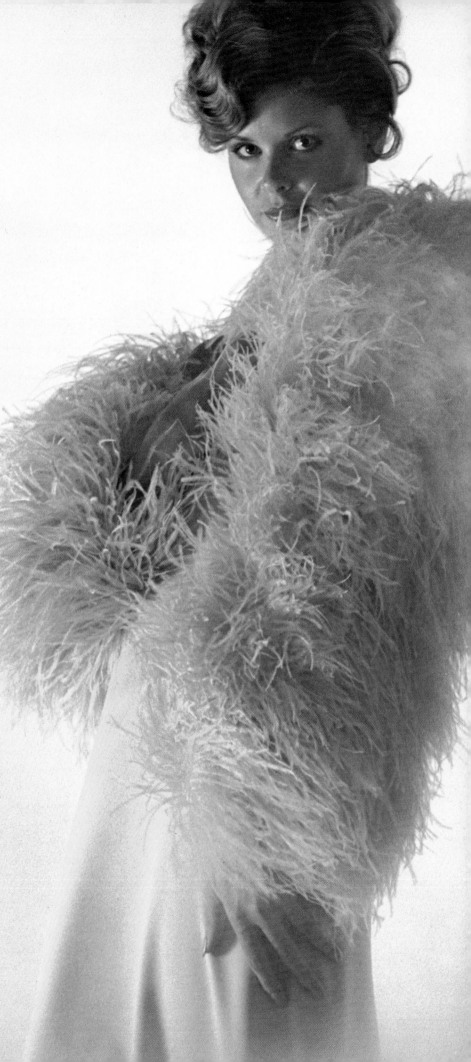

ATTACHING A PERMANENT STRIP OF FEATHERS

1. Complete the garment according to your pattern instructions.

2. Make a row of basting stitches ½ inch in from the edge to which you will attach the feather strip—in this case, the neckline.

5. Turn the garment wrong side out. Using thread that matches the color of the feathers, make a series of four or five small fastening stitches (Appendix) over the bastings at one end of the strip. Space the stitches close together and sew through the fabric and over the base of the feather strip. Make the stitches firm enough to hold the feathers in place, but not so tight that they pucker the fabric.

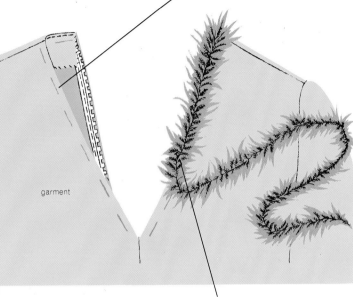

garment

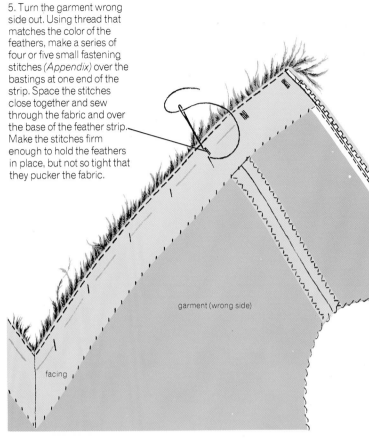

garment (wrong side)

facing

3. With the garment turned right side out, align the base of the feather strip—the cord to which the individual feathers are attached—with the row of basting stitches made in the previous step. Leave 1/2 inch of cord extending at both ends, and trim the strip.

4. Pin the feather strip to the garment, catching the cord and the garment fabric.

6. When you have completed the first group of stitches, fasten off the thread and remove the pin.

7. Continue to make groups of fastening stitches at 1- to 1 1/2-inch intervals. Remove the pins as you go.

8A. If the edge of the garment has an opening, turn under the extended ends of the cord and sew them to the garment with whipstitches (Appendix). If the opening has a zipper, keep the feathers out of the way of the zipper teeth and sew through the placket fabric only.

8B. If the edge of the garment has no opening, such as a hem, overlap the ends of the strip and sew them together with a whipstitch.

9. Remove the bastings made in Step 2.

10. Turn the garment right side out. To hide the threads of the fastening stitches and fluff up the feathers, use the eye end of a large needle to pull out the individual feather vanes that are caught by the fastening stitches.

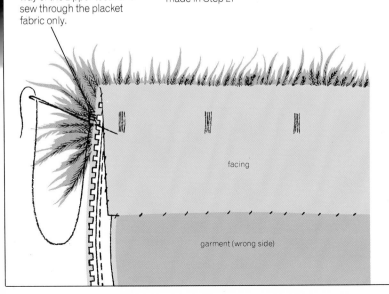

facing

garment (wrong side)

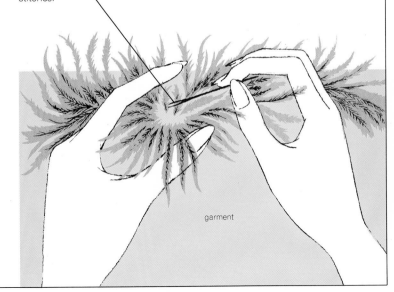

garment

ATTACHING A REMOVABLE STRIP OF FEATHERS

1. Complete the garment according to your pattern instructions.

2. With the garment turned right side out, make a row of basting stitches 1 inch in from the edge to which you will attach the feather strip —in this case, the hem.

3. To mark the position of the thread loops—which will hold the feather strip—start by placing a pin at a right angle to the basting stitches.

4. Using a tape measure, continue to insert pins, as you did in the previous step, at 3-inch intervals around the edge.

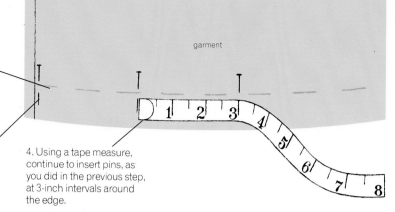

5. Thread a needle with a double strand of buttonhole twist that matches the color of the feathers. Knot the ends.

6. To form the foundation stitches for the thread loop, bring the needle up from the wrong side next to one of the pins and 1/2 inch below the bastings.

7. Draw the needle through. Then insert the needle next to the pin and 1/2 inch above the bastings.

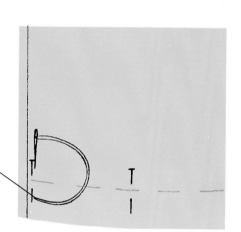

8. Draw the threads through to the wrong side and pull them until they are only slightly loose. Remove the pin.

9. Make a second foundation stitch by repeating Steps 6-8.

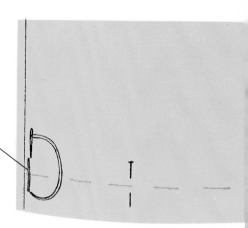

10. Bring the needle up at the bottom of the foundation threads. Slip the eye end of the needle under all four strands and make a series of closely spaced blanket stitches (Appendix) around them. Pull the stitches tight.

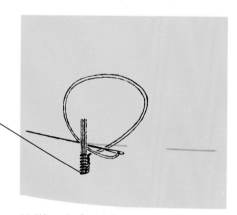

11. When the foundation threads are completely covered, secure the threads on the wrong side with fastening stitches (Appendix).

12. Repeat Steps 5-11 to make thread loops at each pin marking. Remove the basting.

13. Draw the feather strip through the loops—as though you were putting on a belt—until the feathers completely encircle the edge.

14. Trim the cord that forms the base of the feather strip, leaving 1/2 inch extending at each end.

15. Finish the ends of the feather strip as described in Steps 8A or 8B for attaching a permanent strip of feathers (page 95). Then pull the individual feathers from under the thread loops as in Step 10.

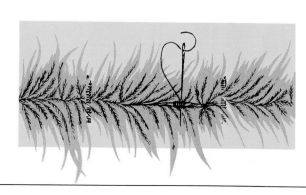

ATTACHING SINGLE SEQUINS

1. Determine the position for the sequins, then mark the points on the wrong side of the fabric with chalk dots.

2. Make several tiny fastening stitches (*Appendix*) at one of the chalk marks. Use a slender needle that slips easily through the hole in the sequin and beeswax-coated thread that matches the color of the sequin.

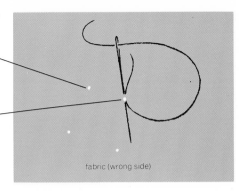

fabric (wrong side)

3. Turn the fabric wrong side down. Bring the needle up from the wrong side, and pull the thread through. Then insert the needle through the hole of the sequin, and slide the sequin, wrong side down, onto the thread.

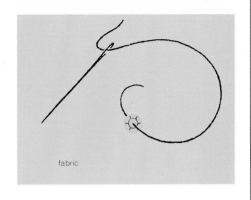

fabric

4. Hold the sequin flat against the fabric, and insert the needle at the right-hand edge. If you are left-handed, insert the needle at the left-hand edge. Bring the needle up again through the hole.

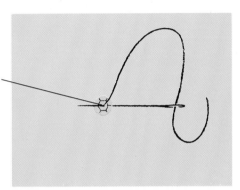

5. Pull the thread through, and insert the needle directly opposite the point at which the needle was inserted in the previous step.

6. Pull the thread through to the wrong side, and secure it as you did in Step 2.

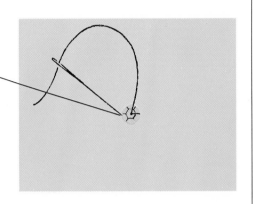

ATTACHING A SEQUIN WITH A BEAD

1. Follow the instructions in Steps 1-3 for attaching single sequins (*above*). If the sequin or bead you are working with is very tiny, use an extra-slender beading needle.

2. Insert the needle through the hole in the bead. Slide the bead onto the thread.

3. Hold the sequin flat against the fabric, and insert the needle through the hole at the center of the sequin.

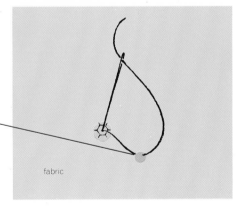

fabric

4. Pull the thread through to the wrong side of the fabric until the bead lies flat against the sequin. Secure the thread on the wrong side with fastening stitches (*Appendix*).

1. Mark the guide line for the design with basting stitches. To apply the first sequin, follow the instructions in Steps 2-4 for attaching a single sequin *(page 97)*. If you are right-handed, start at the right-hand end of the guide line. If you are left-handed, start at the left-hand end and reverse the direction of all stitches.

2. Insert the needle to the wrong side of the fabric at the left-hand edge of the sequin and bring it up on the guide line, making a stitch that equals one half the diameter of the sequin.

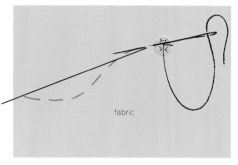

3. Place the second sequin wrong side up and insert the needle through the hole in the center. String the sequin onto the thread. Insert the needle again at the left-hand edge of the first sequin and bring it out on the guide line, making a stitch equal to the diameter of the sequin.

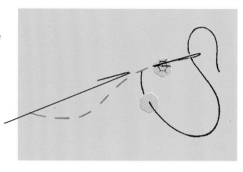

4. Pull the thread through and, at the same time, flip the second sequin over so that it is wrong side down and overlaps the first sequin.

5. Continue to add sequins by repeating Steps 3 and 4 until you reach the end of the guide line.

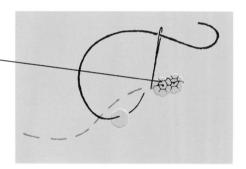

6. As you make the last stitch, bring the needle up at the point at which it emerged in the previous stitch.

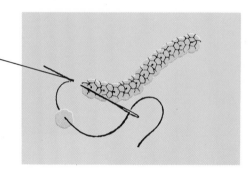

7. Flip the last sequin in place. Then insert the needle at the left-hand edge of the sequin. Pull the threads through to the wrong side, and secure them with fastening stitches *(Appendix)*. Remove the basting.

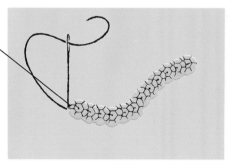

ATTACHING A PRESTRUNG STRIP OF SEQUINS

1. Mark the guide line for the design with basting stitches.

2. Remove enough sequins at the beginning of the strip so that about 4 inches of the foundation threads are left free.

3. Pass the foundation threads through the eye of a needle large enough to accommodate them. Then insert the needle at the beginning of the guide line for your design, and pull the threads through to the wrong side of the fabric. Start at the right-hand end if you are right-handed; begin at the left-hand end if you are left-handed.

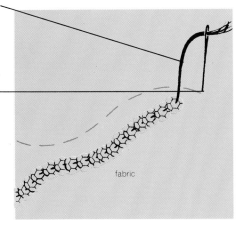

fabric

4. Turn the fabric wrong side up. Knot the foundation threads in pairs. Then clip off the ends close to the fabric.

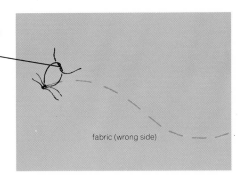

fabric (wrong side)

5. Thread a regular sewing needle with a new strand of thread that matches the color of the sequins. Use fastening stitches (Appendix) to secure the thread on the wrong side of the fabric just beside the knots made in Step 4.

6. Turn the fabric wrong side down. Bring the thread up from the wrong side just below the guide line for the design and between the first two sequins.

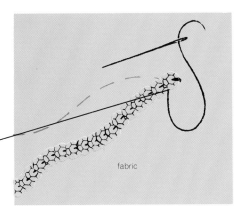

fabric

7. Insert the needle just above the guide line at a point directly opposite the point where the thread emerged in the previous step. Without pulling the thread through, bring the needle up below the guide line, between the second and third sequins.

8. Pull the thread through, anchoring the foundation threads of the strip to the fabric.

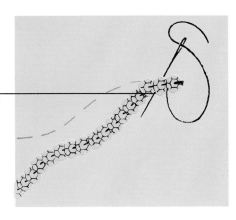

9. Repeat Steps 7 and 8 across the row until the guide line is completely covered.

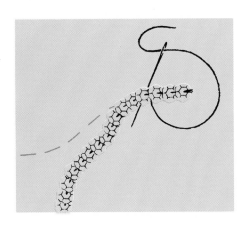

10. When you reach the end of the row, secure your last stitch on the wrong side of the fabric. Then repeat Steps 2-4 to secure the foundation threads. Remove the basting.

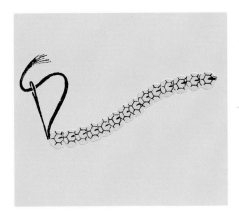

ATTACHING SINGLE BEADS

1. Mark the position for the beads as in Step 1 for attaching single sequins *(page 97)*.

2. Thread a slender beading needle with a double strand of beeswax-coated thread that matches the color of the bead. Secure the thread on the wrong side of the fabric with fastening stitches *(Appendix)*.

3. Bring the needle up from the wrong side at the point where you wish the left-hand end of the bead—the right-hand end if you are left-handed—to be *(arrow)*. Pull the thread through. Pass the needle through the bead holes, and string the bead onto the thread.

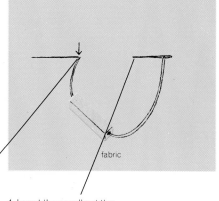

fabric

4. Insert the needle at the point where you wish the other end of the bead to be located. Bring the needle out just beside the hole from which it emerged in the previous step, as shown.

5. Pull the thread through, making sure the bead is facing wrong side down and lies securely against the fabric. Do not pull the thread so tight that it puckers the fabric.

6. Insert the needle just beside the hole from which it emerged in Step 4. Draw the thread through to the wrong side. Secure the thread with fastening stitches.

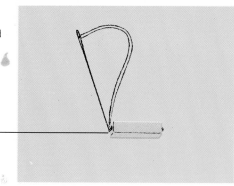

MAKING A ROW OF BEADS

1. Mark the guide line for the beads with basting stitches.

2. Repeat Steps 2 and 3 for attaching single beads *(above)*. Then insert the needle at the point where you wish the other end of the first bead to be located. Bring the needle out exactly a bead length away from the point at which the thread first emerged.

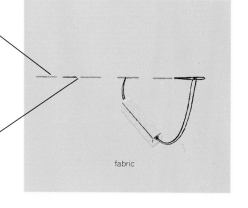

fabric

3. Pull the thread through so that the first bead faces wrong side down and lies securely against the fabric. Do not pull the thread so tight that it puckers the fabric.

4. String a second bead. Then insert the needle at the left-hand end of the first bead (the right-hand end if you are left-handed). Bring it out a bead length away from the hole from which it emerged in Step 3.

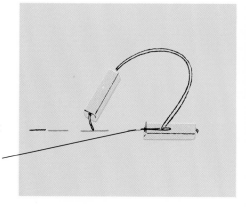

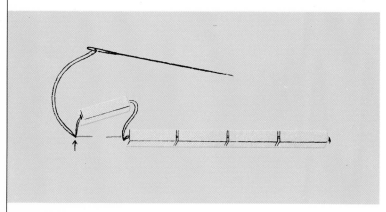

5. Continue to add beads until you reach the end of the row. As you make the last stitch, insert the needle as in Step 4, but bring it up at the point where it last emerged *(arrow)*. Pull the thread through.

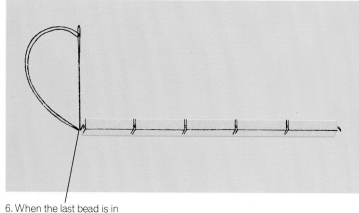

6. When the last bead is in place, insert the needle at the end of the bead row. Pull the thread through to the wrong side, and secure it with fastening stitches *(Appendix)*. Remove the basting.

ATTACHING A BAND OF SEQUINS AND BEADS

1. Measure the length of the edge of the garment to which you will attach the band; trim the band to fit.

2. To secure the loose beads and sequins at each end of the band, thread a slender beading needle with a double strand of beeswax-coated thread that matches the color of the foundation threads of the band.

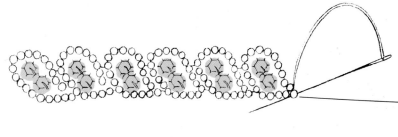

3. Secure the threads on the wrong side of the band with fastening stitches (Appendix). Then bring the needle and thread up from the wrong side of the band. Weave the thread through the holes in the sequins and beads, catching the backing and any loose foundation threads of the band as you go. Fasten off the thread on the wrong side of the band.

4. With the garment wrong side down, make a row of basting stitches along the edge at a distance from the edge where you wish the top of the band to lie.

5. Pin the band to the garment, aligning the top edge to the basting made in the previous step. Use short beading pins, if available.

6. Thread the needle with another double strand of thread, as in Step 2. Secure the thread on the wrong side of the garment at one end of the band.

7. Making tiny stitches and using a stabbing motion, tack the band securely to the garment. Working across the band, place the stitches more or less at random, with some stitches going over the foundation threads of the band and others going through the holes of the sequins and beads. Remove the pins as you sew.

8. When you reach the end of the band, fasten off the thread on the wrong side of the garment. Remove the basting stitches.

ATTACHING A STRIP OF BEADED FRINGE

1. Measure the length of the edge of the garment to which you will attach the strip of beaded fringe, and trim the strip to fit.

2. To finish the ends of the strip, start by removing about 1/2 inch of beads from one end of the strip so that the backing is exposed.

3. Thread a beading needle with a double strand of thread that matches the color of the beads and is coated with beeswax. Secure the thread on the wrong side of the strip with fastening stitches (Appendix).

4. Bring the needle up from the wrong side. Then weave the thread in and out of the holes in the beads at the end, catching the backing fabric and any loose foundation threads.

5. Turn the strip wrong side up. Fold over the end of the strip, and sew it to the backing with whipstitches (Appendix). Repeat on the other end of the strip.

6. With the garment wrong side down, make a row of basting stitches along the edge at a distance from the edge where you wish the top of the strip to lie.

7. Pin the strip to the garment, aligning the top edge with the basting made in the previous step. Use small beading pins, if available.

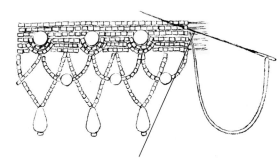
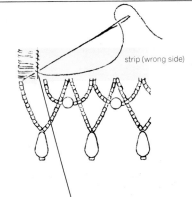
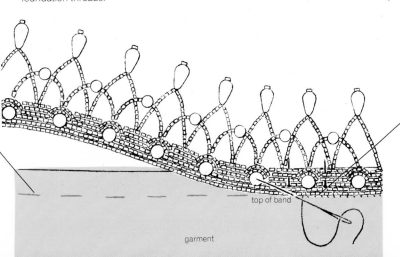

8. Using thread that matches the color of the strip and a regular sewing needle, sew the strip to the garment with tiny, invisible slip stitches (Appendix). Remove the pins and the basting stitches.

9. If you are making a continuous strip of fringe, sew the ends together with whipstitches.

101

4
DAINTY BOUDOIR LUXURIES

When journalist Alexandra Anderson slithered out to the dance floor at a 1974 New York charity ball, wearing a satin slip of a dress with the briefest of panties beneath, she caused a sensation. Her outfit did not amount to much; in fact, it was barely there, and cost next to nothing. She had picked up the delicate, cream-colored sheath for four dollars at a thriftshop; the wispy panties cost even

MUCH ADO OVER NOTHINGS IN LINGERIE

less. Yet, topped off with a loop of pearls and worn with assurance, Alexandra's little combination of nothings easily outshone all the elegant, bejeweled gowns around her.

Besides stealing the show, Ms. Anderson's outfit closed a 5,000-year-old circle in the concept and use of women's underthings. The dress she had chosen turned out to be a real slip with adjustable straps, the kind of boudoir garment that less venturesome women had been keeping carefully concealed by outer clothing—or by carefully closed doors. With Alexandra Anderson's daring appearance, such delicate underwear returned to the realm of outerwear where, in fact, it had begun. Egyptian ladies of 1500 B.C., as recorded on friezes and wall paintings, dressed for court in filmy petticoats and diaphanous capes. And even Ms. Anderson's modish briefs bore a remarkable resemblance to loincloths that Sumerian women wore in 3000 B.C. The further fact that Ms. Anderson wore no brassiere would have seemed only common sense to the ladies of ancient times, when cloth was too precious to wear for any reason but beauty—which nobody confused with artificial shaping or false modesty.

Between its preclassic origins and its modish rediscovery, however, ladies' underwear not only disappeared from view but lost its delicacy. The vestiges of these unhappy changes also have their roots in the preclassic era. While Egyptian women flaunted the grace of their natural shapes in the simplest see-through costumes, ladies on the island of Crete were beginning to reshape their own silhouettes with waist-whittling corsets and hip-swelling hooped skirts made of metal and rush.

Worse yet, by the time of Julius Caesar the priggish matrons of Rome decided that no decent woman would lie around her villa with nothing underneath her tunic. Thereupon they commenced to swathe themselves in layers of underdraperies that met their new standards of propriety. Much later, in the Renaissance, these deplorable notions were compounded by the replacement of flowing gowns with fitted dresses whose function was to emphasize some part of the body.

To achieve whatever silhouette might be currently modish—in one century a swelling bust, in another a wasp waist or an ample stomach or a protruding derrière—women devised structural outer garments called bodys that were either laced or padded or stiffened with paste. But there was neither mystique nor illusion in these generally bizarre items, and besides they looked terrible.

Clever women soon put such contrivances out of sight. Tucked away from prying eyes, bodices and corsets could push here and pull there without spoiling the fantasy that the inner woman was every bit as enticing as her outer shape suggested.

Soon women replaced their unreliable paste-stiffened pads with rigid materials that accomplished more dramatic results. During the Elizabethan Age, for example, ladies spread their skirts like wings over drum-shaped scaffolds called farthingales, elaborate structures made of whalebone, wire, wood or wickerwork. A Spanish tailor's book of 1589 suggests that an ideal farthingale should be 13 hand spans (some 10 feet) in circumference, although he conceded that under some circumstances even more breadth might be permissible.

After farthingales, in 1625 came the hip-enhancing bum rolls, shaped like life preservers and made of cork or stuffed cloth. Panniers, or false hips, were next. Oblong rings of wood, metal or cane suspended from the waist on cords or tapes, panniers extended the hips at either side while flattening the back and front. These were followed by crinolines, circular versions of the panniers that domed the hips like a bell.

By the time Victoria was crowned Queen, women were flourishing crinolines—now called hoops—that measured 15 feet or more in circumference. And gentlemen were complaining that such gear was devised not to attract admirers but to keep them at bay. In a dialogue reported by *Godey's Lady's Book,* an exasperated husband tells a friend: "I caught my Jenny by surprise this morning in her wrapper and *without hoops;* I got the first kiss I've had since whalebone skirts came into fashion."

By now, too, in order to further emphasize the heroic swell of their hoops, women were cinching their waists with whalebone or steel-reinforced corsets. A corset was considered to fit properly if, upon first being put on, the lacing eyelets at either side of the lady's spine missed touching by two inches before they were lashed tight. Getting the rows to come together usually required some outside help—a strong pair of hands behind, and perhaps a sturdy bedpost in front to cling to while the waist was being squeezed down to 20 inches or less. If the constriction tended to give the lady the vapors, so be it. That astonishingly small waist made any sacrifice worthwhile.

Hoops and corsets were only part of the

Outlandish fashions of former days demanded that women wear extravagant understructures like those shown here in silhouette below their matching costumes. Pictured from left to right are Mary Todd Lincoln with a hip-swelling 1860s hoop, English actress Lily Langtry with an 1880s bustle, American singer Lillian Russell with an 1890s waist cincher and American movie star Patsy Ruth Miller with a columnar girdle of the 1920s.

19th Century underwardrobe that sealed a woman of fashion almost hermetically within a cocoon of cloth and stiffeners. Simply putting on underthings could take hours.

First milady had to slip into a loosely fitted knee-length chemise, then she had to be laced into a shoulder-to-thigh corset, after which she climbed into billowing pantaloons that puffed out the bottom of the chemise. After covering the corset top with a camisole to camouflage the lines of protruding corset stays, she was pushed headfirst between the rings of her hoop, and draped with as many as four separate petticoats. Only then could she turn to donning a gown and bedecking herself with bangles.

Just when it seemed that fashion had achieved the apex of complexity and bulk in undergarments—which by this time had acquired the merited name of "unmentionables"—women adopted one more bizarre shaping device: the bustle. Popularized in the 1880s, the bustle was a plump fabric-covered wire cage that sat just above a lady's posterior—and assured grand exits. It also pulled the layers of chemise, pantaloons and petticoats against the knees and pushed all the excess fabric out behind.

At last, just before the turn of the century, women rebelled against the whole bulky uncomfortable business. Corsets became looser and began to shrink so that they covered the waist alone. Women then dispensed with bustles and all their other cages. Feeling braver as time passed, they proceeded to shed the rest of their cocoons as well. The leadership for this final stage of emancipation came, naturally enough, from Paris, which by Edwardian times was already established as the seat of power for the world of high fashion.

A major step in the return to delicacy occurred in 1912 when the haute couture designer Paul Poiret invented the brassiere. At first a shoulder-to-waist garment worn over a chemise, the brassiere quickly shrank to become a mere bandeau covering otherwise naked breasts. Then during World War I, the last of the corsets were superseded by hip-hugging girdles that provided flexible support with elastic, rather than with unyielding steel, stays and lacing. At the same time, as women started working in factories or hospitals and driving ambulances, hems rose to provide freedom of movement. The trend went on into the 1920s, when knee-length tubular styles replaced floor-length bouffant ones for daytime.

Underwear continued to shrink. Petticoats became slim, and pantaloons were cut off at mid-thigh or higher—or the pantaloons were combined with camisoles as one-piece cami-knickers. The smaller these underthings became, the more enchantingly delicate they looked and felt. For the first time in perhaps 2,000 years, women could actually enjoy wearing their underclothes. And talking about them, too. The new wave of underthings, and the other light and lacy boudoir items such as negligees and peignoirs that came along with them, ceased to be unmentionable. Instead, they became very much mentioned under the Frenchified term "lingerie."

The garments, like those of preclassic times, had little or no shape of their own —until a lady put them on and gave them *her* shape. All that had been bone and lace and steel was now gone. And what had been stiff and padded was now soft and lightweight. By 1964 when the American innovator Rudi Gernreich devised the ultimate in delicate brassieres to complement his futuristic outerwear styles, the only shaping he used was a pair of tiny angled darts. And the transparent nylon tricot he chose for the material was so close to nothing that the brassiere was inevitably nicknamed the no-bra bra.

With this bit of daring ingenuity, Gernreich set the stage for the totally braless look so charmingly flaunted by Alexandra Anderson when she brought underwear full cycle at the charity ball. Since then, not only slips but also nightgowns have become conspicuous articles of evening outerwear at restaurants and theaters in America's more sophisticated metropolitan centers.

Meanwhile, at-home wear such as lounging pajamas and robes has moved down from the bedroom to the dining and living rooms for parties. The basic materials for this excitingly revived line of delicate things are slinky, synthetic nylons and filmy rayons. But classic natural fabrics like silk satin are also in vogue. And so, too, are the delicate traditional handstitches and embroidery like that shown overleaf; or the lace inserts, open thread work and cutaway appliqués described on the following pages.

The return to natural shapes in fashion after World War I freed women to wear softly structured underthings of diminishing size. A slip of the early 1920s *(left)* reached below the knee, while the so-called teddy of the 1940s was cut off at mid-thigh. By the 1960s slips shrank to mini length or disappeared in favor of a camisole and short knickers. Finally the ensemble dwindled to a bra and bikini pants, ending ultimately with no bra at all.

Sleight of hand with embroidery

To accent lingerie and other gossamer finery, nothing less than the most fragile-looking embroidery will do. The work depends on delicate stitches like those described on these pages: five techniques for bordering sleeves, necklines and the like—and two for edging the hems and folds of a garment.

The two edging stitches shown opposite—knot stitch and knotted closed-buttonhole edging—can be snubbed in close to the fabric to form a crisp edge, or worked more loosely to create delicate scallops.

The border stitch known as shadow stitch (*overleaf*) is meant for sheers and finished on both the front and the back of the fabric. Thus, some parts of each stitch are seen partially veiled, and look like shadows. The other four border stitches—arrowhead, fern, feather and sheaf—can all be applied to any lightweight material, in single rows of tracery or combined row on row to form wider, more complex motifs. Like the edges, borders are best sewed with cotton or silk embroidery thread of a weight and color compatible with the fabric to be decorated.

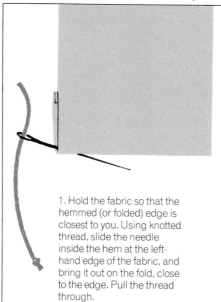

1. Hold the fabric so that the hemmed (or folded) edge is closest to you. Using knotted thread, slide the needle inside the hem at the left-hand edge of the fabric, and bring it out on the fold, close to the edge. Pull the thread through.

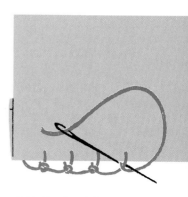

2. Insert the needle 1/16 inch above the folded edge and 1/4 inch to the right of the hole from which the thread emerged in Step 1. Bring the needle out on the folded edge, and slide the thread emerging from the previous stitch under it, as shown. Pull the thread through loosely, leaving a loop.

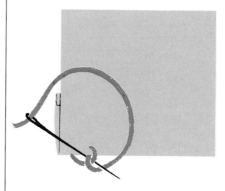

3. Without inserting it into the fabric, slip the needle from left to right under the middle and right-hand threads of the loop. Then slide the thread extending from the loop under the needle, as shown. Pull the thread through tightly to form a knot.

4. Working from left to right, repeat Steps 2 and 3 every 1/4 inch along the length of the hemmed edge. Secure the last stitch by making a small fastening stitch (*Appendix*) on the wrong side of the hem. Clip the excess thread.

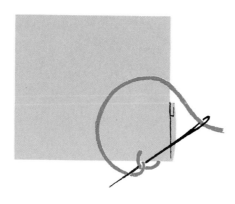

IF YOU ARE LEFT-HANDED...
Follow the directions in Steps 1-4, but proceed from right to left, as shown.

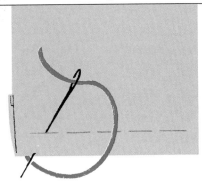

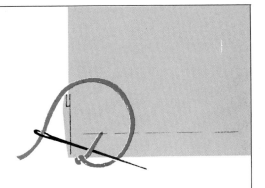

1. Mark a guide line on the fabric by making a row of basting stitches 1/4 inch from—and parallel to—the hemmed (or folded) edge. Then hold the fabric so that the hemmed edge is closest to you. Using knotted thread, slide the needle inside the hem at the left-hand edge and bring it out on the fold, close to the edge.

2. Insert the needle on the guide line 1/8 inch to the right of the hole made in Step 1. Bring the needle out close to the folded edge, just to the right of the hole made in Step 1. Pull the thread through to form a diagonal stitch.

3. Without inserting it into the fabric, slip the needle from left to right under the diagonal stitch. Then slide the thread extending from the completed stitch under the needle, as shown. Pull the thread through, pulling it toward you tightly to form a looped knot along the folded edge of the fabric.

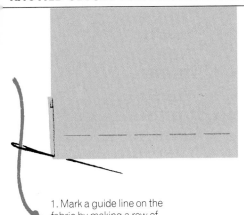

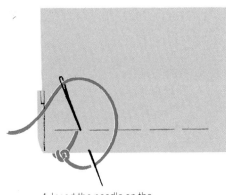

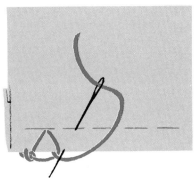

4. Insert the needle on the guide line just to the right of the top of the previous diagonal stitch. Bring the needle out close to the folded edge, 1/4 inch to the right of the bottom of the previous diagonal stitch. Slide the thread extending from the completed stitch under the needle, as shown, and pull the thread through.

5. Insert the needle on the guide line 1/4 inch to the right of the top of the previous stitch. Bring the needle out close to the folded edge, just to the right of the bottom of the previous stitch. Slide the thread extending from the completed stitch under the needle, and pull the thread through.

6. Without inserting it into the fabric, slip the needle from left to right under the last two completed diagonal stitches. Then slide the thread extending from the previous stitch under the needle, as shown. Pull the thread through, pulling it toward you tightly to form a looped knot along the folded edge of the fabric.

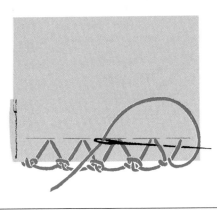

7. Make similar stitches along the length of the hemmed edge by repeating Steps 4-6. Secure the last stitch by making a small fastening stitch (Appendix) on the wrong side of the hem. Clip the excess thread, and remove the basted guide line.

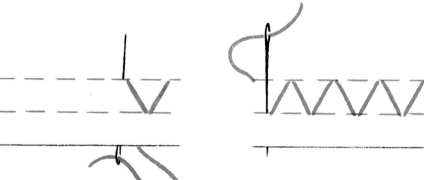

1. Mark guide lines on the fabric by making two parallel rows of basting stitches separated by a distance equal to the desired length of the stitches. Then, using knotted thread, bring the needle up from the wrong side of the fabric at the right-hand end of the upper guide line. Pull the thread through.

2. Insert the needle on the lower guide line one stitch-length to the left of the hole made in Step 1. Bring the needle up on the upper guide line one stitch-length to the left of the point at which the needle was inserted. Pull the thread through to form a diagonal stitch.

3. Insert the needle on the lower guide line, just to the left of the bottom of the diagonal stitch. Pull the thread through to the wrong side of the fabric to complete the arrowhead shape.

4. To make the next stitch, bring the needle up on the upper guide line, just to the left of the previous stitch, as shown. Then repeat Steps 2 and 3.

5. Make similar stitches from right to left until you reach the left-hand end of the guide lines. Complete the last stitch as shown in Step 3, and pull the thread through to the wrong side of the fabric.

6. End off on the wrong side of the fabric by slipping the needle underneath the nearest stitch and sliding the thread under the needle, as shown. Then pull the thread through tightly, creating a small knot. Clip the excess thread, and remove the basted guide lines.

IF YOU ARE LEFT-HANDED...
Follow the directions in Steps 1-6, but proceed from left to right, as shown.

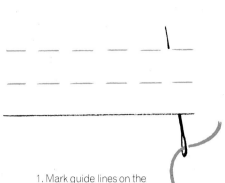

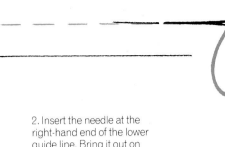

1. Mark guide lines on the fabric by making two parallel rows of basting stitches separated by a distance equal to the desired length of the stitches. Then, using knotted thread, bring the needle up from the wrong side of the fabric at the right-hand end of the upper guide line. Pull the thread through.

2. Insert the needle at the right-hand end of the lower guide line. Bring it out on the lower guide line about 1/16 inch to the left of the point at which it was inserted, as shown. Pull the thread through to form the first vertical stitch.

3. Insert the needle on the upper guide line about 1/16 inch to the left of the previous stitch. Bring the needle out on the upper guide line about 1/16 inch to the left of the point at which it was inserted. Pull the thread through to form the second vertical stitch.

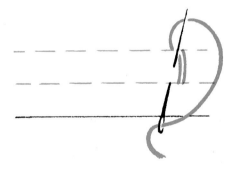

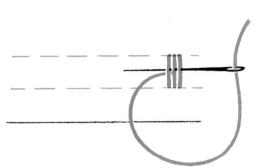

4. Insert the needle on the lower guide line about 1/16 inch to the left of the previous stitch. Bring the needle out midway between the guide lines, just to the left of the last completed stitch, as shown. Pull the thread through to form the third vertical stitch.

5. Slide the needle from right to left under the three vertical stitches, as shown, without inserting it into the fabric. Pull the thread through tightly, gathering the three vertical stitches into a bunch.

6. Repeat Step 5. Then reinsert the needle into the fabric in the hole from which the thread emerged in Step 4. Pull the thread through to the wrong side of the fabric.

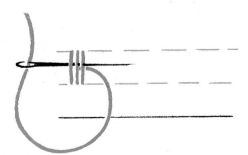

7. Working from right to left, repeat Steps 1-6 to make similar stitches at the desired intervals until the guide lines are covered. End off on the wrong side of the fabric, following the directions for the arrowhead stitch (left), Step 6.

IF YOU ARE LEFT-HANDED...
Follow the directions in Steps 1-7 but proceed from left to right, as shown.

THE SHADOW STITCH: For decorative lines and borders on sheer fabrics

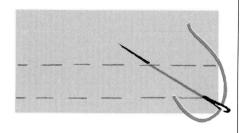

THE FEATHER STITCH: For lines and fillings

1. Mark guide lines on the fabric by making two parallel rows of basting stitches separated by a distance equal to the desired length of the stitches. Then, using knotted thread, bring the needle up from the wrong side of the fabric 1/8 inch from the right-hand end of the lower guide line. Pull the thread through.

2. Insert the needle on the lower guide line 1/8 inch to the right of the hole from which the thread emerged in Step 1. Slant the needle upward and bring it out on the upper guide line 1/16 inch to the left of the hole from which the yarn emerged in Step 1. Pull the thread through.

1. Mark a guide line on the fabric by making a single row of basting stitches. Then, using knotted thread, bring the needle up from the wrong side of the fabric at the top and about 1/8 inch to the left of the guide line. Pull the thread through.

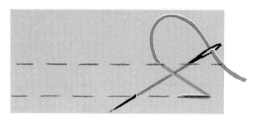

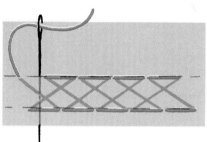

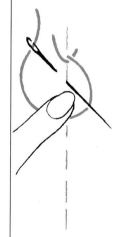

3. Insert the needle on the upper guide line 1/8 inch to the right of the hole from which the thread last emerged. Slant the needle downward and bring it out on the lower guide line 1/8 inch to left of the previous stitch made on the lower guide line. Pull the thread through, creating an X-shaped stitch on the wrong side of the fabric.

4. Repeat Steps 2 and 3 to make similar stitches from right to left until the guide lines are covered. On the last stitch, insert the needle on the upper guide line 1/8 inch to the right of the hole from which the thread last emerged, and pull the thread through to the wrong side of the fabric. End off as shown in the arrowhead stitch *(page 112, Step 6).*

2. Make a counterclockwise loop, and hold down the thread loop with your thumb, as shown. Insert the needle about 1/8 inch to the right of the guide line and about 1/8 inch lower than the hole made in Step 1. Bring the needle out on the guide line 1/8 inch below the point at which it entered the fabric. Pass the needle over the thread held down with your thumb, and pull the thread through.

3. Make a clockwise loop, and hold down the thread loop with your thumb, as shown. Insert the needle about 1/8 inch to the left of the guide line and about 1/8 inch lower than the hole from which the thread last emerged. Bring the needle out on the guide line 1/8 inch below the point at which it entered the fabric. Pass the needle over the thread loop held down with your thumb, and pull the thread through.

IF YOU ARE LEFT-HANDED...
Follow the directions in Steps 1-4, but proceed from left to right, as shown.

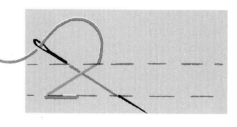

4. Make similar stitches by repeating Steps 2 and 3 until the guide line is covered. After making the last stitch, push the needle through to the wrong side of the fabric just below the last loop. End off as shown for the arrowhead stitch *(page 112, Step 6).*

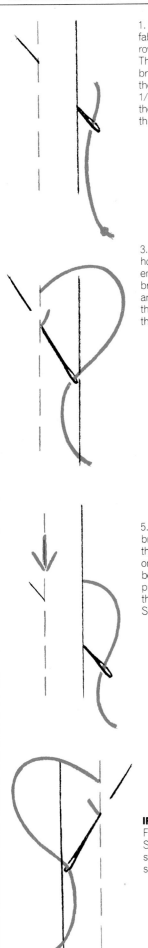

1. Mark a guide line on the fabric by making a single row of basting stitches. Then, using knotted thread, bring the needle up from the wrong side of the fabric 1/4 inch below the top of the guide line. Pull the thread through.

2. Insert the needle 1/8 inch above and 1/8 inch to the right of the hole from which the thread emerged in Step 1. Bring the needle out at the top of the guide line, and pull the thread through.

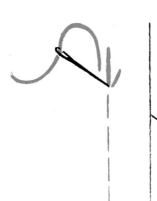

3. Insert the needle in the hole from which the thread emerged in Step 1, and bring it up 1/8 inch above and 1/8 inch to the left of this point. Pull the thread through.

4. Complete the first fern stitch by reinserting the needle in the hole from which the thread emerged in Step 1 and pulling the thread through to the wrong side of the fabric.

5. Begin the next stitch by bringing the needle up from the wrong side of the fabric on the guide line, 1/4 inch below the bottom of the previous fern stitch. Pull the thread through. Then repeat Steps 2-4.

6. Working vertically, make similar stitches until the guide line is covered. Complete the last stitch as shown in Step 4, and pull the thread through to the wrong side of the fabric. End off as shown in the arrowhead stitch (*page 112, Step 6*).

IF YOU ARE LEFT-HANDED...
Follow the directions in Steps 1-6, but make each stitch from left to right, as shown.

In supporting roles—straps and elastics

The support function of both straps and elastic strips in lingerie is as prosaic as that of a farmer's galluses. But straps need not look prosaic, and elastics need not be visible at all.

The simplest design for straps —and the most elegant—is the bias-cut style, shown here in a daintily narrow version, made out of the same fabric as the garment. Because the fabric is cut on the bias, the strap has some natural flexibility. Where more support is needed, straps cut on the straight of the grain and reinforced with satin or grosgrain ribbon will lie flat against the body. Instructions for both start on the opposite page.

Elastic offers maximum give and security—not only for straps but also for waistbands on slips and formal-wear pajamas. Though elastics with decorative edges can be applied so as to be visible, regular kinds should be encased in a garment tunnel *(pages 120-121).* To avoid cutting the elastic in sewing, use a Size 14 ballpoint needle, and zigzag the stitches so they will give with the stretch.

BIAS STRAPS

A STITCHING THE STRAP

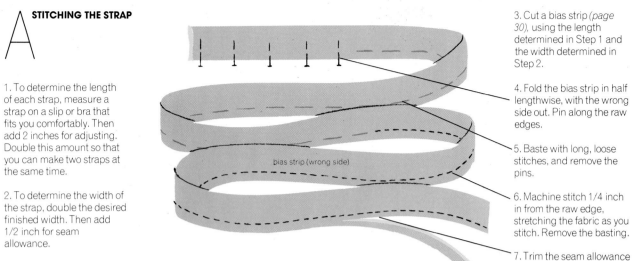

bias strip (wrong side)

1. To determine the length of each strap, measure a strap on a slip or bra that fits you comfortably. Then add 2 inches for adjusting. Double this amount so that you can make two straps at the same time.

2. To determine the width of the strap, double the desired finished width. Then add 1/2 inch for seam allowance.

3. Cut a bias strip (*page 30*), using the length determined in Step 1 and the width determined in Step 2.

4. Fold the bias strip in half lengthwise, with the wrong side out. Pin along the raw edges.

5. Baste with long, loose stitches, and remove the pins.

6. Machine stitch 1/4 inch in from the raw edge, stretching the fabric as you stitch. Remove the basting.

7. Trim the seam allowance to 1/8 inch.

B TURNING THE STRAP

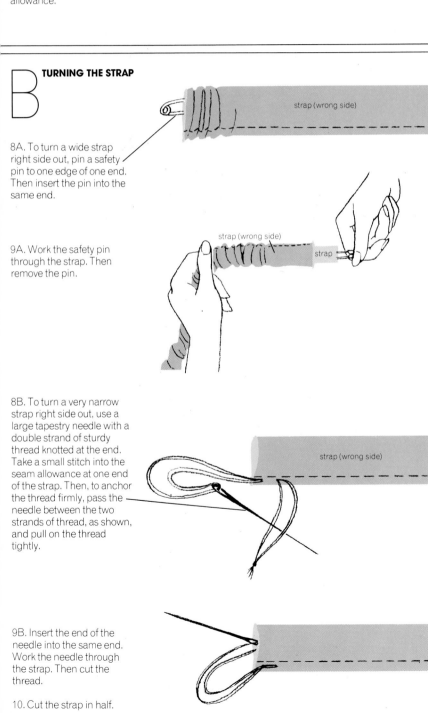

strap (wrong side)

strap (wrong side)

strap

strap (wrong side)

8A. To turn a wide strap right side out, pin a safety pin to one edge of one end. Then insert the pin into the same end.

9A. Work the safety pin through the strap. Then remove the pin.

8B. To turn a very narrow strap right side out, use a large tapestry needle with a double strand of sturdy thread knotted at the end. Take a small stitch into the seam allowance at one end of the strap. Then, to anchor the thread firmly, pass the needle between the two strands of thread, as shown, and pull on the thread tightly.

9B. Insert the end of the needle into the same end. Work the needle through the strap. Then cut the thread.

10. Cut the strap in half.

C ATTACHING THE STRAPS

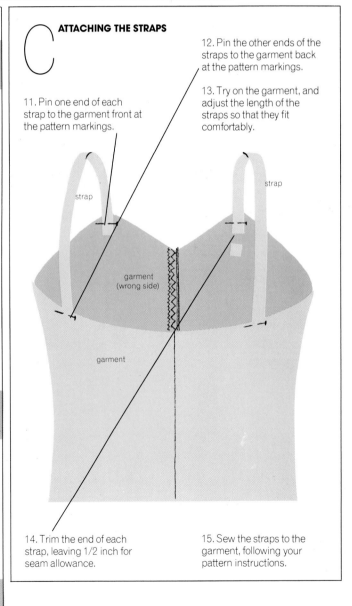

strap

strap

garment (wrong side)

garment

11. Pin one end of each strap to the garment front at the pattern markings.

12. Pin the other ends of the straps to the garment back at the pattern markings.

13. Try on the garment, and adjust the length of the straps so that they fit comfortably.

14. Trim the end of each strap, leaving 1/2 inch for seam allowance.

15. Sew the straps to the garment, following your pattern instructions.

SELF-FABRIC STRAPS WITH RIBBON

A CUTTING OUT THE STRAP

1. To determine the length of each strap, measure a strap on a slip or bra that fits you comfortably. Then add 2 inches for adjusting. Double this amount so that you can make two straps at the same time.

2. From ribbon that is the desired final width of the strap, cut a piece the length you determined in Step 1. Choose ribbon that is a shade lighter than your garment fabric. For a lightweight fabric, such as crepe, use satin ribbon. For a stiffer fabric, such as taffeta, use lightweight grosgrain ribbon.

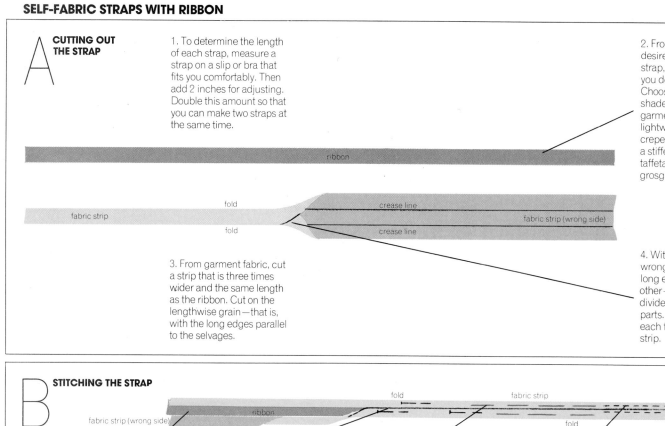

3. From garment fabric, cut a strip that is three times wider and the same length as the ribbon. Cut on the lengthwise grain—that is, with the long edges parallel to the selvages.

4. With the fabric strip wrong side up, turn up both long edges—one over the other—so that the strip is divided into three equal parts. Press a crease along each fold. Then open the strip.

B STITCHING THE STRAP

5. With the strip wrong side up, lay the ribbon between the two creased folds.

6. Turn up both long raw edges and then turn them up again so that the folds meet at the center of the enclosed ribbon. Pin.

7. Baste the strip to the ribbon next to the outside folded edges, and remove the pins.

8. Machine stitch 1/16 inch from the center folded edges. Remove the bastings.

9. Cut the strap in half.

10. Attach the straps, following the instructions for attaching bias straps (*page 117, Box C*).

ELASTIC EDGING

A PREPARING THE ELASTIC

1. To determine the length of the elastic edging, put the elastic around the appropriate body area—the waist in this example. Stretch it until it is both secure and comfortable. Then allow 1 inch for joining the overlapping ends.

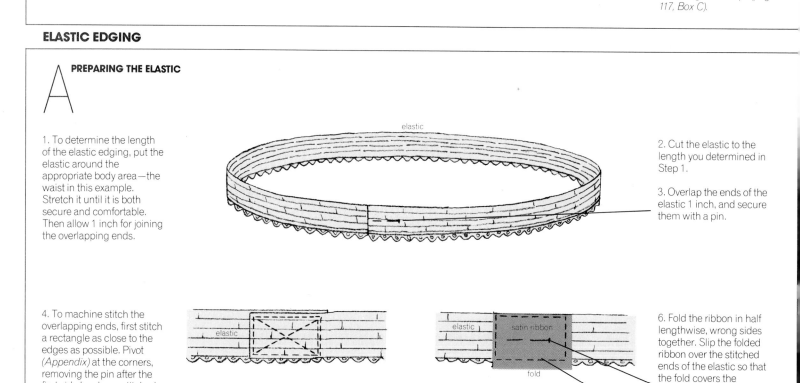

2. Cut the elastic to the length you determined in Step 1.

3. Overlap the ends of the elastic 1 inch, and secure them with a pin.

4. To machine stitch the overlapping ends, first stitch a rectangle as close to the edges as possible. Pivot (*Appendix*) at the corners, removing the pin after the first side has been stitched. Then stitch diagonally, sewing a second time over one side of the rectangle.

5. To cover the overlapping ends of the elastic, cut a piece of satin ribbon 1 1/2 inches long and twice the width of the elastic plus 1/2 inch.

6. Fold the ribbon in half lengthwise, wrong sides together. Slip the folded ribbon over the stitched ends of the elastic so that the fold covers the decorative edge of the elastic. Secure with a pin.

7. Machine stitch 1/16 inch inside all four edges.

B ATTACHING THE ELASTIC TO THE GARMENT

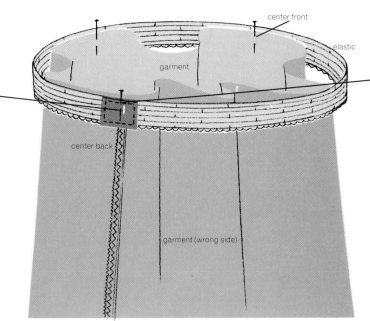

8. Divide the continuous elastic strip into four equal parts, marking with a pencil or chalk. Make the first mark at the ribbon that you attached in Steps 5-7.

9. With the garment wrong side out, divide the raw edge where the elastic will be attached into four equal parts, marking with a pencil or chalk. Make the first mark at the center back.

10. Place the elastic strip around the garment and align the nondecorative edge of the elastic with the raw edge of the garment.

11. Match the mark on the ribbon with the center back of the garment, and pin.

12. Match the opposite mark on the elastic with the center front of the garment, and pin. Then, stretching the elastic, match the other two marks on the elastic with the marks on the garment edge, and pin.

13. If the pins are more than 6 inches apart, stretch and pin the elastic midway between the pins.

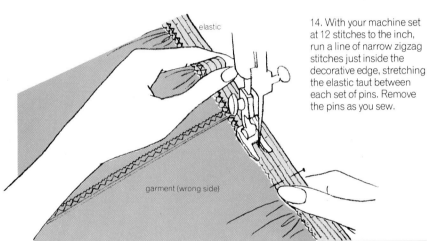

14. With your machine set at 12 stitches to the inch, run a line of narrow zigzag stitches just inside the decorative edge, stretching the elastic taut between each set of pins. Remove the pins as you sew.

C FINISHING THE ELASTIC EDGING

15. Turn the garment right side out.

16. Trim the garment seam allowance so that it is 1/8 inch inside the nondecorative edge of the elastic.

17. Fold the elastic over the seam allowance so that it is against the outside of the garment.

18. Make a line of machine zigzag stitches just inside the nondecorative edge, stretching the elastic as you did in Step 14.

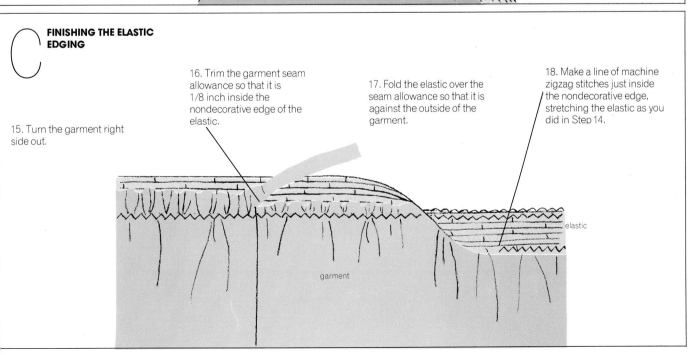

CONTINUOUS CASING WITH ELASTIC

A MAKING THE CASING

1. To determine the depth for the casing, measure the width of the elastic you plan to use. Then add 1/4 inch for clearance and 1/4 inch for the seam allowance.

2. With the garment wrong side out, turn up the garment edge that you are putting the elastic in by the amount determined in Step 1. Press.

3. Turn under the raw edge 1/4 inch, and pin at 1-inch intervals.

4. Baste near the inner folded edge and remove the pins.

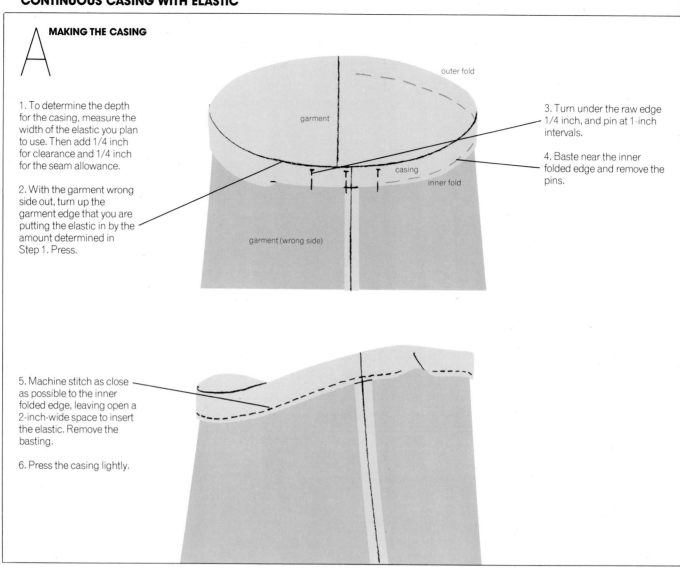

5. Machine stitch as close as possible to the inner folded edge, leaving open a 2-inch-wide space to insert the elastic. Remove the basting.

6. Press the casing lightly.

B INSERTING THE ELASTIC

7. To determine the length of the elastic, put the elastic around the appropriate body area, and stretch it until it is both secure and comfortable. Allow 1 inch for joining the ends.

8. Cut the elastic to the length you determined in the previous step.

9. Attach a small safety pin to one end of the elastic. Insert the pinned end of the elastic into the open space you left in the casing, and work it through the casing. Remove the pin.

10. Join the overlapping ends of the elastic, following the instructions for elastic edging (page 118, Steps 3 and 4).

11. Finish machine stitching the opening in the inner folded edge of the casing.

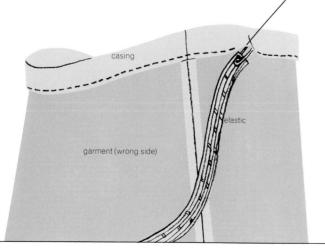

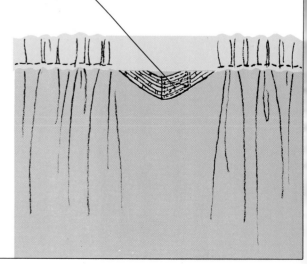

THE OPEN-ENDED CASING WITH ELASTIC

A MAKING THE CASING

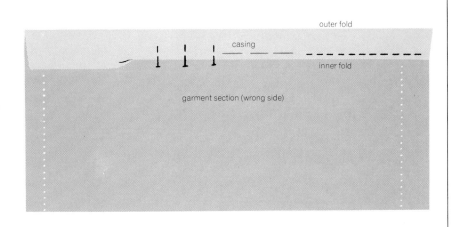

1. To make the casing, follow the instructions for the continuous casing with elastic *(opposite, Steps 1-6),* but stitch from one edge of the garment section to the other without leaving an opening.

outer fold

casing

inner fold

garment section (wrong side)

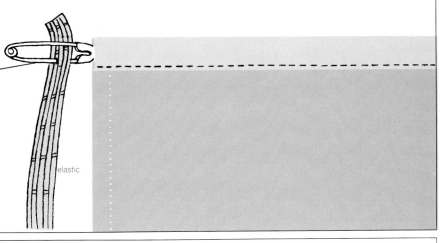

2. Without cutting the elastic to its final length, attach a small safety pin to one end of the elastic.

3. Insert the pinned end of the elastic into one end of the casing, and work it through. Remove the pin.

elastic

B INSERTING THE ELASTIC

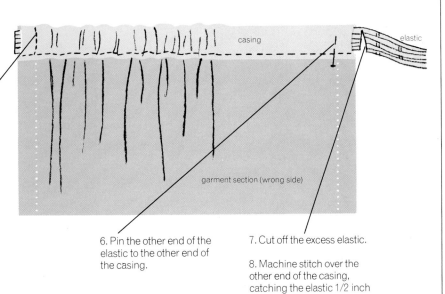

4. Align one end of the elastic with one end of the casing, and machine stitch over the end of the casing, catching the elastic 1/2 inch from the end.

5. Holding the casing up to the appropriate body area, stretch the elastic until it is both secure and comfortable.

casing

elastic

garment section (wrong side)

6. Pin the other end of the elastic to the other end of the casing.

7. Cut off the excess elastic.

8. Machine stitch over the other end of the casing, catching the elastic 1/2 inch from the end. Remove the pin.

The airy art of cutaway appliquéing

In conventional appliquéing, pieces are cut to shape—then sewed in place. But in cutaway appliqué, the steps are reversed: a design is stitched on uncut fabric; the excess material around, and often behind, the design then is scissored away to unveil the appliqué. The result appears to float on the base fabric, so that sheers remain transparent and lace inserts—like the side panel in the shorts at left—keep their intriguing openness.

Cutaway appliquéing uses both straight stitches to outline shapes, and fine or satin zigzag machine stitches to form attractive edges around those shapes. On delicate fabrics, the stitches should be kept narrow and fine looking, especially where they have to follow intricately looped and swirled lines like those along the rims of laces. Instructions for sewing and scissoring cutaway appliqué start on the opposite page.

122

LACE INSET APPLIQUÉ

A PREPARING THE APPLIQUÉ PIECE

1A. If you are using lace fabric, cut a rectangular piece of the fabric containing the design you wish to appliqué. Make sure the piece is at least 1 inch larger all around than the design outline. If the lace fabric is soft, cut a piece of tulle or organza the same size as the lace piece for backing.

1B. If you are inserting a lace border piece, cut a length that is 1 inch longer at each end than the area you want to appliqué. Then, for backing, cut a piece of tulle or organza 1 inch larger on all sides than the lace piece.

2. With the wrong sides together, pin the lace piece to the backing.

3. Baste the pieces together about 1/4 inch inside the design outline. Remove the pins.

lace fabric

backing fabric

B ATTACHING THE APPLIQUÉ PIECE

4. Pin the appliqué piece on the outside of the garment.

5. Baste the piece to the garment about 1/4 inch outside the design outline. Remove the pins.

6. With your machine set at 20 stitches per inch, sew along the design outline. Pivot *(Appendix)* at the corners or on curves. If the lace motif has a raised outline edge, stitch just outside the edge.

7. Reset your machine to a very fine—or satin—zigzag stitch of narrow-to-medium width.

8. Following the outline of the design, slowly stitch directly on the straight stitching and, if any, the raised edge of the lace motif. To avoid gaps in the stitching, pivot only when the needle is on the outside of the curves or corners.

9. Pull the loose thread ends to the wrong side of the garment and tie them off. Remove the bastings.

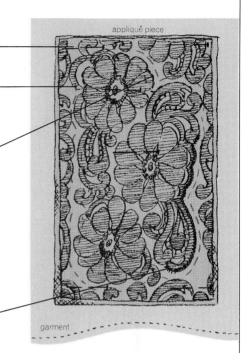

appliqué piece

garment

C FINISHING THE APPLIQUÉ

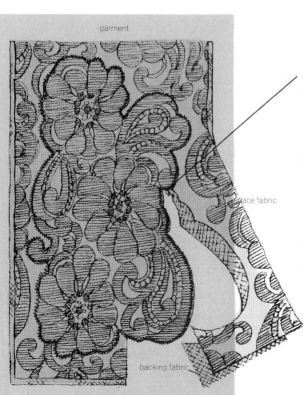

garment

lace fabric

backing fabric

10. Using embroidery or manicure scissors, trim away the excess fabric along the edges of the appliqué piece, close to the zigzag stitching, without cutting into it. Be careful not to cut into the garment fabric underneath.

11. Turn the garment wrong side out.

12. Cut out the garment fabric within the zigzag-stitched area. To do this, pinch both layers of the appliqué piece to hold it away from the garment fabric, and make a small snip in the garment fabric in the center of the area. Then cut away the rest of the fabric as close to the zigzag stitching as possible without cutting into it.

13. Lightly press the appliqué with a warm dry iron.

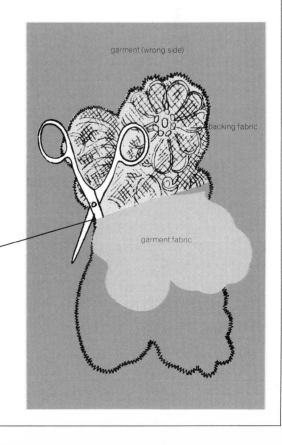

garment (wrong side)

backing fabric

garment fabric

SHEER INSET APPLIQUÉ

A PREPARING THE APPLIQUÉ PIECE

1. To make a pattern for the appliqué, draw or trace a design on a sheet of paper. Make sure that the design is simply an outline, and that the lines are dark enough to show through sheer fabric. If you want to enlarge or reduce the design, follow the instructions on page 127.

2. Cut a rectangular piece of sheer fabric at least 1 inch larger all around than the design outline.

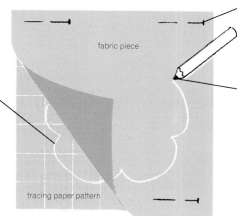

3. Lay the fabric piece wrong side down over the pattern and pin it in place.

4. Using a sharp, light-colored dressmaker's pencil, trace the outline of the design for the appliqué onto the fabric. Remove the pins, and set aside the paper pattern.

5. For backing, cut another piece of sheer fabric the same size as the marked one.

6. With the wrong sides together, pin the marked piece to the backing.

7. Baste 1/4 inch inside the design outline. Remove the pins.

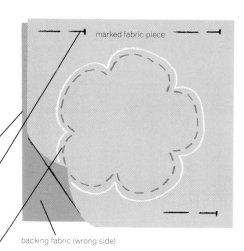

B ATTACHING THE APPLIQUÉ

8. Attach and finish the sheer inset appliqué, following the instructions for lace inset appliqué (page 123, Boxes B and C).

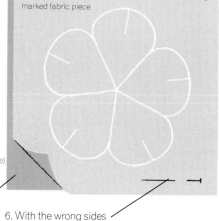

SIMPLE THREE-DIMENSIONAL APPLIQUÉ

A PREPARING THE APPLIQUÉ PIECE

1. To make a pattern for the appliqué, draw or trace a design on a sheet of paper. Make sure the lines are dark enough to show through sheer fabric. If you want to enlarge or reduce the design, follow the instructions on page 127. Note that the design can have lines for stitching within the outline.

2. Cut a rectangular piece of sheer fabric at least 1 inch larger all around than the design.

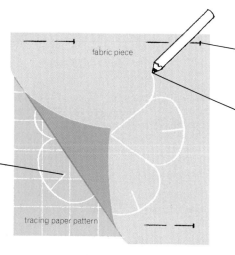

3. Lay the fabric piece wrong side down over the pattern, and pin it in place.

4. Using a sharp, light-colored dressmaker's pencil, trace the design for the appliqué onto the fabric. Make sure to include any internal lines. Remove the pins, and set aside the pattern.

5. For backing, cut another piece of sheer fabric the same size as the marked one.

6. With the wrong sides together, pin the marked piece to the backing.

B SEWING THE APPLIQUÉ PIECE

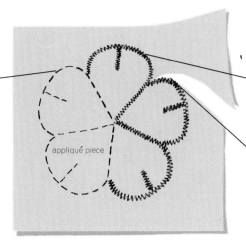

7. With your machine set at 15 to 20 stitches per inch, sew along all lines in the design. Begin at a point near the center, and try to make your stitching as continuous as possible. Pivot (Appendix) at corners and on curves.

8. Reset your machine to a very fine—or satin—zigzag stitch of narrow-to-medium width.

appliqué piece

9. Slowly zigzag stitch directly on the straight stitching. To avoid gaps in the stitching, pivot only when the needle is on the outside of the curves or corners.

10. Using embroidery or manicure scissors, trim away the excess fabric along the edges of the appliqué piece as close to the zigzag stitching as possible without cutting into it.

C ATTACHING THE APPLIQUÉ

11. Pin the completed appliqué piece in position on the outside of the garment. Do not pin in the center area where you plan to sew the appliqué to the garment.

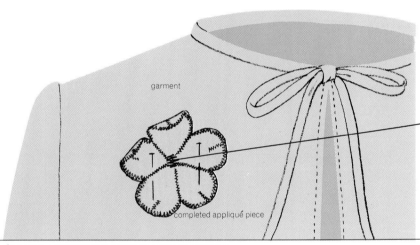

garment

completed appliqué piece

12. With your machine still set for a very fine—or satin—zigzag stitch, sew the center of the appliqué to the garment. If you want to create a rounded shape with the stitching, stitch slowly while adjusting the stitch-width control—as smoothly and gradually as possible—from narrow to wide and then back to narrow. Remove the pins.

13. Pull the loose ends of the thread to the wrong side of the garment, and tie them off.

THREE-DIMENSIONAL APPLIQUÉ WITH CUTAWAYS WITHIN THE DESIGN

A STITCHING AROUND THE AREA TO BE CUT AWAY

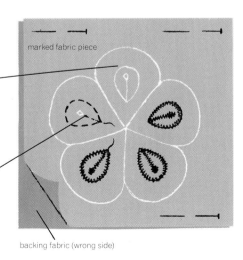

marked fabric piece

backing fabric (wrong side)

1. Prepare the appliqué piece following the instructions for simple three-dimensional appliqué (Box A, left). Make sure to outline the areas where the backing is to be cut away.

2. With your machine set at 15 to 20 stitches per inch, sew around all the lines in the design, beginning with the outlines closest to the center. If there is to be decorative stitching inside an area, such as the stems in the flower shown here, stitch along them at the same time. Pivot (Appendix) on curves and at corners.

3. Reset your machine to a very fine—or satin—zigzag stitch of narrow-to-medium width.

4. Slowly zigzag stitch directly over the straight stitching. At the same time, complete any decorative stitching inside an area, such as the tips of the stems. To avoid gaps in the stitching, pivot only when the needle is on the outside of the curves or corners.

5. Trim the outer edges of the appliqué piece, following the directions for making a simple three-dimensional appliqué (Box B, Step 10, above).

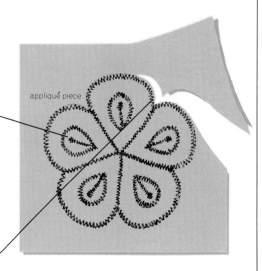

appliqué piece

continued

6. In each area to be cut away, insert a pin in the upper layer of fabric to hold it away from the backing.

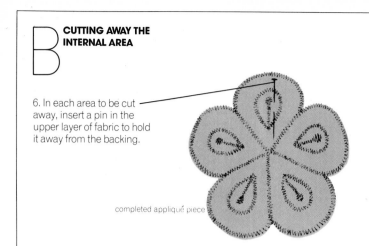

completed appliqué piece

7. Turn the appliqué piece over and snip the backing fabric with embroidery or manicure scissors, just above the pin protecting the top layer.

8. Very carefully cut away the backing fabric as close to the zigzag stitching as possible without cutting into it.

9. Attach the appliqué to the garment, following the instructions for the simple three-dimensional appliqué *(page 125, Box C).*

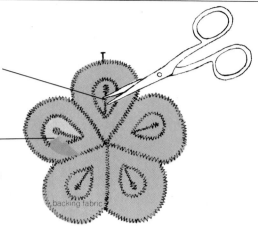

backing fabric

APPLIQUÉ WITH DECORATIVE ZIGZAG STITCHING OF VARIED WIDTH

A ATTACHING THE APPLIQUÉ

1. Prepare the appliqué piece following the directions for simple three-dimensional appliqué *(page 124, Box A).*

2. Pin the appliqué piece to the outside of the garment.

3. With your machine set at 20 stitches per inch, sew along all lines in the design. Begin near the center, making your stitching as continuous as possible. Pivot *(Appendix)* at corners and on curves. Remove the pins as you sew.

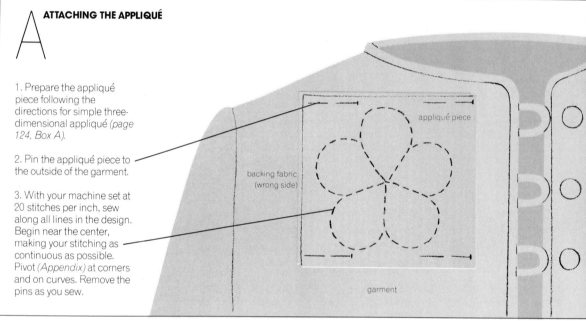

appliqué piece

backing fabric (wrong side)

garment

B MAKING THE DECORATIVE ZIGZAG STITCHING

4. Draw light pencil lines to mark each area along the lines of stitching that will be filled in with zigzag stitches of varying widths.

5. With your machine set to a very fine—or satin—zigzag stitch, slowly stitch in each marked area while adjusting the stitch-width control, as smoothly and gradually as possible, from narrow to wide and then back to narrow. Begin at the center of the design. Make sure the stitching covers the pencil markings.

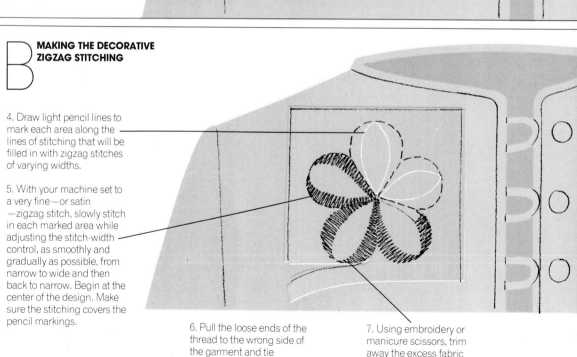

6. Pull the loose ends of the thread to the wrong side of the garment and tie them off.

7. Using embroidery or manicure scissors, trim away the excess fabric along the edges of the appliqué piece, just outside the line of machine stitching.

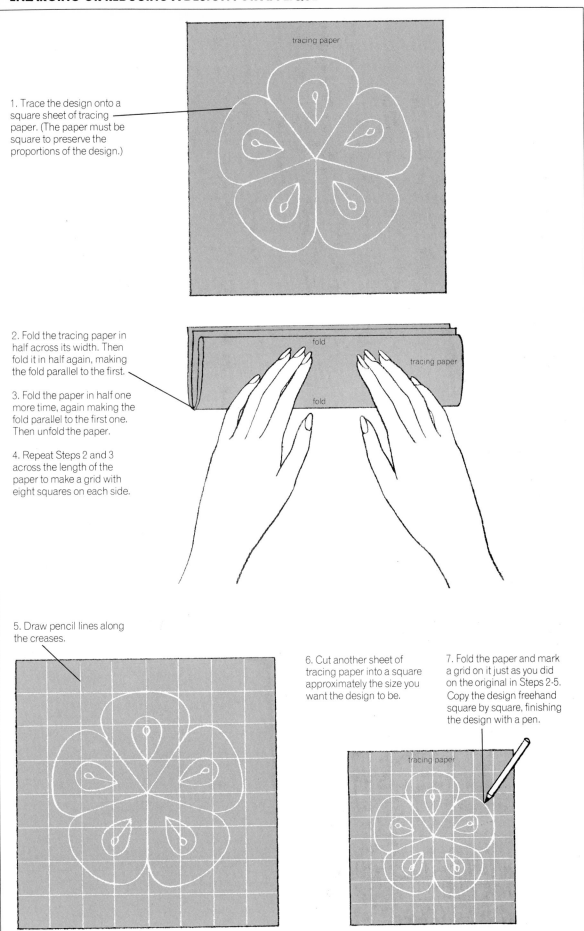

1. Trace the design onto a square sheet of tracing paper. (The paper must be square to preserve the proportions of the design.)

2. Fold the tracing paper in half across its width. Then fold it in half again, making the fold parallel to the first.

3. Fold the paper in half one more time, again making the fold parallel to the first one. Then unfold the paper.

4. Repeat Steps 2 and 3 across the length of the paper to make a grid with eight squares on each side.

5. Draw pencil lines along the creases.

6. Cut another sheet of tracing paper into a square approximately the size you want the design to be.

7. Fold the paper and mark a grid on it just as you did on the original in Steps 2-5. Copy the design freehand square by square, finishing the design with a pen.

See-through thread works

Lattices of threads, called fagoting or drawn work, create delicate linear designs between fabrics—or within them. Fagoting, for example, bridges a seam between hemmed edges with a see-through pattern of decorative stitches. It can substitute for any plain seam—straight or curved—that joins two fabric pieces of equal length without any easing or gathering. Or it can be introduced to garments with no seams, as on the yoke of the pajama blouse seen here, which has been cut apart and reassembled with fagoting.

Drawn work, on the other hand, forms bridges within a piece of fabric—in the version called hemstitching, along the top of a hem. Several adjacent rows of warp or weft are drawn out of a fabric, then the remaining cross threads are secured in small, even bunches.

Both kinds of openwork can be done in color-contrasting or matching thread. Fagoting works on almost any fabric, but drawn work is best reserved for evenly woven cloth where threads can be counted without too much eyestrain. Instructions for both openwork techniques appear on the following pages.

ADJUSTING A PATTERN FOR FAGOTING ALONG A SEAM

1. Decide how wide you want the fagoting to be —usually between 1/8 and 1/2 inch, depending on the fabric and the effect desired.

2. On one pattern piece, measure in from the seam line half of the desired fagoting width, and draw a new seam line parallel to the original seam line.

3. Draw a new cutting line 1/2 inch outside the new seam line. Make sure to mark any notches.

4. Trim the pattern along the new cutting line.

5. Repeat Steps 2-4 on the corresponding seam line of the adjacent pattern piece.

ADJUSTING A PATTERN FOR INTERIOR FAGOTING

1. Decide how wide you want the fagoting to be —usually between.1/8 and 1/2 inch, depending on the fabric and the effect desired.

2. At the point on the garment pattern piece where you want the fagoting to be, draw two parallel lines separated by the desired fagoting width. These lines will be the fagoting seam lines.

3. Cut the pattern apart midway between the lines.

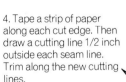

4. Tape a strip of paper along each cut edge. Then draw a cutting line 1/2 inch outside each seam line. Trim along the new cutting lines.

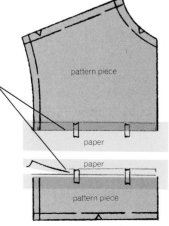

PREPARING THE FABRIC FOR FAGOTING

1. Using dressmaker's carbon paper and a tracing wheel, trace one of the adjusted seam lines for the fagoting onto a sheet of stiff paper. If the pattern was designed to be placed on folded fabric, make sure to double the length of the seam line. Mark any notches with short lines, as shown.

2. Remove the pattern, then draw a second line parallel to the first. The space between the lines should equal the desired width of the fagoting.

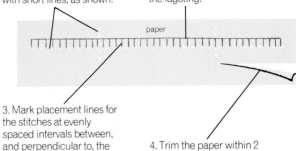

3. Mark placement lines for the stitches at evenly spaced intervals between, and perpendicular to, the two lines.

4. Trim the paper within 2 inches of the marked area.

5. Mark any notches across the seam lines of the fabric pieces with small running stitches (Appendix).

6. If necessary, trim the seam allowances to 1/2 inch.

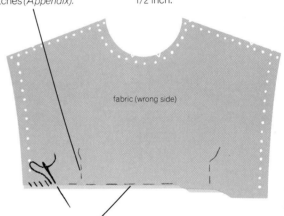

7. With the fabric wrong side up, make a narrow hem along each edge to be fagoted. Start by turning up the seam allowance 1/4 inch. Then turn up the seam allowance along the seam line. Baste in place.

8. Slip stitch (Appendix) along the inner folded edge, and remove the basting. Press.

9. With the wrong sides down, pin the fabric pieces to the paper strip, aligning the hemmed edges with the parallel lines and matching notches.

10. Baste the fabric pieces to the paper strip 1/8 inch from the hemmed edges. Remove the pins.

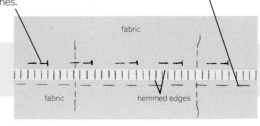

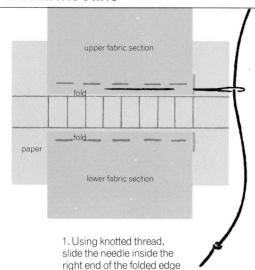

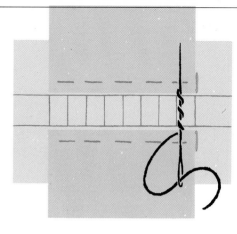

1. Using knotted thread, slide the needle inside the right end of the folded edge of the upper fabric section; bring the needle out just above the fold at the first stitch placement mark. Pull the thread through.

2. Insert the needle into the wrong side of the lower fabric section at the same stitch placement mark. Bring it out just below the folded edge. Pull the thread through.

3. Slant the needle upward vertically and twist it around the vertical stitch two or three times, as shown. Pull the thread through.

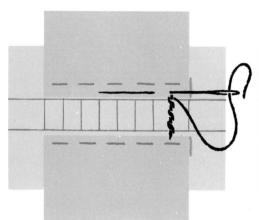

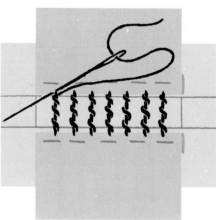

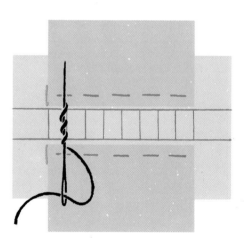

4. Insert the needle into the upper fabric section in the hole from which it emerged in Step 1. Slanting the needle horizontally to the left, slide it inside the folded edge of the fabric and bring it out just above the fold at the next stitch placement mark.

5. Repeat Steps 2-4 as many times as necessary to complete the line of fagoting, ending with Step 3. Then insert the needle into the hole in the upper fabric section, as in Step 4, but this time draw the thread through to the wrong side of the fabric. Remove the bastings, and secure the fagoting by making a small fastening stitch (Appendix) on the wrong side of the fabric.

IF YOU ARE LEFT-HANDED...
Follow the directions in Steps 1-5, but proceed from left to right, as shown.

TRELLIS FAGOTING

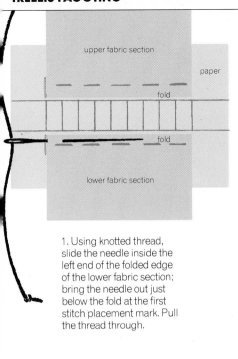

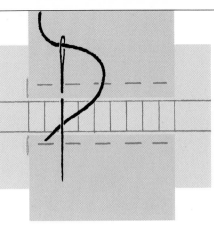

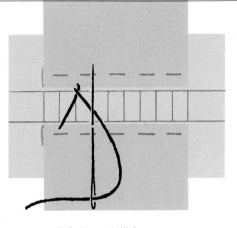

1. Using knotted thread, slide the needle inside the left end of the folded edge of the lower fabric section; bring the needle out just below the fold at the first stitch placement mark. Pull the thread through.

2. At the next stitch placement mark to the right, insert the needle through all layers to the wrong side of the upper fabric section just above the fold. Slant the needle downward vertically and bring it up just below the edge of the upper fold. Slide the thread extending from the previous stitch under the needle, as shown, and pull the thread through.

3. At the next stitch placement mark to the right, insert the needle through all layers to the wrong side of the lower fabric section just below the fold. Slant the needle upward vertically, and bring it up above the edge of the bottom fold. Slide the thread extending from the previous stitch under the needle, as shown, and pull the thread through.

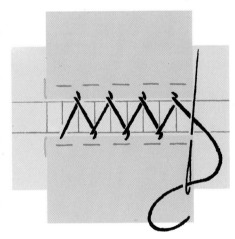

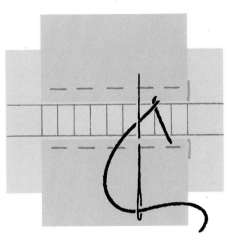

4. Working to the right, repeat Steps 2 and 3 as many times as necessary to complete the row of fagoting. Then remove the bastings, and secure the fagoting by making a small fastening stitch (Appendix) on the wrong side of the fabric.

IF YOU ARE LEFT-HANDED...
Follow the directions in Steps 1-4 above, but proceed from right to left, as shown.

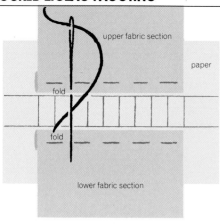

upper fabric section

paper

fold

fold

lower fabric section

1. Start by following the instructions in Steps 1 and 2 of trellis fagoting.

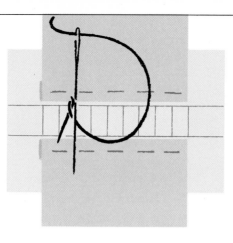

2. Reinsert the needle into the hole in the upper fabric section made in the previous step. Slant the needle downward vertically and bring it up just below the edge of the upper fold. Slide the thread extending from the previous stitch under the needle, as shown, and pull the thread through.

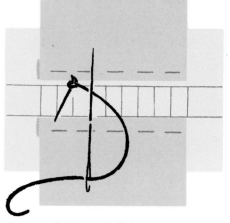

3. At the next stitch placement line to the right, insert the needle through all layers to the wrong side of the lower fabric section just below the fold. Slant the needle upward vertically and bring it up just above the edge of the lower fold. Slide the thread extending from the previous stitch under the needle, as shown, and pull the thread through.

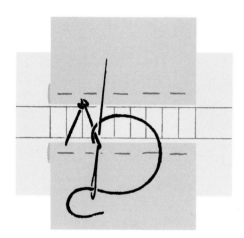

4. Reinsert the needle into the lower fabric section in the hole made in the previous step. Slant the needle upward vertically and bring it up just above the edge of the lower fold. Slide the thread extending from the previous stitch under the needle, as shown, and pull the thread through.

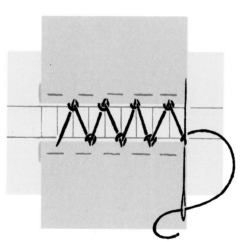

5. Make similar stitches as many times as necessary to complete the row of fagoting. Remove the bastings and secure the fagoting by making a small fastening stitch (*Appendix*) on the wrong side of the fabric.

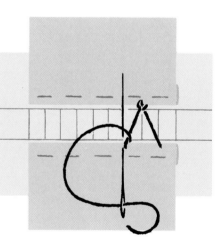

IF YOU ARE LEFT-HANDED...
Follow the directions in Steps 1-5, but proceed from right to left, as shown.

LACED KNOT STITCH

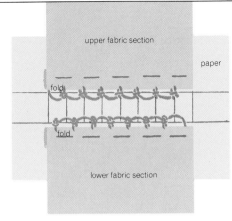

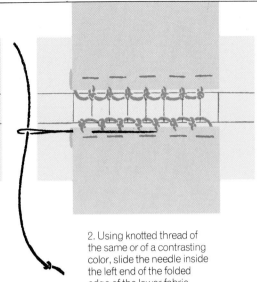

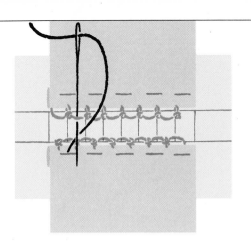

1. Make a row of knot stitches along each folded edge of the fabric, following the instructions on page 110. Along one edge, align the stitches with the stitch placement lines marked on the paper. Along the other edge, stagger the stitches so that they are midway between the stitch placement lines, as shown.

2. Using knotted thread of the same or of a contrasting color, slide the needle inside the left end of the folded edge of the lower fabric section. Bring the needle out just below the fold and midway between the first two knots of the row of knot stitches.

3. Slant the needle downward vertically and insert it under the first loop of the upper row of knot stitches. Slide the thread extending from the previous stitch under the needle, as shown. Pull the thread through.

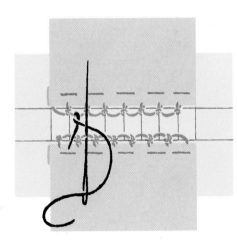

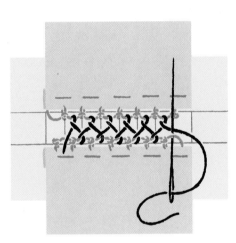

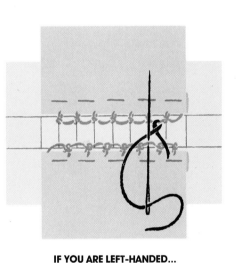

4. Slant the needle upward vertically and insert it under the second loop of the lower row of knot stitches. Slide the thread extending from the previous stitch under the needle, as shown. Pull the thread through.

5. Working to the right, repeat Steps 3 and 4 as many times as necessary to complete the row of fagoting. Remove the bastings, and secure the thread by making a small fastening stitch (Appendix) on the wrong side of the fabric.

IF YOU ARE LEFT-HANDED...
Follow the directions in Steps 1-5, but proceed from right to left, as shown.

STRAIGHTENING FABRIC FOR HEMSTITCHING

1. Spread the fabric wrong side up on a flat surface. Make a small cut near the edge to be hemstitched, and snag a thread with a pin.

2. Gently pull on the thread so that it shows up as a puckered line along the hem edge.

3. Trim the hem edge along the puckered line.

4. Repeat along any other edge to be hemstitched.

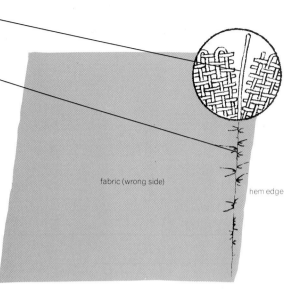

fabric (wrong side)

hem edge

5. If the grain of the fabric needs to be straightened, fold the fabric in half, wrong side out, and pin it together along the edges at 5-inch intervals, using rustproof pins. As you pin, smooth the fabric toward the fold with your hands.

6. Using a steam iron, start ironing at the pinned edges and move toward the fold. Continue moving in parallel paths until you have ironed the entire length of the fabric. As you press, stop periodically and pull the fabric diagonally to straighten the grain.

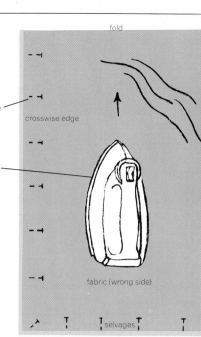

fold

crosswise edge

fabric (wrong side)

selvages

PREPARING TO HEMSTITCH ALONG ONE EDGE

1. To determine where to begin drawing out threads from the fabric, double the desired finished width of the hem, then add 1/4 inch.

2. With the fabric wrong side up, measure in from the hem edge the distance you determined in Step 1, and draw a chalk line parallel to the edge. Use one thread as a guide for the line.

3. Midway along the length of the chalk line, use a pin to snag the thread that you used as a guide for drawing the line.

4. Pull the thread up slightly, and clip it with an embroidery scissors. Be careful not to cut into any other surrounding threads.

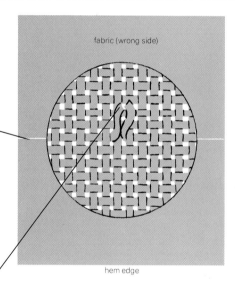

fabric (wrong side)

hem edge

5. To draw out the clipped thread, start by inserting a pin under the thread 1/4 to 1/2 inch to one side of the clip. Gently pull up the thread until you have eased the clipped end out of the fabric.

6. Continue drawing out the thread in this manner, working from the center out toward the side edge. Cut off the end of the drawn thread at intervals if it becomes too long to draw out easily.

7. Draw out the other half of the clipped thread in the same manner.

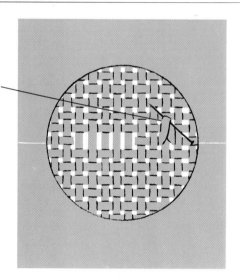

8. Working away from the hem edge, repeat Steps 3-7 to draw out one or more additional threads. The number of threads drawn out will depend on the weight of the fabric and the desired width of the drawn-thread area.

9. With the fabric still wrong side up, turn up the hem edge 1/4 inch. Press.

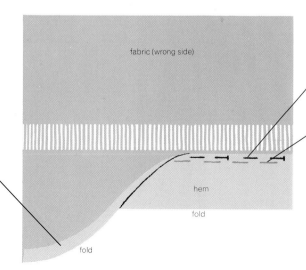

fabric (wrong side)

hem

fold

fold

10. Turn the hem up again, to within one thread of the drawn area. Pin the hem in place.

11. Baste 1/8 inch in from the first folded edge and remove the pins. Press.

1. Along both edges to be hemstitched, follow the directions for drawing threads given in preparing to hemstitch along one edge, Steps 1-8 (left). However, draw out threads only to the point at which the chalk lines intersect, and leave a long enough end on each drawn strand to thread it on a needle.

2. To finish the edges of the small open square formed by the intersection of the drawn areas, thread the drawn strands, one at a time, on a needle. Then, following the grain, use a running stitch (Appendix) to weave each thread back into the fabric.

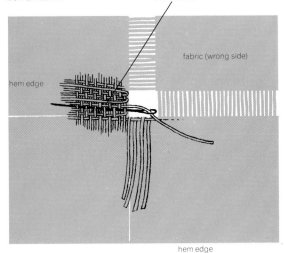

3. Fold the corner of the fabric diagonally to within 1/8 inch of the open square formed by the drawn threads. Press.

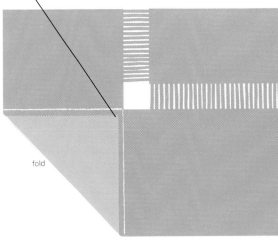

4. Open up the corner, and trim it off along the diagonal crease.

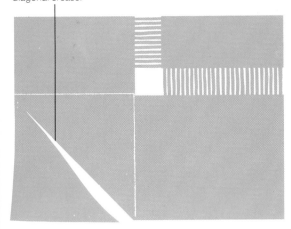

5. Turn up the diagonal edge of the hem 1/4 inch, and press.

6. Turn up the long edges 1/4 inch, and press.

7. Fold up each hem to within one thread of the drawn area, and press. Pin the hems in place.

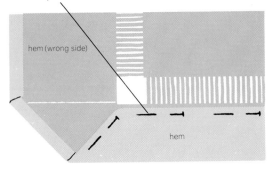

8. Baste 1/8 inch from the inner folded edges.

9. Slip stitch (Appendix) the corners together and remove the pins.

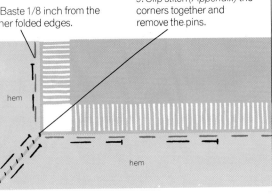

PLAIN HEMSTITCHING

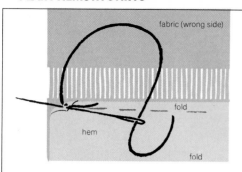

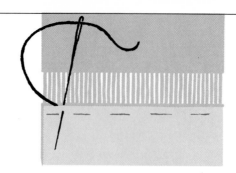

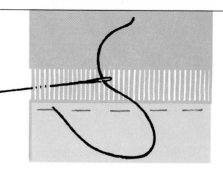

1. Place the fabric wrong side up, with the basted hem closest to you. Then, at the left side of the work, turn back the folded edge of the hem, and make a small fastening stitch (*Appendix*), sewing through the inner layer of the fold only.

2. Insert the needle in the wrong side of the folded hem, close to the fastening stitch. Bring the needle out just below the fold.

3. Slide the needle horizontally from right to left under the desired number of vertical threads in the drawn area. Pull the thread through, making sure to pull it taut in order to separate the group of drawn threads you have gathered.

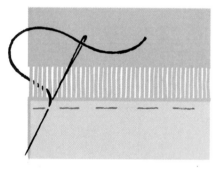

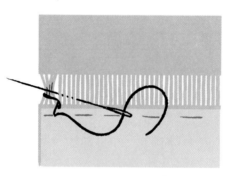

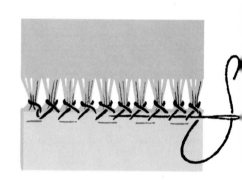

4. Slant the needle downward vertically and insert it into the wrong side of the hem, just to the right of the group of drawn threads you have just gathered. Bring the needle out of the hem, just below the fold. Secure the stitch by pulling the thread taut.

5. Working to the right of the previous stitch, repeat Steps 3 and 4 across the hem, ending with Step 4.

6. Secure the last stitch of the row by repeating Step 4. Then run the thread back under the finished hemstitches for about 1 inch, as shown. Clip the end of the thread close to the fabric and remove the basting.

IF YOU ARE LEFT-HANDED...
Follow the directions in Steps 1-6 with the following exceptions: begin at the right edge and work to the left, and slide the needle under the drawn threads from left to right, as shown.

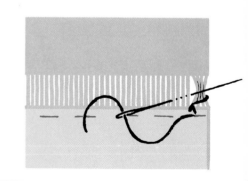

LADDER HEMSTITCHING

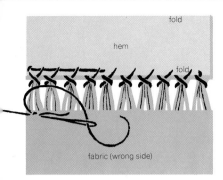

1. With the wrong side of the fabric up, complete a row of plain hemstitching (opposite) across the hemmed edge of the drawn area. Then turn the work so that the hemmed edge is away from you. Make a small fastening stitch (Appendix) near the left edge of the fabric, just below the drawn area.

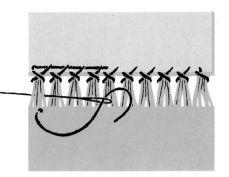

2. Slide the needle horizontally from right to left under the first group of drawn threads on the left. Pull the thread through tightly.

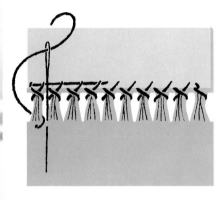

3. Slant the needle downward vertically, and insert it from under the fabric, just below the drawn area, as shown. Pull the thread through to the wrong side of the fabric. Secure the stitch by pulling the thread toward you tightly.

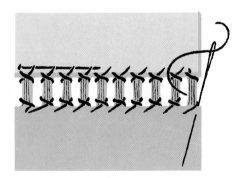

4. Working to the right of the previous stitch, repeat Steps 2 and 3 across the drawn area, ending with Step 3, as shown. Make sure to gather the same group of drawn threads in each stitch that was gathered in the original row of hemstitching.

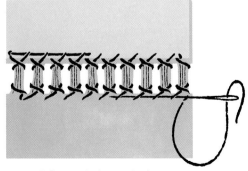

5. Secure the last stitch of the row by repeating Step 3. Then run the thread back under the finished hemstitches for about 1 inch, as shown. Clip the end of the thread close to the fabric.

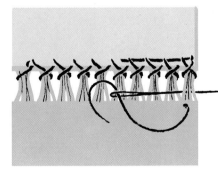

IF YOU ARE LEFT-HANDED...
Follow the directions in Steps 1-5 with the following exceptions: begin at the right edge and work to the left, and slide the needle under the drawn threads from left to right, as shown.

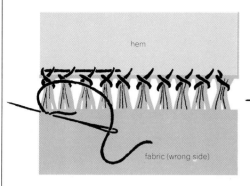

1. With the wrong side of the fabric up, complete a row of plain hemstitching (page 136) across the hemmed edge of the drawn area. Make sure to group an even number of threads. Then turn the work so that the hemmed edge is away from you, and make a small fastening stitch (Appendix) near the left edge of the fabric, just below the drawn area.

2. Slide the needle horizontally from right to left under the left half of the first group of drawn threads on the left. Pull the thread through tightly.

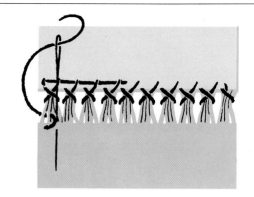

3. Slant the needle downward vertically, and insert it from under the fabric, just below the drawn area, as shown. Pull the thread through to the wrong side of the fabric. Secure the stitch by pulling the thread toward you tightly.

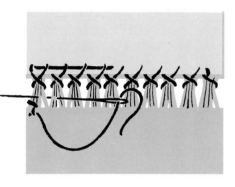

4. Working to the right of the previous stitch, slide the needle horizontally from right to left under the left half of the next group of drawn threads and the other half of the previous group, as shown. Pull the thread through. Secure the stitch by pulling the thread toward you tightly.

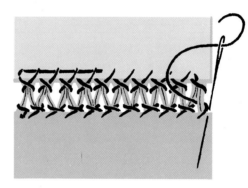

5. Working to the right, repeat Steps 3 and 4 across the row until you have gathered all but half of the last group of drawn threads. Gather the last half group by repeating Steps 2 and 3.

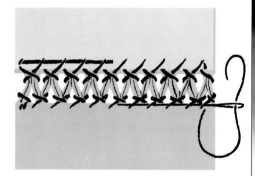

6. Secure the last stitch of the row by repeating Step 3. Then run the thread back under the finished hemstitches for about 1 inch, as shown. Clip the end of the thread close to the fabric.

IF YOU ARE LEFT-HANDED...
Follow the directions in Steps 1-6 with the following exceptions: begin at the right edge and work to the left, and slide the needle under the drawn threads from left to right, as shown.

CLUSTERED HEMSTITCHING

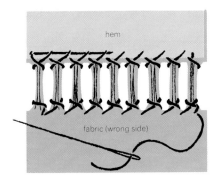

1. With the wrong side of the fabric up, make a wide drawn area—from 3/8 inch for finely woven fabrics up to 3/4 inch for coarser weaves. Then make ladder hemstitching (*page 137, Steps 1-4*) across the drawn area; end by repeating Step 3 at the right edge of the work, as shown, to secure the last stitch. Do not run the thread back under the finished stitches or cut it off.

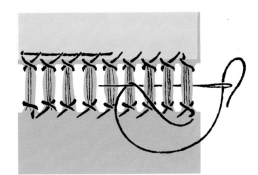

2. Insert the needle horizontally from right to left under the first three groups of ladder stitches on the right. Slide the thread over and around the needle in a counterclockwise direction, as shown. Holding the fabric so that the ladder stitches being clustered remain fairly taut, pull the thread through tightly.

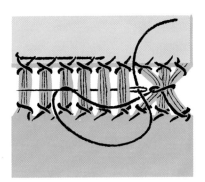

3. Working to the left, repeat Step 2 across the row. Make sure to gather three groups of drawn threads each time.

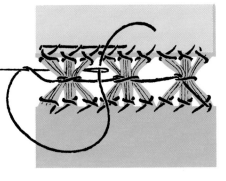

4. Secure the last stitch of the row by repeating Step 2 around the cluster.

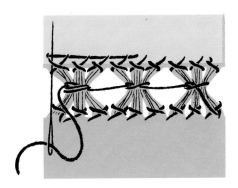

5. To end off, slant the needle upward toward the hemmed edge, and slide it under the last hemstitch, as shown. Then run the needle back under the finished hemstitches for about 1 inch. Clip the end of the thread close to the fabric.

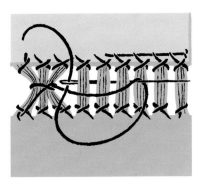

IF YOU ARE LEFT-HANDED…
Follow the directions in Steps 1-5 above, but proceed from left to right, as shown.

Gossamer gardens of stitchery

Flowers and butterflies—appliquéd in place or appliquéd separately, cut out and then stitched on—create a gossamer garden for a sheer pillow sham. Using techniques shown on pages 123-127, each piece is fashioned from two layers of organdy or of dotted Swiss and organdy. This method helps keep the flowers fresh looking, and one layer can be cut away from sections in the butterflies' wings to give them subtle variations in shading. Detailed instructions appear overleaf.

Instructions for appliquéing the pillow sham

The appliquéd ruffle-edged pillow sham shown on pages 140-141 covers a standard-sized bed pillow. To make a sham of this size, you will need 3 yards of lawn or organdy 45 inches wide for the sham and its ruffle. You will also need 1/2 yard of organdy and a small piece—about 8 inches square —of dotted swiss for the appliqués. Use mercerized cotton thread (No. 50) and a fine, Size 11 sewing-machine needle.

Cutting the pillow sham front and back: To determine the size of the sham front, measure the length and width of your pillow. Then add 1/2 inch all around for seam allowances. Cut the sham front from the lawn, with the length of the piece along the lengthwise grain of the fabric. Cut a sham back that is the same width as the sham front but 3 inches longer to provide for an overlap in the opening that will be in the middle of the back.

Preparing the appliqué patterns: Copy the design for the butterfly and the three flowers, given in actual size on the upper half of the opposite page, onto tracing paper.

Making the three-layered flower appliqués: Following the instructions for preparing and sewing the simple three-dimensional appliqué *(pages 124-125, Boxes A and B)*, make two appliqués each of the large, medium-sized and small flowers from organdy. Stack the appliqué pieces into two sets of triple-layered flowers, alternating the position of the petals so that each petal will be visible. Pin the flowers together, and set them aside for attachment later.

Making the three-dimensional flower appliqués: Again following the instructions provided for simple three-dimensional appliqué, prepare and sew—but do not attach—four small flower appliqués from the piece of dotted swiss. Then make three more small three-dimensional flower appliqués from organdy. Work in the same manner as you did on the dotted swiss, but instead of making a zigzag satin stitch of even width, follow the technique for making zigzag stitches of varied width described in Steps 3-5 for appliqué with decorative zigzag stitching *(page 126)*.

Making the butterfly appliqués: Following the instructions for three-dimensional appliqués with cutaways *(pages 125-126)*, prepare and sew—but do not attach—two butterfly appliqués from organdy. Sew the antennae with a zigzag satin stitch of even width, the body area with varied width. The areas to be cut away are tinted in the butterfly design on the opposite page. Make sure to trim carefully around the antennae.

Making the flat flower appliqués: Following the instructions for appliqué with decorative zigzag stitching, appliqué five small organdy flowers directly to the sham front. The position of the flowers is indicated by the letter A on the diagram at the bottom of the facing page. Make sure the appliqués that are nearest the edges of the sham front are at least 1 1/2 inches inside the edges. This distance will allow for a 1/2-inch seam allowance and a 1-inch margin between the appliqués and the seam.

Attaching the three-dimensional appliqués: Following the diagram showing the position of the appliqués on the sham front, attach the triple-layered flowers (labeled B in the diagram), the small organdy flowers (C), the small dotted-swiss flowers (D) and the butterflies (E). Follow the instructions for the simple three-dimensional appliqué, *(page 125, Box C)*.

Preparing and attaching the ruffle: To determine the length of the ruffle, measure the perimeter of the sham front. Then multiply by two. From the remaining lawn, cut and join 9-inch-wide bias strips until you have a continuous circular strip of the length you determined above. Follow the instructions on pages 30-31 for making a bias strip. Fold the circular strip in half lengthwise so that the wrong side is together. Hand baste the raw edges of the strip together 1/8 inch inside the edge. Make two parallel lines of machine basting—at 6 stitches to the inch—along the raw edge. Make the first line 1/4 inch from the edge and the second line 3/8 inch from the edge. Remove the hand basting.

Gather the ruffle by pulling the loose ends of the bobbin thread until the strip will fit around the sham front. Pin the gathered ruffle around the edges of the appliquéd side of the sham front, aligning the raw edges. Hand baste the ruffle to the front just inside the edges, and remove the pins. Machine stitch 3/8 inch from the edges, making sure to keep the gathers evenly distributed. Remove the hand basting but not the machine bastings.

Attaching the sham back: Cut the sham back in half crosswise. Finish the center cut edges with a narrow hem by turning up each edge 1/4 inch twice, and machine stitching along it. With the appliquéd side of the sham front facing up, pin the back sham pieces wrong side up to the front, aligning the outer edges. Make sure to overlap the hemmed edges of the sham back pieces at the center. Also make sure the ruffle is completely tucked in between the front and the back. Baste around the edges and remove the pins. Machine stitch 1/2 inch from the edges all around. Remove the basting. Trim the seam allowances to 1/4 inch. Clip the corners diagonally.

Finishing the pillow sham: Turn the sham right side out through the back opening. Press the sham lightly, being careful not to press the folded edge of the ruffle.

The butterfly and flowers above are actual-size designs for the appliqués. The diagram below shows the position of the appliqués.

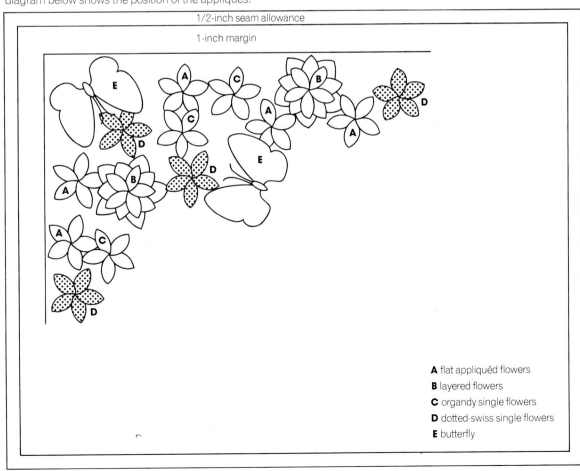

1/2-inch seam allowance

1-inch margin

A flat appliquéd flowers
B layered flowers
C organdy single flowers
D dotted-swiss single flowers
E butterfly

A look of stained glass

Varicolored sheers, juxtaposed in cutaway appliqués, create filmy tissues that have the clarity of stained glass. This gossamer triangle, which can be tied as a scarf *(left)* and draped as a stole *(below),* demonstrates how such appliqués work: Dark-colored organza is laid over light-colored, the two are stitched together as described on page 124, and then the light background is cut out from within the designs to leave the darker areas transparently clear. Instructions appear overleaf.

145

Cutting and stitching the appliqué stole

To make the stole with sheer inset and border appliqué, pictured on the preceding pages, you will need 1 1/2 yards of light-colored organza, 45 inches wide, for the background fabric and an equal amount of dark-colored organza for the appliqués. Use a fine Size 11 sewing-machine needle and cotton-covered polyester thread or mercerized cotton thread, No. 50, in a color that matches the dark-colored fabric.

Making the patterns for the appliqué: For each of the four appliqué designs shown on grids *(below and opposite)*, mark a piece of tracing paper with a grid of 1-inch squares. For the larger designs, tape together sheets of tracing paper if necessary. Copy the designs freehand onto your enlarged grid, square by square. Finish the designs in ink so that they will be dark enough to show through the sheer fabric that you will use for the appliqués.

Preparing the stole: Cut a 45-inch square piece of the light-colored background fabric. Fold the piece in half diagonally, wrong sides together, to form a double-layered triangle. Baste the layers together near the cut edges. Then as a guide for positioning the appliqués, baste through the center of the triangle, at a right angle to the folded edge. To baste this center guideline, fold the stole in half and mark the fold with pins. Then unfold the stole, and baste along the pin markers. Remove the pins as you sew.

Preparing the border: Cut two rectangular pieces of the dark-colored appliqué fabric. Each piece should measure 10 by 48 inches. Fold each piece in half lengthwise, wrong sides together. Baste near the long cut edge.

To trace the design onto the borders, pin one of the border pieces to the border pattern with the folded edge of the fabric along the long straight edge of the design. Using a dressmaker's pencil, trace the design onto the fabric. At each end of the border, add 1 inch for seam allowance. Remove the pattern, and trim off the ends of the border. Turn the pattern over and trace the design onto the other border piece in the same way.

To make the mitred corners between the border pieces, remove just enough of the basting so that you can open the ends. Then baste the two pieces together, wrong sides out, along the V-shaped center seam line. Machine stitch on the seam line, and remove the basting. Make a very fine — or satin — zigzag stitch of narrow width directly over the straight stitching. Then trim the seam allowances close to the zigzag stitching.

To close each of the outer ends of the border, remove the basting near the end. Then turn the end wrong side out, and baste along the seam line. Stitch and trim the seam as you did the mitred corner.

Appliquéing the border to the stole: Pin the border to the stole, making sure to match the corners, and align the folded edge of the border with the cut edge of the stole. Baste the border to the stole 1/4 inch outside the scalloped line, and remove the pins. Stitch along the scalloped line, and then trim away the border fabric above the stitching and the stole fabric under the border, following the instructions for lace inset appliqué *(page 123, Steps 6-12).*

Making the appliquéd shapes: Appliqué one teardrop shape and two of each free-form shape to the stole, following the instructions for sheer inset appliqué on page 124. The position of the appliqués is indicated on the diagram on the opposite page. Make sure to center the teardrop shape on the basted center line.

Finishing the stole: Remove all bastings; lightly press the stole with a warm, dry iron, being careful not to crease the folded edges of the stole.

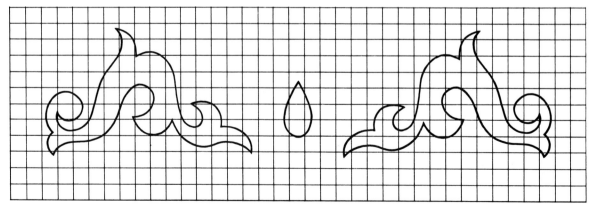

Appliqué designs

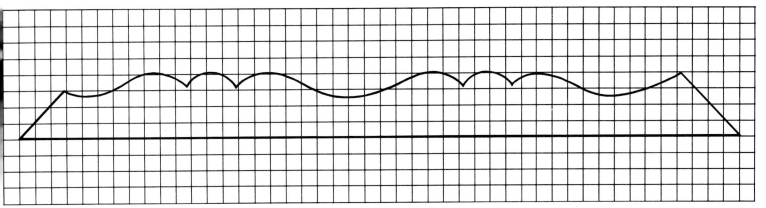

Border design (The left-hand end is the center seam line; the right-hand end is the outer seam.)

Diagram showing the position of the appliqués and border on the stole

Lattices and ladders

Fancy thread work opens up new ways to make plain-weave fabrics and classic patterns interesting. In the crepe overblouse *(left)*, bands of fagoting in a locked zigzag stitch —done in the same color thread as the garment—circle the sleeves and delineate the raglan seams. In the tailored linen-weave blouse *(right)*, hemstitching using ladder stitches of matching thread finishes off the hems of the center-front opening, the sleeves and the pocket. Instructions for adjusting garment patterns to these techniques begin overleaf.

Adding fagoting and hemstitching to the blouses

Both of the blouses shown on the preceding pages are adaptations of commercial patterns. To make the blouse with fagoting, buy any blouse pattern that has a raglan sleeve and use a natural or synthetic crepe fabric. You will need the yardage your pattern advises, plus an additional 1/4 yard for the jewel neckline with double bias binding. This neckline, which has no facing, replaces the pattern's collar and neck facings to keep the fagoting as open as possible. For the fagoting stitches, use silk buttonhole thread in a color that matches the fabric of the garment.

For the blouse with hemstitching, you can use any short-sleeved blouse pattern with a convertible collar. Make sure that the front pattern piece has a facing designed to be cut all in one piece with the front. For fabric, select material that is loosely woven—such as linen or synthetic linen—so that you can draw the threads easily. You will need the yardage your pattern indicates. For the hemstitching, use the same cotton or polyester thread you will use to sew the garment.

Before you start to make either blouse, make the pattern modifications shown in the boxes on the facing page.

THE BLOUSE WITH FAGOTING

Cutting and marking the garment pieces: Set aside any collar or neckline facing pattern pieces. Then follow your pattern instructions to cut and mark the fabric, making allowance for the three separate sections of the modified sleeve pattern *(opposite)*.

Making the fagoting on the sleeves: To join the three sections on each sleeve, follow the directions for preparing fabric for fagoting on page 129. Then sew the sections together, using locked zigzag fagoting *(page 132)*.

Making the fagoting on the raglan seams: To join each sleeve to the blouse front and back, prepare the fabric for fagoting as you did for the sleeve sections. When you make the paper strips for the fagoting this time, transfer the adjusted seam lines from the blouse front and back patterns. Then, when you pin the sleeve to each strip, shape the edge of the sleeve to the seam line. Again, using locked zigzag fagoting, sew the sleeve first to the blouse front and then to the back.

Assembling the blouse: Start by closing the shoulder dart on the sleeve. Then join the blouse fronts to the back by closing the side seams up to the fagoting. Next, close the seams on the sleeves, making sure to sew each sleeve section separately. Hem each sleeve. When you do, turn under the raw edge 1/4 inch so that the fold is just below the lowest row of fagoting on the sleeve. Complete the blouse, except for the neck edge, following your pattern instructions. Then finish the neck edge by making a jewel neckline with double bias binding *(page 81)*.

THE BLOUSE WITH HEMSTITCHING

Cutting and marking the garment pieces: Start by straightening the grain of the fabric *(page 134)*. Then cut and mark the garment pieces according to your pattern instructions. Make sure the lines indicating the point where you will begin to draw out threads for the hemstitching are parallel to the threads in the fabric. After you mark each garment piece to be hemstitched, fold back the pattern along the hemstitching guide line. Then draw a chalk line along the folded edge of the pattern. Use one thread in the fabric as a guide for the line. Mark garment pieces cut from the underlayer of fabric by positioning the pattern pieces on them and drawing a chalk line in the same manner.

Making the hemstitching: On each garment piece to be hemstitched, draw out the threads and turn up the hem, following the instructions for preparing fabric for hemstitching along one edge *(page 134, Steps 3-11)*. On each sleeve, close the underarm seam after you draw out the threads but before you turn up the hem. Hemstitch each garment piece, using the ladder hemstitch *(page 137)*.

Assembling the blouse: Follow your pattern instructions.

MODIFYING THE PATTERN PIECES FOR THE BLOUSE WITH FAGOTING

The sleeve pattern: To mark the three rows of fagoting on the sleeve, start by determining the desired length of the finished sleeve and marking a new hemline on the pattern piece. Make sure the new hemline follows the curve of the original hemline. Then draw a new hem cutting line 2 1/4 inches below the new hemline. To indicate the position of each row of fagoting, draw two parallel lines, 1/2 inch apart. The lowest row should be 2 inches above the hemline, and there should be 2 inches between the rows. Make sure the lines follow the curve of the hemline. Follow the instructions for adjusting a pattern for fagoting in a garment piece on page 129.

To mark the row of fagoting along the two raglan seams at the top of the sleeve, redraw each seam line 1/4 inch inside the original seam line. Follow the instructions for adjusting a pattern for fagoting along an existing garment seam *(page 129)*. Make sure to follow the curve of the original seam line.

The front and back pattern pieces: Redraw the raglan seam line on each pattern piece 1/4 inch inside the original seam line, as you did on the sleeve pattern.

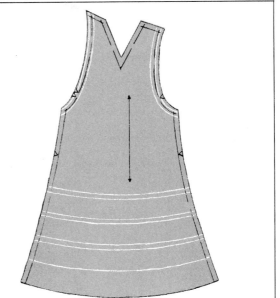

MODIFYING THE PATTERN PIECES FOR THE BLOUSE WITH HEMSTITCHING

To determine the width of the finished hem along all edges to be hemstitched, measure the distance on the front pattern piece between the center-front line and the facing fold line. Then double this measurement.

The front pattern piece: To mark the line where you will start to draw threads for the hemstitching, measure in from the facing fold line the hem width you determined. Then draw a line parallel to the fold line.

To mark the edge of the hem that will replace the facing, measure out from the facing fold line an amount equal to the hem width you determined plus 1/4 inch. Then draw a line parallel to the fold line. Trim along the line.

The sleeve pattern piece: Determine the desired length of the finished sleeve and mark a new hemline on the pattern piece. Make sure the new hemline is parallel to the original hemline.

To mark the hemstitching guide line, measure up from the new hemline the hem width you determined. Then draw a line that is parallel to the new hemline.

To mark the hem edge, measure down from the new hemline an amount equal to the hem width you determined plus 1/4 inch. Then draw a line that is parallel to the new hemline. Trim along the line.

The pocket pattern: To mark the hemstitching guide line, measure down from the top fold line the hem width you determined for the front of the blouse. Then draw a line parallel to the fold line.

To mark the hem edge, measure up from the fold line the hem width you determined plus 1/4 inch, and draw a line parallel to the fold line. Trim along the line.

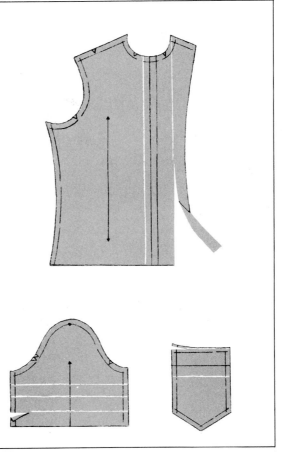

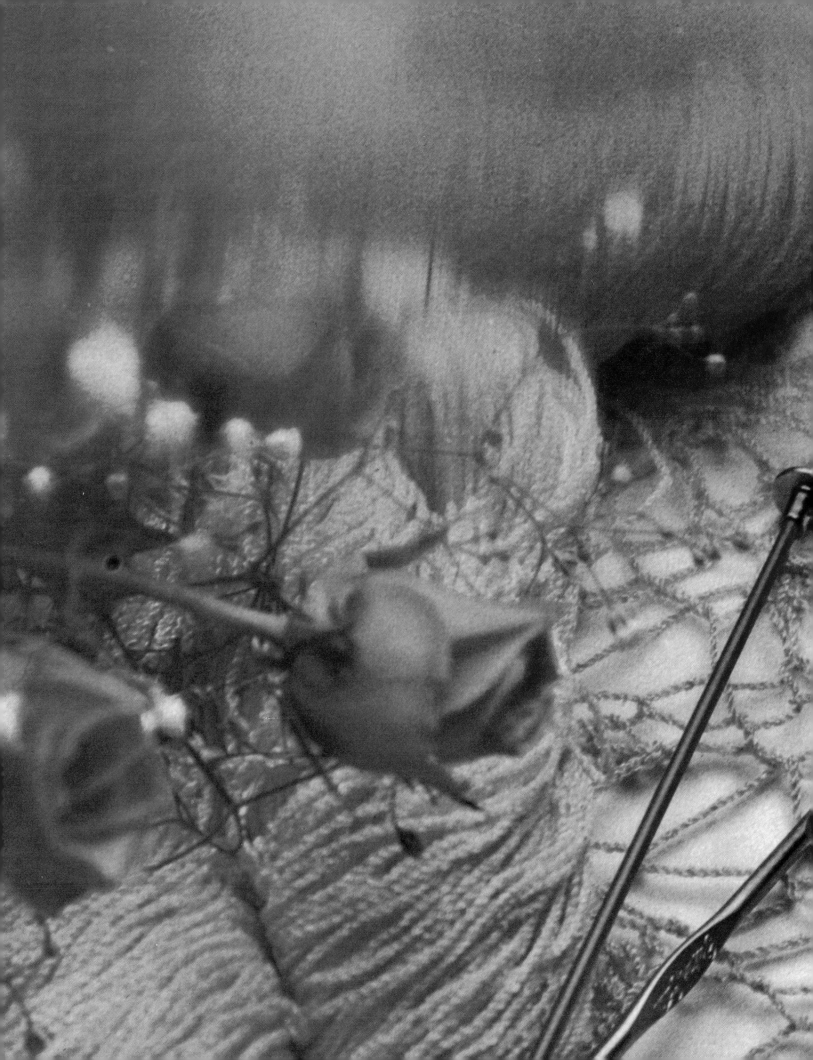

5
ENCHANTING WEBS OF NEEDLEWORK

Since the art of lacemaking first evolved in Europe nearly 500 years ago, it has represented a quintessence of delicacy—both in couture and in craft. Originally the finely patterned netting was knotted or twisted by the most painstaking of all needle techniques, and only the privileged few could afford to wear the results. But in the 19th Century, when the art's practitioners began to dwindle in numbers, crocheters

THE ENDURING LEGACY OF HANDMADE LACE

and knitters devised their own lacemaking techniques. To their delight, the newcomers found they could re-create the old, fragile patterns remarkably well, using crochet and knit methods that were immeasurably easier. In the process, they also changed lace from a luxury into a stylish ornament that everyone could execute and enjoy.

According to some accounts, lace as a craft most probably began in Italy before 1450. But lace was not adopted as haute couture until 1533 when Catherine de Médicis, accompanied by her own lacemaker, left her native Florence to marry the future French King Henry II. Catherine was a natural style setter, and her husband promptly adopted the Italian lace ruffs she wore. Always eager to please, Henry's court followed suit. But no one in France, save Catherine's personal artiste, could duplicate the complex patterns required: laces worn by the nobility had to be imported.

At first Italy was the center of the lace trade—as it had probably been the source of lacemaking skills. Venice was a major purveyor of needlepoint lace, or *point de Venise,* a crisp netting created with a needle by working silk or linen threads in variations of the loop or buttonhole stitch. Milan and Genoa—and later towns in Flanders—supplied a softer variety known as bobbin lace, pillow lace or bone lace. Actually a sophisticated form of braiding, or passementerie, bobbin lace was fabricated by working dozens of threads from separate bobbins around and between scores of straight pins or slivers of bone, arranged in a design and anchored in a firm cushion.

French aristocrats soon made a cult of displaying lace; they collected laces of various types and argued the merits of each example in the same way their modern counterparts discuss wines. Though a few French lacemakers were beginning to ply the craft, native laces, still coarse by comparison, seldom earned a kind word in such debates. Use of the foreign frippery reached prodigious proportions between 1570 and 1650. During the reigns of Henry III and Henry IV, so wide did the Frenchman's ruff become that the wearer's head seemed cut off from his shoulders—an illusion that prompted wits to dub the ruffs John the Baptist platters. Henry III's sister was so deeply upholstered in lace that she needed a two-foot-long spoon to eat her soup.

Such excesses were discouraged by the plainly dressed Henry IV, but the French proclivity for ostentation was too strong to quell for long. By the time of Louis XIV's accession in 1643, lace was a necessity of life for blue blood and *bourgeois gentilhomme* alike; no man could decently venture forth to greet the day without it.

Lace trimmed his underwear, his collars, his cuffs, his boot tops, his garters, even his suit of armor. It embellished his women in great poufs of snowy finery, seen and unseen. It made splendid the bed in which he slept, the coach in which he traveled and the coffin in which he was buried. Families of means flirted with financial ruin to obtain choice examples of lacework; wellborn nuns risked excommunication to wear filmy lace slips under their pious habits. Royal personages swaddled themselves in literally dozens of yards of the stuff.

Finally, to stem the ruinous drain of royal and noble capital, Jean Baptiste Colbert as Louis' financial minister determined to stop the importing—if not the wearing—of lace. Money squandered abroad, Colbert reasoned, could be kept at home if French lace were improved to the point where Frenchmen would buy it. Colbert accordingly lured Flemish and Italian master craftsmen to France to teach his countrymen their professional secrets. "Fashion is to France what the mines of Peru are to Spain," he cheerfully proclaimed as he created a royal lace company, granting it a 10-year monopoly and a substantial subsidy. Towns like Alençon and Argentan, where lacemakers with modest skills already worked, were chosen as nurseries for the infant industry.

Because court taste preferred the look of needlepoint to that of bobbin lace, Venetian artists were the most urgently sought; Colbert lured some 30 lacemaker-instructors out of Venice. The Venetian Senate, outraged at the defection of such workers and the theft of Venice's business, ordered them home with the warning: "If any craftsman

disobey, his nearest of kin will be put in prison, but if he obstinately decides to continue living abroad, an emissary will be commissioned to kill him."

For all the menace of its proclamation, however, the Senate was only blustering. The Venetian lacemakers remained in France to teach undisturbed. Within a short time Colbert pronounced the results fit for king and country.

The French Revolution brought the lace industry to an abrupt halt in 1789. Lace was too closely associated with the deposed aristocracy to continue in favor; some 30 major lace houses, descendants of Colbert's shops, closed down. In England,

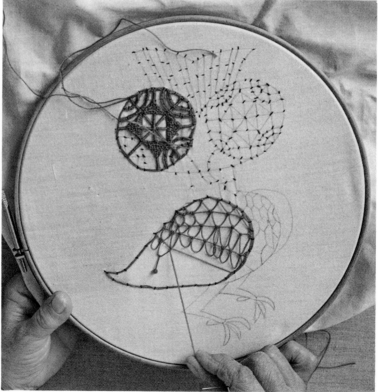
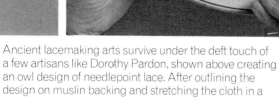

Ancient lacemaking arts survive under the deft touch of a few artisans like Dorothy Pardon, shown above creating an owl design of needlepoint lace. After outlining the design on muslin backing and stretching the cloth in a hoop, she traces the design with small hanger stitches *(center)* and then runs thread under and around them to create the lace. When finished *(right),* she frees the lace from its backing by simply cutting the hangers.

meanwhile, machines were invented that produced yards of lace in the time it had taken to make an inch by the old methods.

But just when it seemed that handmade lace might disappear altogether, a new form was born out of another sector of needlecraft. This time it was crocheters who supplied the dainty work fashion demanded. During the great famine of the 1840s, sisters in several Irish nunneries conceived the idea of producing traditional lace patterns by crochet as a means of generating income for their convents and for impoverished Irish peasants; lace became an Irish industry. Soon women in other parts of Europe and in America began to follow the Irish example as patterns adapted to crochet and, later, to knit were published.

Today, traditional lace is something to inherit and cherish or to see in museums; rarely can it be bought new. The skills that produced this great and historic art-craft are kept alive by such groups as the International Old Lacers, a worldwide organization of some 900 members, including the craftsmen shown below. Most needleworkers, however, find crochet lace—and knit lace, too—just as rewarding to create. And, as the projects on the following pages demonstrate, there is very little in traditional lacemaking that cannot be imitated with crochet hooks or knitting needles.

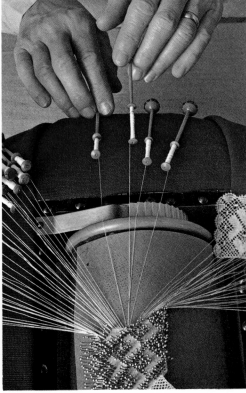

Bobbin lace, shown above in the expert hands of Gunvor Jorgensen, is made on a padded frame called a pillow. Pillows vary in shape and size, but most combine an outer rim to hold the bobbins with a revolving center section designed to hold the pattern. Pins are stuck through that part of the pattern being worked on and the threads twisted around the pins, as pictured at center. The finished lace and its printed pattern appear at right.

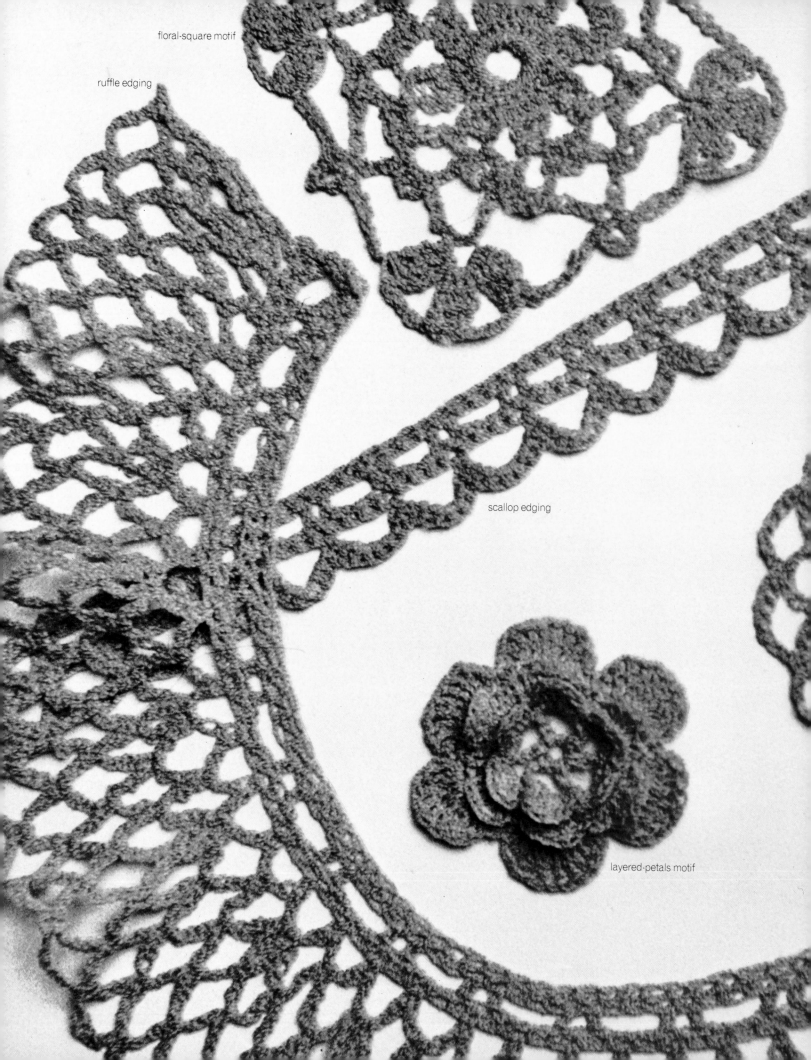

floral-square motif

ruffle edging

scallop edging

layered-petals motif

Traceries in crochet

Crochet lace is simply crocheting done with light yarns and airy patterns, employing stitches already in the technical vocabulary of the beginning craftsman. Shown here are motifs suitable for large works and decorative edgings. The layered-petals motif was used for the over-blouse pictured on pages 170-171; floral square and ruffle edging were used for the shawl shown on page 174. The additional motifs and edgings can be used for similar projects to create different looks. A practice run, making each of the swatches *(directions, pages 162-165),* will help in the choosing of the most attractive combinations.

arabesque motif

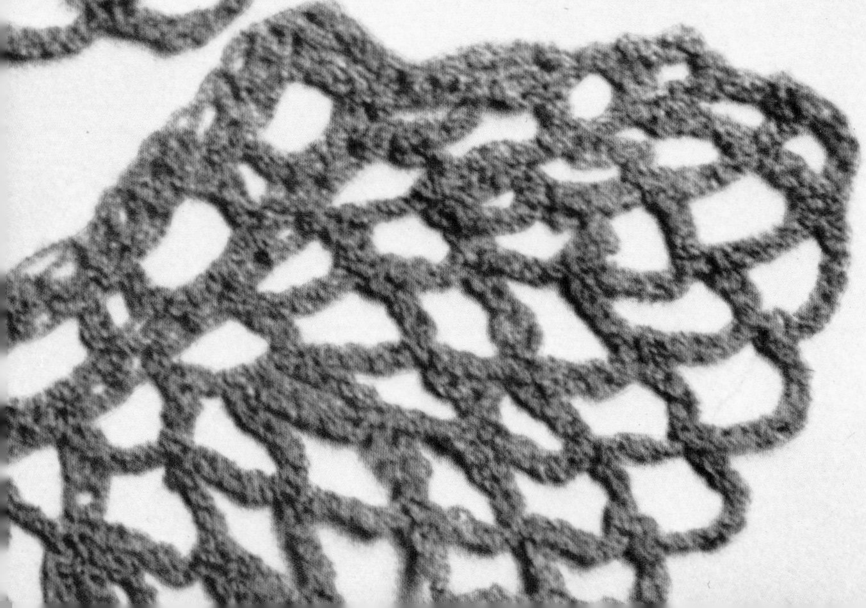

pinwheel motif

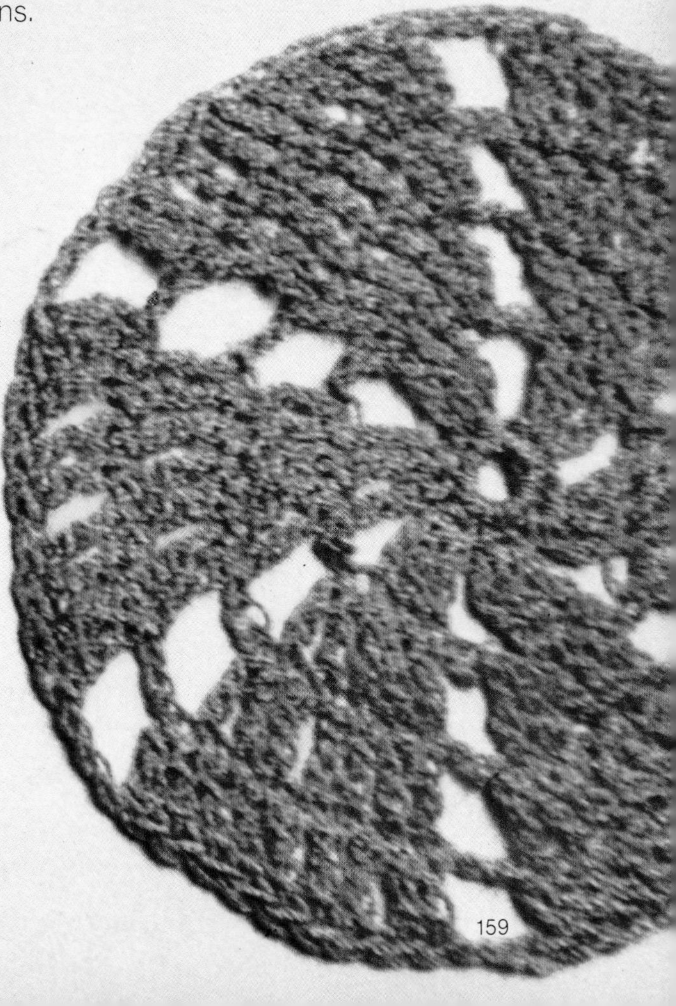

Filigrees in knitwork

Fine openwork created with knitting needles is called knit lace. And as the lacy exercises here show, the designs can be worked in squares or strips for use in big projects and small ones. The swatch bands *(center)*, conceived as fabric insertions, feature the diamond design—which spirals around the dress on pages 178-179—and the ripplet. Squares of spider web *(top, far right)* edged with fishnet *(below)* make up the shawl on page 175. The arrowhead square and two-tier edging might join to produce a rectangular wrap. Instructions begin on page 165.

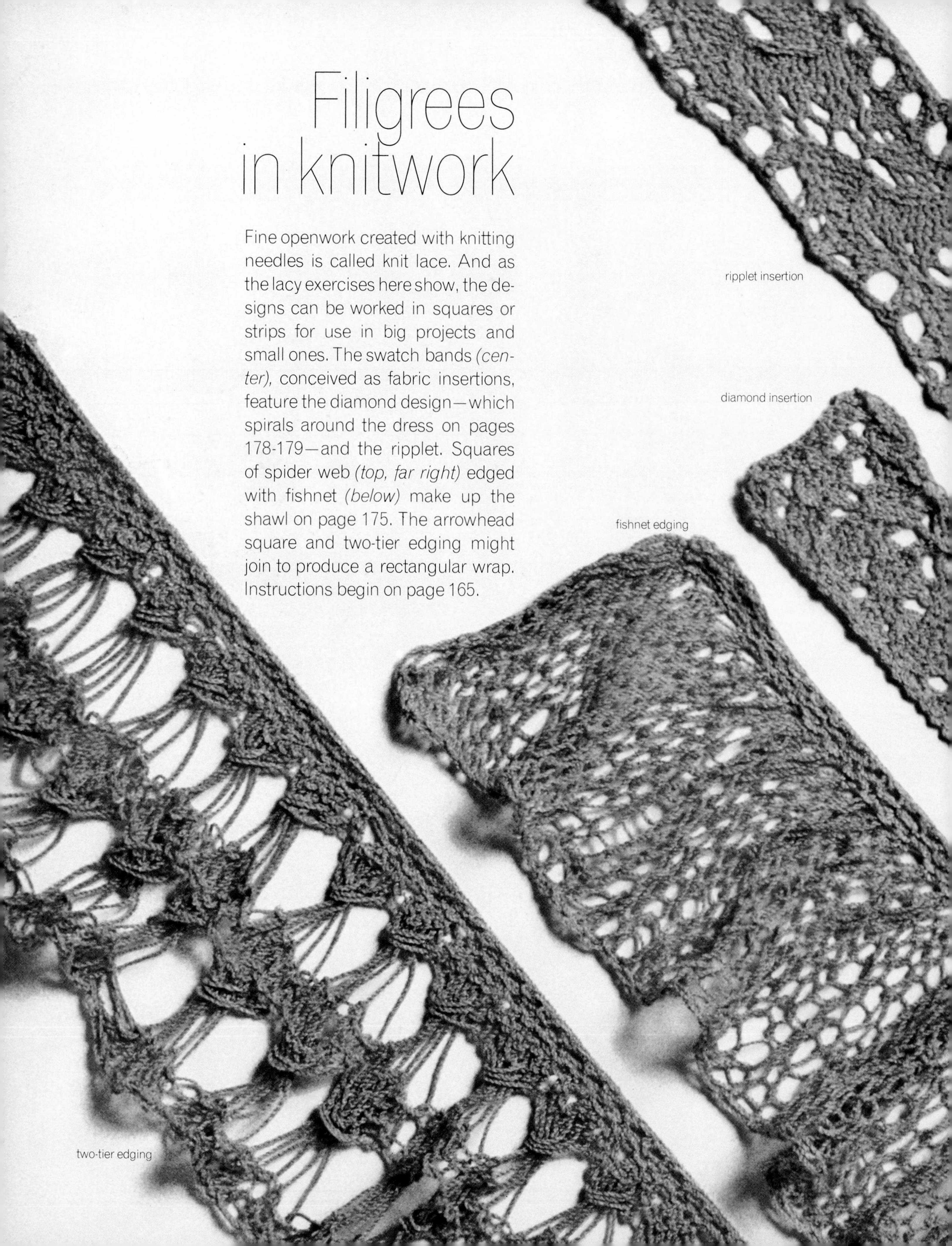

ripplet insertion

diamond insertion

fishnet edging

two-tier edging

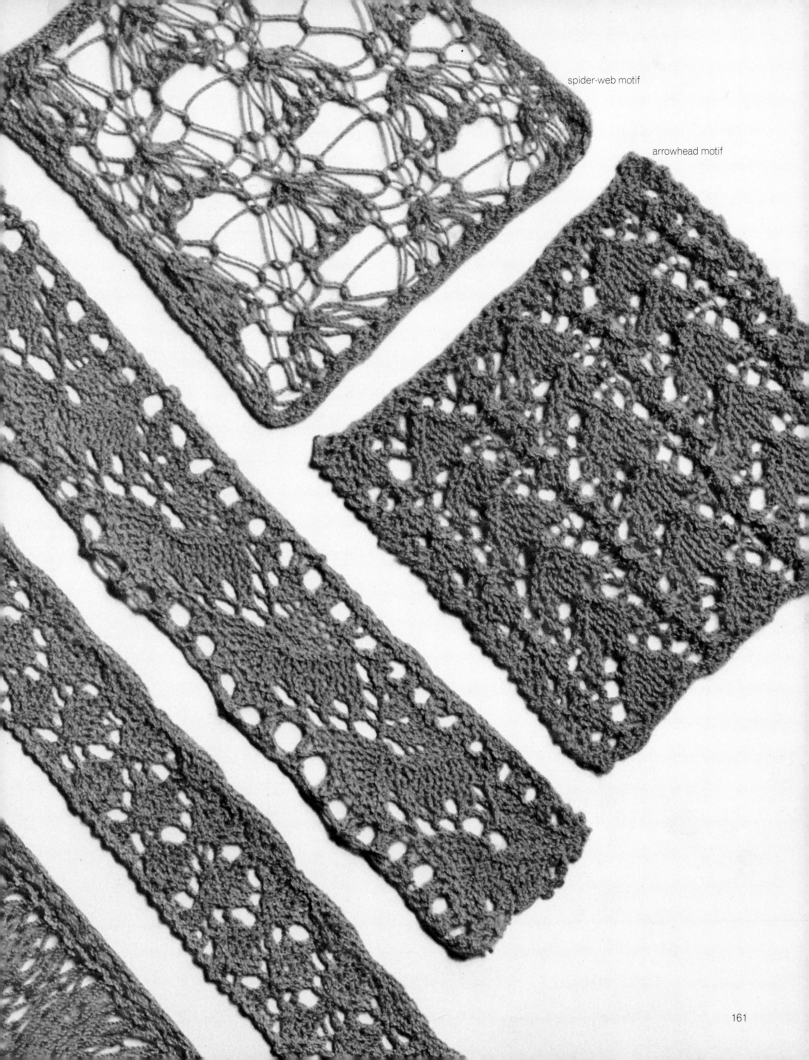

spider-web motif

arrowhead motif

Crocheting and knitting the lace patterns

The following instructions are for crocheting and knitting the lacy motifs, edgings and insertions that are shown on pages 158-161. All of the samples were made from a thin, nubby, wool-and-rayon yarn. The size of the crochet hook or knitting needles varies with the individual pattern, and is given in each set of directions.

In this book, the crochet and knitting instructions describe each procedure fully in simple terms. Most books, as well as magazines and commercial patterns, however, use a shorthand of standard abbreviations for their directions. The ones translated below are the basic terms you will encounter in most other instructions.

CROCHETING ABBREVIATIONS

HK—hook	**HDC**—half double crochet
CH—chain	**DC**—double crochet
ST—stitch	**TRC**—triple crochet
SL ST—slip stitch	**SK**—skip
SC—single crochet	**LP**—loop
REP—repeat	**SP**—space

—starting point for a sequence of steps to be repeated. When instructions tell you to "rep from," read back to find the point (*) from which you must begin to repeat the sequence of steps.

KNITTING ABBREVIATIONS

K—knit	**REP**—repeat
P—purl	**PAT**—pattern
ST—stitch	**SL**—slip stitch
YO—yarn over	**PSSO**—pass slipped stitch over
INC—increase	**BEG**—beginning
DEC—decrease	**MC**—main color

—starting point for a sequence of steps to be repeated. When instructions tell you to "rep from," read back to find the point (*) from which you must begin to repeat the sequence of steps.

CHECKING THE GAUGE

All knitting and crocheting instructions begin with the stitch gauge, that is, the number of stitches to the inch in each row—and often the number of rows to the inch—you must have if your finished project is to have the correct measurements.

To check the gauge, all you need to do is make sure that your needle or hook and yarn produce the desired number of stitches to the inch. Knit or crochet a sample swatch measuring at least 4 by 4 inches, and use the yarn and needle or hook size recommended in the directions. (If two sizes of needles or hooks are required, use the larger size to measure your gauge.)

Remove the swatch from the needles or hook without binding off, and lay it on a flat surface. Count the number of stitches to the inch across the swatch, using a ruler; this figure is your stitch gauge for the pattern. Then count the number of vertical rows to the inch; this is your row gauge. If the gauge calls for fewer stitches to the inch, use larger needles or hook; if it calls for more stitches to the inch, use smaller ones. This change will also adjust the rows-to-the-inch gauge.

THE CROCHET SWATCHES
LAYERED-PETALS MOTIF

Use a Size E aluminum crochet hook, and work in a gauge of 6 single crochet stitches to 1 inch. Begin the pattern at the center by making 5 chain stitches, and then making a slip stitch in the first chain stitch to form a ring (*drawing 1*).

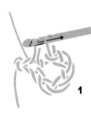

Round one: Chain 6. Now repeat this sequence—make 1 double crochet in the center of the ring, then chain 3—5 times. End the round by making a slip stitch in the third chain stitch of this round.

Round two: In the first space, make 1 single crochet stitch, 1 half double crochet stitch, 3 double crochet stitches, 1 half double crochet stitch, and 1 single crochet stitch. These stitches form the first petal (*drawing 2*). Make five more petals, one in each space around the circle.

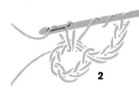

Round three: Repeat this sequence—chain 4, then hold the chain behind the first petal, and make 1 single crochet stitch in the first single crochet stitch of the next petal *(drawing 3)*—5 times. Then chain 4.

Round four: Repeat this sequence—into the next space make 1 single crochet stitch, 1 half double crochet stitch, 5 double crochet stitches, 1 half double crochet stitch, and 1 single crochet stitch—6 times. This completes the second round of petals.

Round five: Repeat this sequence—chain 5, then hold the chain behind the next petal, and make 1 single crochet stitch in the first single crochet stitch of the next petal—5 times. Chain 5.

Round six: Repeat this sequence—into the next space, make 1 single crochet stitch, 1 double crochet stitch, 7 triple crochet stitches, 1 double crochet stitch, and 1 single crochet stitch—6 times. This completes the third round of petals. Finish the motif by making a slip stitch in the first single crochet stitch of this round. Fasten off.

FLORAL-SQUARE MOTIF

Use a Size I aluminum crochet hook, or whatever size hook will give you a gauge of 11 single crochet stitches to 2 inches. Begin the pattern at the center by making a chain of 6 stitches and then making a slip stitch in the first chain stitch to form a ring, as shown for the layered-petals motif *(drawing 1)*.

Round one: Chain 4. Then make a cluster. To do this, start by following this sequence: Bring the yarn over the hook twice (as if to triple crochet) and insert the hook into the middle of the ring. Bring the yarn over the hook and draw it through the ring *(drawing 4)*. Bring the yarn over the hook

again and draw it through two loops. Bring the yarn over the hook, and draw it through two more loops. You will now have two loops remaining on the hook. Repeat this se-

quence one more time. You will now have three loops on the hook. To complete the cluster, bring the yarn over the hook once more, and draw it through all three loops. This is a cluster at the beginning of a round *(drawing 5)*. For all clusters that do not occur at the beginning of a round, fol-

low the sequence described above 3 times. At the end of the third sequence, you will have four loops to draw the yarn through. Chain 5. Now make seven additional clusters in the ring, with 5 chain stitches between each cluster. To end the round, chain 5, and make 1 slip stitch in the top of the first cluster *(drawing 6)*.

Round two: Make 1 slip stitch in each of the first and second

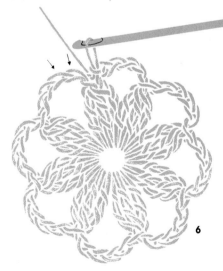

chain stitches of the first chain 5 of round one (indicated by arrows in drawing 6). Then make 1 single crochet stitch in the same chain-5 space. Chain 3, and make 1 more single crochet stitch in the same space. Now repeat this sequence—chain 5, make 1 single crochet stitch in the next space, chain 3, make 1 single crochet stitch in the same space—7 times. To complete this round, chain 2, and make 1 double crochet stitch in the first single crochet stitch at the beginning of round two.

Round three: Chain 3. Now make 1 single crochet stitch in the space formed by the double crochet *(drawing 7).* Then repeat this sequence—chain 9, make 1 single crochet stitch in the next chain-5 space, chain 3, and make 1 single crochet stitch in the same space—7 times. Chain 4, and make 1 triple crochet stitch in the double crochet stitch made at the end of round two.

Round four: To make the motif square, follow this sequence: Chain 6. Then make a cluster (as you did in round one) in

7

the fifth chain stitch of the next chain 9. Chain 5, and make another cluster in the same stitch in which you made the first cluster. Chain 5, and make a third cluster in the same stitch. Chain 6.

In the fifth chain of the next chain 9, make 1 single crochet stitch. Chain 5, and make another single crochet stitch in the same chain stitch as the first single crochet stitch. This forms the first corner and one side of the square and completes the sequence.

Repeat the sequence two more times. Then, to make the fourth corner, repeat the sequence again, but after the third cluster proceed as follows: Chain 6, and make 1 single crochet stitch in the triple crochet stitch of the last round. Chain 5, and make 1 single crochet stitch in the same triple crochet stitch. Fasten off.

PINWHEEL MOTIF

Use a Size E aluminum crochet hook, and work in a gauge of 6 single crochet stitches to 1 inch. Begin the pattern at the center by making 6 chain stitches and then making a

slip stitch in the first chain stitch to form a ring as shown for the layered-petals motif in drawing 1, page 162.

Round one: Chain 1, then make 12 single crochet stitches into the center of the ring. End the round by making a slip stitch in the first single crochet stitch of the round.

Round two: Chain 4. Then make 2 triple crochet stitches in the same single crochet stitch in which you made the slip stitch. Repeat this sequence—chain 3, skip 1 single crochet stitch, and make 3 triple crochet stitches in the next single crochet stitch—5 times. To complete the round, chain 3, and make a slip stitch in the fourth chain stitch of this round.

Round three: Chain 4, and make 1 triple crochet stitch in the same chain stitch in which you made the last slip stitch. Then repeat this sequence—make 1 triple crochet stitch in the next triple crochet stitch, 2 triple crochet stitches in the next triple crochet stitch, chain 3, and make 2 triple crochet stitches in the next triple crochet stitch—5 times. Make 1 triple crochet stitch in the next triple crochet stitch. Make 2 triple crochet stitches in the next triple crochet stitch. Chain 3, and end the round with a slip stitch in the fourth chain stitch of this round.

Round four: Chain 4, and make 1 triple crochet stitch in the same stitch in which you made the last slip stitch. Then repeat this sequence—make 1 triple crochet stitch in each of the next 3 triple crochet stitches, 2 triple crochet stitches in the next triple crochet stitch, chain 3, and make 2 triple crochet stitches in the next triple crochet stitch—5 times. Then make 1 triple crochet stitch in each of the next 3 triple crochet stitches.

Make 2 triple crochet stitches in the next triple crochet stitch. Chain 3, and end the round with a slip stitch in the fourth chain stitch of this round.

Round five: Chain 4, and make 1 triple crochet stitch in the same stitch in which you made the last slip stitch. Then repeat this sequence—make 1 triple crochet stitch in each of the next 5 triple crochet stitches, 2 triple crochet stitches in the next triple crochet stitch, chain 3, and make 2 triple crochet stitches in the next triple crochet stitch—5 times. Make 1 triple crochet stitch in each of the next 5 triple crochet stitches.

Then make 2 triple crochet stitches in the next triple crochet stitch. Chain 3, and end this round with a slip stitch in the fourth chain of this round. Fasten off.

ARABESQUE MOTIF

Use a Size G aluminum crochet hook or whatever size will give you a gauge of 6 single crochet stitches to 1 inch. Begin at the center of the pattern by making a chain of 6 stitches and then making a slip stitch in the first chain stitch to form a ring, as shown for the layered-petals motif *(drawing 1, page 162).*

Round one: Make 12 single crochet stitches in the center of the ring. End the round with a slip stitch in the first single crochet stitch.

Round two: Chain 4. Then follow this sequence: Bring the yarn over the hook twice (as if you were going to make a triple crochet stitch) and insert the hook into the same single crochet stitch in which you made the slip stitch. Bring the yarn over the hook again, and draw it through the single crochet stitch, as shown for the floral-square motif (drawing 4, page 163). Bring the yarn over the hook, and draw it through two more loops. There are now two loops remaining on the hook.

Repeat the entire sequence described above. There will now be three loops remaining on the hook. Now bring the yarn over the hook once more, and draw it through all three loops as for the floral-square motif (drawing 5, page 163). This forms the first cluster. Chain 5.

Make one cluster in each of the next 11 single crochet stitches, with 5 chain stitches between each cluster. (For all of these clusters, which are not at the beginning of a round, follow the sequence described above 3 times. At the end of the third sequence you will have four loops to draw the yarn through.)

Chain 1, and end the round by making 1 double crochet stitch in the top of the first cluster.

Round three: Repeat this sequence—chain 6, and make 1 single crochet stitch in the next chain-5 space—11 times. Then chain 2, and make 1 double crochet stitch in the last double crochet stitch of round two.

Round four: Repeat the sequence—chain 7, and make 1 single crochet stitch in the next chain-6 space—11 times. Chain 7, and end by making a slip stitch in the last double crochet of the previous round. Fasten off.

RUFFLE EDGING

Use a Size I crochet hook or whatever size you need to work in a gauge of 11 single crochet stitches to 2 inches. Make a foundation chain of any multiple of 4 stitches plus 1 that measures the desired length of the edging you will be making. Then chain 1, and turn.

Row 1: Make 1 single crochet stitch in the second chain from the hook. Then make 1 single crochet stitch in each chain stitch across the row. When you reach the end of the row, chain 3, and turn.

Row 2: Make 1 double crochet stitch in the first single crochet stitch. Then repeat the sequence—chain 2, skip 2 single crochet stitches, make 1 double crochet stitch in each of the next 2 single crochet stitches—across the row. Chain 1, and turn.

Row 3: Make 1 single crochet stitch in each double crochet stitch and in each chain stitch across the row. Then chain 5, and turn.

Row 4: Repeat this sequence—skip 1 single crochet stitch, make a single crochet stitch in the next single crochet stitch, then chain 5—across the row. End with 1 single crochet stitch in the last single crochet stitch of the previous row. Chain 7, and turn.

Row 5: Repeat this sequence across the row—make 1 single crochet stitch in the next chain-5 space, chain 7, and make 1 single crochet stitch in the same space; then chain 7, make 1 single crochet stitch in the next space and chain 7. At the end of the row chain 3, and make a double crochet stitch in the last chain-5 space. Chain 7, and turn.

Row 6: Repeat this sequence—make 1 single crochet stitch

in the next chain-7 space, then chain 7—across the row. At the end of the row, chain 3, and make 1 double crochet stitch in the last space. Chain 7, and turn.

Rows 7, 8 and 9: Repeat this sequence across each of the rows: make 1 single crochet stitch in the next chain-7 space, then chain 7. At the end of each row, chain 3, and make 1 double crochet stitch in the last space. Then, in rows 7 and 8 only, chain 7, and turn. In row 9, fasten off at the end of the row.

SCALLOP EDGING

Use a Size G aluminum crochet hook or whatever size will give you a gauge of 11 single crochet stitches to 2 inches. Make a foundation chain of any multiple of 16 stitches plus 12 that measures the desired length of your edging. Then chain 1, and turn.

Row 1: Make 1 single crochet stitch in the second chain stitch from the hook. Then make 1 single crochet stitch in each chain stitch across the row. Chain 3, and turn.

Row 2: Make 1 double crochet stitch in the first single crochet stitch. Then repeat the sequence—chain 2, skip the next 2 single crochet stitches, make 1 double crochet stitch in each of the next 2 single crochet stitches—across the row. End by making 1 double crochet stitch in the last stitch of the previous row. Chain 1, and turn.

Row 3: Make 1 single crochet stitch in each double crochet stitch and in each chain stitch across the row. At the end of the row, chain 6, and turn.

Row 4: Repeat this sequence—skip the next 3 single crochet stitches, then make 1 single crochet stitch in the next single crochet stitch, and chain 6—across the row. End by making 1 single crochet stitch in the last single crochet stitch of the previous row. Chain 1, and turn.

Row 5: Repeat this sequence—make 1 single crochet stitch in the next single crochet stitch, then make 6 single crochet stitches in the next chain-6 space—across the row. End by making a slip stitch in the first chain stitch of the previous row. Fasten off.

THE KNIT SWATCHES
SPIDER-WEB MOTIF

Using Size 11 needles and a gauge of 7 stitches to 2 inches, cast on 17 stitches.

Row 1: Knit 2 stitches; then bring the yarn between the needles to the front of the work (called yarn over) and knit 1 stitch (drawing 1).

Repeat the sequence of yarn over, knit 1 stitch, across

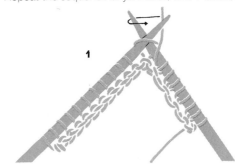

the row until there are 3 stitches left on the needle. Bring the yarn over; then knit each of the 3 stitches.

Row 2: Purl 3 stitches. Then repeat this sequence—drop the yarn over that was formed in the last row from the left needle, then purl the next stitch *(drawing 2)*—across the row. Purl the last 2 stitches in the row.

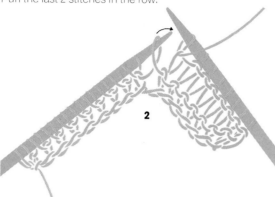

Row 3: Knit 1 stitch. Then follow this sequence: Holding the yarn behind the work, insert the right needle into the next stitch as if to purl, and slip it onto the right needle without working it *(drawing 3)*. Then slip a second stitch in the

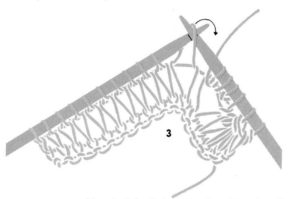

same manner. Now knit 2 stitches together *(drawing 4)*, and pass the 2 slipped stitches over the knit stitch and off

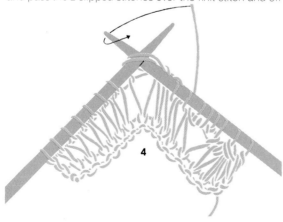

the right needle *(drawing 5)*. Knit the next stitch, but leave it on the needle. Bring the yarn between the needles to the front of the work, and purl 1 stitch in the same place as the knit stitch *(drawing 6)*, still without dropping the stitch from the left needle. Knit 1 more and purl 1 more in the same stitch. Then complete the sequence by dropping the old

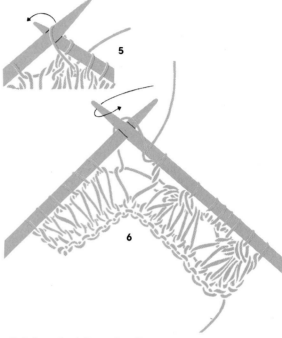

stitch from the left needle. (Remember to hold the yarn at the back of the work before slipping the next 2 stitches.) Repeat the sequence above—slip 2, knit 2 together, pass the slipped stitches over; then knit 1, purl 1, knit 1, and purl 1 all in the same stitch—across the row. End by knitting the last stitch.

Row 4: Purl each stitch across the row.

Row 5: Repeat row 1.

Row 6: Repeat row 2.

Row 7: Knit 1 stitch. Then follow this sequence: knit 1, purl 1, knit 1, and purl 1 all in the next stitch. Holding the yarn at the back of the work, insert the right needle as if to purl, and slip the next 2 stitches onto the right needle. Knit the next 2 stitches together, and pass the slipped stitches over the knit stitch. Repeat the sequence described above across the row. Knit the last stitch in the row.

Row 8: Purl each stitch across the row. To complete the motif, repeat the sequence of rows 1 through 8 once more. Then bind off with a knitted row *(Appendix)*.

ARROWHEAD MOTIF
Using Size 5 needles and a gauge of 5 stitches to 1 inch, cast on 31 stitches.

Row 1: Knit the stitches across the row.

Row 2: Repeat row 1.

Row 3: Knit each of the first 2 stitches. Then follow this sequence: Bring the yarn between the needles to the front of the work, called yarn over (*drawing 1, page 165*). Insert the right needle into the next stitch as if to purl, and slip it from the left to the right needle without working it (*drawing 3*). Knit 2 stitches together (*drawing 4*).

Pass the slipped stitch over the knit stitch and off the right needle (*drawing 5*).

Then bring the yarn between the needles to the front of the work to yarn over, and knit each of the next 5 stitches.

Repeat this sequence until 5 stitches are left.

Then yarn over, slip 1 stitch, knit 2 stitches together, and pass the slipped stitch over the knit stitch. Yarn over, and knit each of the last 2 stitches.

Row 4: Knit each of the first 2 stitches. Then purl each stitch across the row until there are 2 stitches left. Knit the remaining 2 stitches.

Row 5: Repeat row 3.

Row 6: Knit each of the first 2 stitches. Then purl each stitch across the row until there are 2 stitches left. Knit the last 2 stitches.

Row 7: Knit each of the first 2 stitches. Then follow this sequence: Knit 3 stitches, yarn over, slip 1 stitch, knit 1 stitch, pass the slipped stitch over the knit stitch, knit 1 stitch, knit 2 stitches together, and bring the yarn over the right needle again.

Repeat this sequence across the row until there are 5 stitches left on the needle.

Knit each of these last 5 stitches.

Row 8: Knit each of the first 2 stitches. Then purl each stitch across the row until there are 2 stitches left. Knit the remaining 2 stitches.

Row 9: Knit each of the first 2 stitches. Then follow this sequence: Yarn over, slip 1 stitch as if to purl, knit 2 stitches together, pass the slipped stitch over the knit stitch, yarn over, and knit 1 stitch.

Repeat this sequence until there are 5 stitches left.

Then yarn over, slip 1 stitch, knit 1 stitch, pass the slipped stitch over the knit stitch, and knit each of the last 3 stitches.

Row 10: Knit each of the first 2 stitches. Then purl each stitch across the row until there are 2 stitches left. Knit the remaining 2 stitches.

To complete the motif, repeat the sequence of rows 3 through 10 five times more. Then knit all of the stitches across the next row, repeat that row once more, and bind off (*Appendix*).

FISHNET EDGING

Using Size 13 needles and working in a gauge of 5 stitches to 2 inches, cast on twice the number of stitches that you will need to achieve the desired length of the piece at the sewed-on edge.

Then follow the sequence of knitting all the stitches across the first row and purling all the stitches across the next row (this is commonly known as the stockinette stitch), until the piece measures 3 inches in depth. Bind off (*Appendix*).

To complete the ruffle, use a Size F crochet hook, and make a row of single crochet stitches (*Appendix*) along the starting row, decreasing by crocheting every two stitches as one (*Appendix*). Fasten off.

TWO-TIER EDGING

Using Size 8 needles and working in a gauge of 4 stitches to 1 inch, cast on any multiple of 6 stitches that will give you the desired length at the sewed-on edge.

Row 1: Knit each stitch across the row.

Rows 2 and 3: Repeat row 1.

Row 4: Knit 1 stitch and leave it on the needle. Bring the yarn between the needles to the front of the work and purl 1; then move the yarn between the needles to the back of the work and knit 1 more—all in the same stitch (*drawing 6*). Repeat this sequence in each of the stitches across the row.

Row 5: (NOTE—For this row and all the rest of the edging, use Size 11 needles.)

Knit each stitch across the row.

Row 6: Knit each stitch across the row, but wrap the yarn

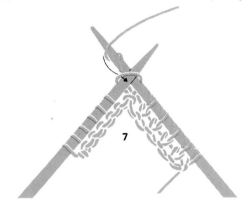

twice around the needle instead of once before completing each stitch (*drawing 7*).

Row 7: Follow this sequence: Slip the first stitch onto

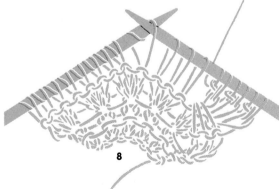

the right needle, dropping the extra loop that follows it (*drawing 8*).

Then slip the next 5 stitches in the same way, dropping the extra loop that follows each one.

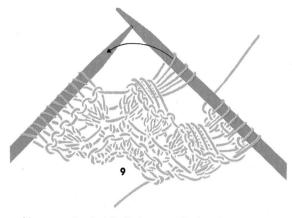

9

Now pass the first 3 stitches over the last 3 stitches, and slip the remaining 3 stitches back onto the left needle (drawing 9).

Knit first into the front and then into the back of the first stitch before dropping it from the needle (drawing 10). Now

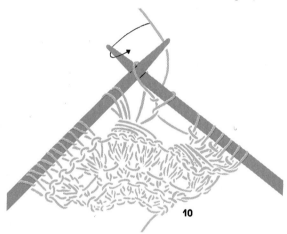

10

knit into the front and back of the next 2 stitches. Repeat this sequence across the row.

Row 8: Repeat row 5. To complete the edging, repeat the sequence of rows 5 through 8 twice more. Then bind off as if to purl on the next row.

DIAMOND INSERTION

Using Size 13 needles and working in a gauge of 5 stitches to 1 inch, cast on any multiple of 6 stitches plus 1 that will give you the desired length of your insertion.

Row 1: Knit each stitch across the row.

Row 2: Repeat row 1.

Row 3: Follow this sequence: Knit 1 stitch. Bring the yarn between the needles to the front of the work, called yarn over (drawing 1, page 165).

Insert the right needle into the next stitch as if to purl, and slip it onto the needle without working it (drawing 3, page 166). Knit 1 stitch; then pass the slipped stitch over the knit stitch and off the right needle (drawing 5, page

166). Knit 1 stitch; then knit 2 stitches together (drawing 4, page 166) and yarn over. Repeat the sequence across the row. End by knitting the last stitch.

Row 4: Purl each stitch across the row.

Row 5: Knit each of the first 2 stitches. Then follow this sequence—yarn over, slip 1 stitch, knit 2 stitches together, pass the slipped stitch over the knit stitch, yarn over, and knit each of the next 3 stitches. Repeat the sequence across the row until there are 2 stitches left; knit each of the 2 stitches.

Row 6: Purl each stitch across the row.

Row 7: Knit 1 stitch, and then knit 2 stitches together. Now repeat this sequence—yarn over, knit 1 stitch, yarn over, slip 1 stitch, knit 1 stitch, pass the slipped stitch over the knit stitch, knit 1 stitch, and knit 2 stitches together—until there are 4 stitches left. Yarn over, and knit 1 stitch. Yarn over, slip 1 stitch, and knit 1 stitch. Pass the slipped stitch over the knit stitch. Knit the last stitch.

Row 8: Purl each stitch across the row.

Row 9: Knit 2 stitches together. Then repeat the sequence —yarn over, knit each of the next 3 stitches, yarn over, slip 1 stitch, knit the next 2 stitches together, pass the slipped stitch over the knit stitch—across the row.

At the end of the row, yarn over, knit 3 stitches, yarn over, slip 1 stitch, knit 1 stitch, and pass the slipped stitch over the last knit stitch.

Row 10: Purl each stitch across the row. To complete the insertion, repeat the sequence of rows 3 through 9 once more. On the last row bind off with purl stitches.

RIPPLET INSERTION

Using Size 4 needles and working in a gauge of 5 stitches to 1 inch, cast on any multiple of 8 stitches that measures the desired length of your insertion.

Row 1: Knit each stitch across the row.

Row 2: Repeat row 1.

Row 3: Knit 1 stitch. Then follow the sequence—knit 2 stitches together (drawing 4, page 166), bring the yarn between the needles to the front of the work and wrap it once entirely around the right needle, called a double yarn over (drawing 11). Repeat the sequence—knit 2 together and wrap the yarn once entirely around the needle—across the row. Knit the last stitch.

Row 4: Knit 3 stitches. Then follow this sequence—drop the next loop and knit 2—across the row.

Row 5: Follow this sequence: Hold the yarn in front of the

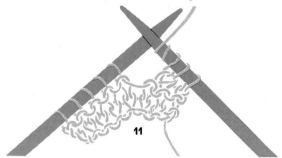

11

right needle (this is how to yarn over at the beginning of a row—drawing 12). Then knit 1 stitch and bring the yarn between the needles to the front (this is how to yarn over in the middle of a row—drawing 1, page 165). Insert the needle in the next stitch as if to purl and slip the stitch onto the right needle without working it (drawing 3, page 166). Knit 1 stitch, then pass the slipped stitch over the knit stitch

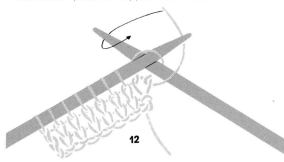

12

(drawing 5, page 166), and knit each of the next 5 stitches. Repeat this sequence across the row.

Row 6: Purl each of the next 4 stitches, purl 2 stitches together (in the same manner you knitted 2 stitches together—drawing 4, page 163), then purl each of the next 3 stitches.
Repeat this sequence of stitches across the row.

Row 7: Follow this sequence across the row: Yarn over, then knit 1 stitch, yarn over, knit each of the next 2 stitches, slip 1 stitch, knit 1 stitch, pass the slipped stitch over the knit stitch, and knit each of the next 3 stitches.

Row 8: Purl each of the first 2 stitches, then purl 2 stitches together, and purl each of the next 5 stitches. Repeat this sequence across the row.

Row 9: Knit 1 stitch, yarn over, knit each of the next 4 stitches, slip 1 stitch, knit 1 stitch, pass the slipped stitch over the knit stitch, then knit 1 stitch and yarn over. Repeat the sequence of stitches across the row. At the end of the row, simply increase 1 stitch (Appendix) instead of the second yarn over; this will keep the correct number of stitches on the needles.

Row 10: Purl 1 stitch, purl 2 stitches together, and then purl each of the next 6 stitches. Repeat this sequence across the row.

Row 11: Knit each of the first 5 stitches, knit 2 stitches together, yarn over, knit 1 stitch, and then yarn over. Repeat this sequence across the row. End the row by increasing 1 stitch instead of a second yarn over.

Row 12: Purl each of the first 3 stitches, purl 2 stitches together; then purl 4 stitches. Repeat across the row.

Row 13: Knit each of the first 3 stitches, knit 2 stitches together, knit each of the next 2 stitches, yarn over, knit 1 stitch, and then yarn over. Repeat this sequence across the row. At the end of the row, increase 1 stitch instead of the second yarn over.

Row 14: Purl each of the first 5 stitches, purl 2 stitches together, and then purl each of the next 2 stitches. Repeat this sequence across the row.

Row 15: Yarn over, knit 1 stitch, knit 2 stitches together, knit each of the next 4 stitches; then yarn over and knit 1 stitch. Repeat this sequence of stitches across the row.

Row 16: Purl each of the first 6 stitches, purl 2 stitches together, and then purl 1. Repeat this sequence across the row.

Row 17: Knit each stitch across the row.

Row 18: Repeat row 17.

Row 19: Repeat row 3.

Row 20: Repeat row 4. Then bind off on the next row with knitted stitches.

A wrapping of stars and flowers

Like the chameleon, the crocheted lace overblouse shown here changes its guise with its background. Demurely pretty atop a cashmere dress *(left)*, it can also be deliciously indiscreet over bare skin *(right)*. The overblouse flaunts a multitude of layered-petals motifs *(page 158)*, joined together where the flowers meet; crocheted stars fill the interstices between them. Single crochet stitches form the belt, cuffs, facing and collar. Instructions for making the garment begin overleaf.

Instructions for crocheting the overblouse

The crocheted lace overblouse, shown on pages 170-171, can be made in either of two size ranges—small for sizes 8 through 12 and large for sizes 14 through 18. To make the small overblouse, you will need 15 two-ounce skeins of a thin, nubby wool-and-rayon yarn, and Sizes E and I aluminum crochet hooks. To make the large overblouse, you will need 18 two-ounce skeins of yarn and Sizes G and I crochet hooks. You will also need 13 small buttons. But do not buy the buttons until you finish the overblouse, because their size will depend on the size of your finished buttonholes.

Making the individual motifs: Crochet 182 identical layered-petals motifs, following the instructions on pages 162-163. If you are making the small overblouse, use a Size E aluminum crochet hook, and work in a gauge of 6 single crochet stitches to the inch. If you are making the large overblouse, use a Size G hook, and work in a gauge of 5 stitches to the inch. Your gauge should produce a motif 3 inches in diameter using the E hook or 3 1/2 in diameter using the G hook. Make a sample motif and check it carefully, so the overblouse will be the correct size.

Joining the motifs: Arrange the motifs to form a body section and two sleeves according to the diagrams below. Sew the motifs together securely with 2 overcast stitches (Appendix) at each point where one or two petals of one motif meet those of an adjacent motif. Make sure to join the body section at the shoulders; the points at which the shoulder motifs should be sewed together are indicated by the curved arrows on the diagram below. Also make sure to close the sleeves by sewing together the motifs along two side edges shown in the sleeve diagram.

Filling in between motifs: Using the same size crochet hook as you used for the layered-petals motif and working in the same gauge, make a star-shaped fill-in motif in the large opening formed by each group of four joined motifs, as shown in the center of the illustration at the bottom of the facing page. To make each fill-in motif, work as follows: Make a chain of 4 stitches; then make a slip stitch into the first chain stitch to form a ring. Now follow this sequence: Chain 3, then make a single crochet stitch in a stitch on the edge of one of the petals that border the space; chain 3 again, and make a single crochet stitch into the center of

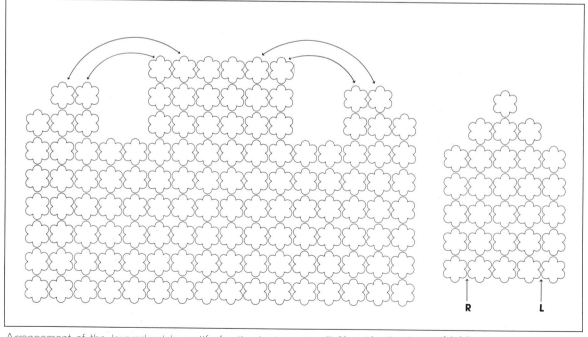

Arrangement of the layered-petals motifs for the body section *(left)* and for the sleeves *(right)*

the ring. This sequence forms one point of the star. Repeat the sequence seven more times so that a star point goes to each one of the petals around the opening. Fasten off.

Filling in the edges: Make partial fill-in motifs, shaped like half of a star, along all the outer edges of the body section and the sleeves, including the armholes and sleeve caps. For most of the edges, where two motifs come together, work in the same manner as you did for the fill-in motifs, but make only four points of the star, instead of eight. In the curves on the armholes and front neckline, where three motifs come together, make six points of the star.

Edging the blouse: Use the same size crochet hook as you used for the motifs to make an edging around the bottom, front and neck edges of the body section. Work in the following manner: Starting with any outside petal, make 1 single crochet stitch in each of the 4 center stitches on the outer edge of the petal. Then chain 4, make a triple crochet stitch into the center of the ring of the next half fill-in motif, and chain 4 again. Repeat this sequence of stitches around the edge of each piece. Where two petals occur next to each other with no half fill-in motif between them, make the 4 single crochet stitches into the first petal, then chain 4, and make 4 more single crochet stitches into the center stitches of the next petal.

On the cuff edge of the right sleeve, make an edging as you did above, but leave a placket opening. To form the opening, start and end the row of edging by making a triple crochet stitch in the center of the half fill-in motif indicated by the arrow marked "R" on the sleeve diagram (*page 172*). Similarly, make an edging on the cuff edge of the left sleeve, starting and ending in the center of the half fill-in motif indicated by the arrow marked "L."

On the armhole edges of the sleeves and the body section, make an edging as you did on the neck, front and bottom edges. Then make 2 more rows of single crochet stitches as follows: *Row 1:* Make 1 single crochet stitch in each single crochet stitch, 3 single crochet stitches in each chain-4 space, and 1 single crochet stitch in each triple crochet stitch. *Row 2:* Make 1 single crochet stitch in each single crochet stitch of the previous row.

Attaching the sleeves: Sew the sleeves to the body section along the single crochet edges, using an overcast stitch.

Making the neck and bottom bands: For this and all subsequent work on the overblouse—no matter which size you are making—switch to the Size I aluminum crochet hook and work in a gauge of 9 stitches to 2 inches.

On the body section, make 6 rows of single crochet stitches along the neck edge and 9 rows along the bottom edge, in the same manner as you did on armhole edges.

Making the front bands: Again working in the same manner as you did on the armhole edges, make 12 rows of single crochet stitches along the left-front edge, including the front edges of the neck and bottom bands. Work the right-front band in the same manner as the left for 6 rows. On the seventh row, work in nine buttonholes, placing the uppermost buttonhole 1/2 inch below the top of the band and the lowest buttonhole 1 inch above the bottom of the band.

Space the remaining seven buttonholes evenly in between. To make each buttonhole, work the row of single crochet stitches until you reach the buttonhole. Then make 2 chain stitches, skip 2 single crochet stitches, and work a single crochet stitch in the next stitch. On the return row make 2 single crochet stitches in the chain-2 space. Continue with the band until you have 12 rows.

Adding the collar: Make a chain of 95 stitches and turn. Make 2 rows of 94 single crochet stitches, with a chain 1 between the rows. Continue to make rows of single crochet stitches, increasing 1 stitch at the beginning and end of the next row and every fourth row thereafter, until you have 106 stitches. Fasten off. Sew the collar to the neck band, using an overcast stitch.

Adding the cuffs: Working in the same manner as you did on the bands, make 15 rows of single crochet stitches on the cuff edge of each sleeve. Begin and end the first row at the triple crochet stitches you made for the placket openings at the points indicated by the arrows on the sleeve diagram (*page 172*). Make a buttonhole on the fourth and 11th rows, placing both approximately 1/2 inch in from the side edge of the cuff.

Finishing the overblouse: Work 1 row of single crochet stitches around all outer edges, making 3 single crochet stitches in each corner stitch as you turn. Block (*Glossary*) the overblouse. Then sew nine buttons on the left-front band and two on each cuff to match the buttonholes.

Making the belt: Make a chain of 228 stitches. Beginning with the second chain stitch from the hook, make 10 rows of 227 single crochet stitches each. Chain 1 between each row. Fasten off at the end of the last row.

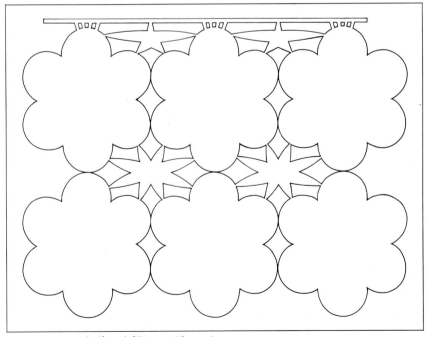

Position of full half and fill-in motifs and edging

Enmeshed in filaments of needlework

Lavish triangles of crochet and knit lace add an elegant—and intriguing—fillip to cover-ups. In the shawl at far left, formed from crocheted floral-square motifs *(page 158),* additional clusters of petals appear where the corners of the squares meet. Two rows of ruffle edging border the shawl. At left, a patchwork of gauzy spider-web motifs with a double layer of fishnet edging *(pages 160-161)* creates the even more fragile knit shawl. Directions for making the wraps begin overleaf.

Crocheting and knitting the shawls

Both the crocheted lace shawl and the knitted one pictured on pages 174-175 are assembled in the same manner. As the two diagrams shown below and opposite indicate, each shawl consists of square motifs sewed together diagonally to form a triangle. Since the upper edge of the triangle would be jagged if only square motifs were used, half motifs are added to straighten it. Two rows of ruffles along the short sides of the triangle complete each shawl.

The following instructions give the details for making each shawl.

THE CROCHETED LACE SHAWL

You will need 12 ounces of a thin, nubby wool-and-rayon yarn and a Size I aluminum crochet hook.

Making the full motifs: Crochet 36 floral-square motifs, following the instructions on page 163. Each motif should be 4 inches square.

Making the half motifs: To give a straight top edge to the shawl, make nine half motifs; use the same hook as you did for the full motifs and work in the same gauge. Work each half motif in the following manner: Chain 6, and make a slip stitch into the first chain stitch to form a ring.
Row 1: Chain 4, and make a cluster in the center of the ring as you did for the full motif *(drawing 5, page 163).* Then repeat this sequence—chain 5, and make another cluster in the ring—3 times. Chain 5, and turn.
Row 2: Repeat this sequence—make 1 single crochet stitch in the next chain-5 space, chain 3, make 1 single crochet stitch in the same space, and chain 5—3 times. Then make 1 single crochet stitch in the top of the last cluster. Chain 9, and turn.
Row 3: Repeat this sequence—make 1 single crochet stitch in the next chain-5 space, chain 3, make 1 single crochet stitch in the same space, and chain 9—3 times. Then make 1 single crochet stitch in the next space, chain 3,

and make 1 single crochet stitch in the same space. Chain 5, and turn.
Row 4: Make a cluster at the beginning of this row by chaining 4 more stitches and making the cluster in the fifth chain stitch from the hook. Then chain 5, and make another cluster in the same stitch. Now chain 6, make 1 single crochet stitch in the fifth chain stitch of the next chain 9. Chain 5, and make 1 more single crochet stitch in the same chain stitch. Chain 6, and make three clusters—with 5 chain stitches between each of them—in the fifth chain stitch of the next chain 9. Chain 6, make 1 single crochet stitch in the fifth chain stitch of the next chain 9; chain 5, and make 1 single crochet stitch in the same stitch. Finish the row by chaining 6, and making two clusters with 5 chain stitches between them—in the fifth chain stitch of the last chain 9. Fasten off.

Assembling the shawl: Arrange the 36 full motifs diagonally, as shown in the diagram at the bottom of this page. With an overcast stitch *(Appendix),* sew the motifs together, joining them only at points where the clusters and the chain-5 loops meet. Then sew the half motifs in place along the top edge of the shawl.

Making the double ruffle: To make the top tier, start with a foundation chain of 289 stitches. Chain 1 more, and turn. Then follow the instructions for the crocheted ruffle edging *(page 165).* For the bottom tier, make a foundation chain of 294 stitches. Then work in the following manner:
Row 1: Make 1 single crochet stitch in the sixth chain from the hook. Then repeat this sequence across the row —chain 5, skip 1 chain stitch, and work 1 single crochet stitch into the next chain stitch. To end the row, chain 3, and make 1 double crochet stitch in the last chain stitch. Chain 7, and turn.
Row 2: Repeat row 5 of the top tier.
Row 3: Repeat row 6 of the top tier. Repeat this last row 10 more times. Fasten off.

Finishing the shawl: Using an overcast stitch, join the two ruffle tiers together by sewing the first row of the bottom tier to the first row of the top tier. Then sew the edge of the

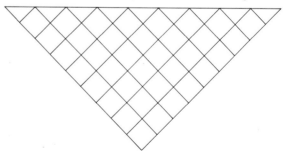

Arrangement of crocheted motifs and half motifs for shawl

top tier to the two short sides of the shawl, fitting the ruffle to the shawl as evenly as possible.

Finish the long top edge of the shawl by making a row of single crochet stitches along it. Block *(Glossary)* the finished shawl.

THE KNITTED LACE SHAWL

You will need 10 ounces of a thin, nubby wool-and-rayon yarn, Sizes 11 and 13 knitting needles, and a Size F aluminum crochet hook.

Making the motifs: Knit 21 spider-web motifs, following the instructions on pages 165-166. Each motif should be 5 inches square.

Making the half motifs: To give a straight top edge to the shawl, make seven half motifs, using the same size needles as you did for the full motifs and working in the same gauge. Make each half motif in the following manner: Cast on 17 stitches, and work rows 1 and 2 of the full motif.

Row 3: Slip the first 3 stitches onto the right needle, knit 2 stitches together, pass the 3 slipped stitches over the knit stitch; then knit 1, purl 1, and knit 1 all in the same stitch. Now repeat the following sequence— slip the next 2 stitches onto the right needle, knit 2 stitches together, and pass the 2 slipped stitches over the knit stitch; then knit 1, purl 1, knit 1, and purl 1 all in the next stitch—2 times. Knit the last stitch.

Row 4: Purl each stitch across the row. You will now have 15 stitches on the needles.

Row 5: Knit 3 stitches together. Then follow this sequence —yarn over, and knit the next stitch—until there are 2 stitches left. Yarn over; then knit the last 2 stitches.

Row 6: Purl 2 stitches. Then follow this sequence—drop the yarn-over loop that was formed in the last row from the left needle, and then purl the next stitch—across the row.

Row 7: Knit 2 stitches together. Then knit 1, purl 1, and knit 1 all in the next stitch. Slip the next 2 stitches onto the right needle, knit 2 stitches together, and pass the 2 slipped stitches over the knit stitch; knit 1, purl 1, knit 1 and purl 1 all in the next stitch. Slip the next 2 stitches onto the right needle, knit 2 stitches together, pass the 2 slipped stitches over the knit stitch; end by knitting the last stitch.

Row 8: Purl each stitch across the row.

Row 9: Repeat row 5.

Row 10: Repeat row 6.

Row 11: Knit 3 stitches together, slip the next 2 stitches onto the right needle, knit 2 stitches together, and pass the 2 slipped stitches over the knit stitch; then knit 1, purl 1, knit 1, and purl 1 all in the next stitch. Knit the last stitch.

Row 12: Purl each stitch across the row.

Row 13: Knit 3 stitches together. Then repeat the following sequence—yarn over, and knit 1 stitch—3 times. Knit the last stitch.

Row 14: Purl 2 stitches. Then repeat this sequence—drop the yarn-over loop formed in the last row, and purl the next stitch—3 times.

Row 15: Knit 1 stitch, slip 1 stitch, knit 2 stitches together, pass the slipped stitch over the knit stitch, and knit the last stitch. Bind off the last 3 stitches with a purl row.

Trimming the motifs: Along all four sides of the full motifs make 16 evenly spaced single crochet stitches. As you turn, make 3 single crochet stitches in each corner stitch. Do the same along each of the two short sides of the half motifs.

Assembling the shawl: Arrange the 21 full motifs diagonally, as shown in the diagram at the bottom of this page. Using an overcast stitch, sew the motifs together. Then sew the half motifs in place along the top edge of the shawl.

Making the double ruffle: This two-tiered ruffle consists of four pieces of fishnet edging—two pieces along each short edge of the shawl. Make each piece with Size 11 needles, following the instructions on pages 167-168. For each of the two top tier pieces, cast on 232 stitches, and work the fishnet pattern until the piece measures 3 inches in depth. Then bind off. For each of the two lower tiers, cast on 232 stitches, and work in the fishnet pattern until the piece measures 6 inches in depth. Then bind off. To join each set of two tiers, put a 3-inch piece of edging on top of a 6-inch piece, and align the side and top edges. Then make a row of single crochet stitches through both top rows of stitches, decreasing *(Appendix)* as you go to gather the edging into a ruffle.

Finishing the shawl: Using an overcast stitch, sew each double ruffle to one side edge of the shawl, joining the top single crochet stitches on the ruffle to the single crochet stitches on the edges of the motifs. Then, at the lower point of the shawl where the ruffles meet, make 2 rows of single crochet stitches along each end of each tier. With an overcast stitch, sew the ruffles together, joining each tier separately. Finish the long top edge of the shawl by making 2 rows of single crochet stitches along it. Block *(Glossary)* the finished shawl.

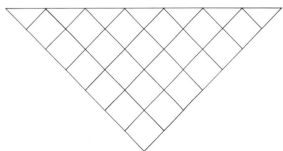

Arrangement of knitted motifs and half motifs for the shawl

Peekaboo bands of knit

With knit lace insertions ribboning its seams, any slip of a dress may become a pretty party gown. In the swirl-pattern style pictured here, bands of diamond insertion—described on page 168—encircle the garment in festive spirals. To create such an effect, lace is lined with organza strips and appliquéd over each of the seams, then the fabric along the seams is trimmed away to make the lace transparent. The straps have similar organza backing, but the lace trim on the hem is unlined. Instructions for inserting lace in garments begin overleaf.

Directions for attaching the knit lace strips

As illustrated by the lace-trimmed dress on pages 178-179, you can insert knitted lace in the seams of a dress or other garment. You can also add it along a hem—or make shoulder straps with it.

Two examples of suitable knitted lace are the diamond and ripplet insertions given on pages 168-169. For each of these insertions, you will need about an ounce of a thin, nubby wool-and-rayon yarn for every 3 feet of lace you wish to make.

If you plan to insert lace in a seam, use a lightweight fabric for the garment. A heavier fabric may cause the lace to lose its shape. Also, use a sheer fabric—instead of the garment fabric—for the facings, so that they will not show through the open lace along the seams.

INSERTING KNITTED LACE ON A SEAM

Preparing the garment pieces: Follow your pattern instructions to close the seam you plan to insert the lace in.

Making the lace insertion: To determine how long you should make the insertion, measure the seam on the garment. Then add 1/2 inch for finishing the ends of the insertion. To determine how many stitches you should cast on, multiply the length you determined above (in inches) by the number of stitches to the inch of your gauge. Add stitches if necessary to obtain a multiple specified in your knitting instructions. Knit the insertion, following the instructions for the diamond or ripplet insertion (pages 168-169) or any other similar knitted lace insertion.

Lining the insertion: To prevent the knitted lace from stretching with the weight of the fabric, make a lining for the insertion. To do this, cut a strip of organza (or other sheer material with strong threads) the same length as the lace insertion but 1/2 inch wider. Make sure to cut the strip so that its length is on the lengthwise grain of the fabric—that is, parallel to the selvages. With the lining strip wrong side up, turn up 1/4 inch along each long side, and press. Turn the lining over so that the wrong side is down, and lay the lace insertion, also wrong side down, on the lining. Baste the two pieces together along the edges.

Attaching the insertions: To attach each insertion, center the lined lace over the finished seam on the outside of the dress, and baste it to the dress just inside the edges of the lace. Machine stitch as close to the edges as possible, and remove the basting. Now turn the dress wrong side out, and cut away the dress fabric underneath the lace, leaving 1/4 inch on each side for a seam allowance. Be careful not to cut the lining. Press the dress and lining seam allowances away from the lace so that they will not show on the finished garment. Finish the edges of the garment pieces, following your pattern instructions.

TRIMMING A HEM WITH KNITTED LACE

Assembling the garment: Follow your pattern instructions to finish the garment except for the hem. Then trim the hem edge to within 1/4 inch of the hemline.

Making the knitted lace: To determine how long you should make the insertion, measure the hem edge of the garment. Then add 1/2 inch for joining the ends of the lace. To determine how many stitches you should cast on, multiply the length you determined above (in inches) by the number of stitches to the inch of your gauge. Add stitches if necessary to obtain a multiple specified in your knitting instructions. Knit the lace, following the instructions for the diamond or ripplet insertion (pages 168-169). Similar lace insertions are also suitable for trimming a hem.

Attaching the lace: Overlap the ends of the lace 1/4 inch, and sew them together with an overcast stitch (Appendix). Then sew the lace to the garment hem, following the instructions for attaching lace with a straight upper edge to a hem (page 70, Steps 2-7).

USING KNITTED LACE FOR STRAPS

Assembling the garment: Follow your pattern instructions to finish the garment except for the straps.

Making the knitted lace: To determine the length of each strap, try on the garment, and measure from the top of the dress in front, over the shoulder, to the top of the dress in back. Then add 1 inch for attaching the strap. To determine the length you should make the knitted lace for each strap, multiply the length you determined above (in inches) by the number of stitches to the inch in your gauge. Add stitches if necessary to obtain a multiple specified in your knitting instructions. Knit the lace, following the directions for the diamond or ripplet insertion (pages 168-169) or any straight-edged knitted lace similar to them.

Lining the strap: Follow the instructions for lining an insertion in a seam (left), but when you baste the lining to the lace, put the wrong sides together so that the turned-up edges of the lining are next to the lace. Then machine stitch the lace to the lining as close to the side edges as possible, and remove the basting.

Attaching the straps: Follow the instructions in Box C on page 117, but do not trim the straps.

GLOSSARY

APPLIQUÉ: The decoration of one piece of fabric with pieces from other fabrics. In conventional appliqué, the pieces from the other fabrics are first cut to shape and then are sewed into place. In cutaway appliqué, two pieces of fabric are sewed together, one on top of the other, with stitches that form a design. One piece of the fabric is then trimmed away outside the stitches, while the other piece of fabric is trimmed away inside the stitches.

BACKSTITCH: To reinforce the beginning or end of a seam by making several machine stitches backward over the seam line.

BALLPOINT NEEDLE: A needle with a smooth, rounded point that enables it to slip gently between the threads of delicate fabrics such as knits and sheers and stretch material.

BASTE: To stitch together pieces of fabrics temporarily, or to indicate pattern markings with thread so that it shows on both sides of a piece of fabric.

BEADING NEEDLE: An extra-slender needle that is used to attach very tiny sequins or beads to fabric or other material.

BIAS: A line in woven fabric that runs diagonal to the threads in the fabric. A 45° bias is called a true bias.

BLOCK: To press newly made knit or crochet items with a warm iron through a damp cloth in order to set their final shape.

CLIP: A small, straight cut that is made into a seam allowance—often up to the line of stitching—in order to help the seam lie flat around curves and at corners.

CROCHETING: The process of making fabric by using a hook to knot strands of yarn into a series of connected loops.

DART: A stitched fabric fold, tapering to a point at one or both ends, that is used to shape fabric around curves.

DRAPE: An unpressed pleat stitched shut at one or both ends, but left open between the ends. Drapes may be made as decorations or as decorative substitutes for darts or other details used for fit.

DRAWN WORK: Decorative open thread work that is made in a piece of fabric by a process in which adjacent parallel threads are drawn out and the remaining crosswise threads are then gathered and secured in small, even bunches.

DRESSMAKER'S CARBON: A heavyweight carbon paper—either white or colored—that is used with a tracing wheel to transfer markings from a pattern to fabric.

EMBROIDERY: The decoration of fabric with a needle and thread, often in several colors and a variety of stitches.

FACING: A piece of fabric that is sewed along the raw edge of an opening, such as a neckline, and then turned to the inside to give the edge a smooth finish. Facings are usually cut from the same cloth as the garment itself.

FAGOTING: Decorative open thread work suspended between two hemmed edges.

FASTENING STITCH: A stitch used to anchor a thread by making three or four stitches, one over the other, in the same place.

GRADING: The act of trimming each seam allowance within a multilayered seam (e.g., one that contains fabric, facing, etc.) to a different width to reduce bulk and make the seam lie flat.

GRAIN: In woven fabric, grain denotes the direction of threads: the warp (the threads running from one cut end to the other) forms the lengthwise grains; the woof, or weft (the threads running across the lengthwise grain from one finished edge to the other), forms the crosswise grain.

GRAIN-LINE ARROW: A double-ended arrow that is printed on a pattern piece to indicate how the piece should be aligned with the grain of the fabric.

HEMSTITCHING: Drawn work that is fashioned along the stitched edge of a hem. See also DRAWN WORK.

KNITTING: The process of making fabric by using two or more pointed needles to knot strands of yarn into a series of connected loops.

LINING: An opaque fabric covering the inside of part or all of a garment.

NAP: On the surface of a fabric, the short fibers that are pulled and brushed in a single direction.

NAP LAYOUT: A specific way of laying out a pattern on fabrics that—because of their surface, nap or printed design—will change in appearance with the direction in which the pattern is placed. When such fabrics are used, all pattern pieces must be laid out and cut in one direction—with the nap, as indicated on the envelopes of commercial patterns.

NOTCH: A V- or diamond-shaped marking made on the edge of a garment piece as an alignment guide; intended to be matched with a similar notch or group of notches on another piece. Also a triangular cut made into the seam allowance of a curved seam to help it lie flat.

PIVOT: A technique for machine stitching around angular corners that involves stopping the machine—with the needle down—at the apex of a corner, raising the presser foot, pivoting the fabric and then lowering the presser foot before continuing to stitch.

PLEATS: Folds that are made in fabric in order to control fullness.

PRESSER FOOT: The part of a sewing machine that holds down fabric while it is being advanced under the needle. An all-purpose, or general purpose, foot has two prongs of equal length and is used for most stitching. A roller presser foot has two rollers with grids to prevent bulky or sheer fabric from sticking or slipping while being stitched. A straight-stitch foot has one long and one short prong and can be used for straight stitching and for stitching fabrics of varying thicknesses. A two-pronged even-feed foot, for use on machines that do zigzag stitching, has teeth on the bottom to move two layers of fuzzy, slippery or heavy fabric at the same speed. A zipper foot has only one prong and is used to stitch zippers and cording.

SELF-BOUND SEAM: A narrow, enclosed seam made by trimming one seam allowance of a seam, then folding over the untrimmed seam allowance, and slip-stitching the folded edge to the stitches of the seam.

TENSION: The degree of tightness of the two threads in machine stitches.

THROAT PLATE: A flat metal piece, set into the base of the machine, with a hole through which a sewing-machine needle passes as it stitches. Most throat plates have guidelines marked on both the left and the right sides to help keep seams straight.

TRACING WHEEL: A small revolving disk that is attached to a handle and used with dressmaker's carbon paper to transfer pattern markings to fabric or to duplicate pattern pieces. Most tracing wheels have serrated edges; however, a plain-edged wheel is often preferable for delicate fabrics.

TUCKS: Stitched-down pleats, arranged either vertically or horizontally, to serve decorative or structural purposes. Tucks may be visible, with the folds sewed to the outside of the garment or hidden, with the folds sewed to the inside of the garment.

UNDERLINING: A tightly woven fabric that is cut in the contours of the main pieces of a garment and then attached to these pieces to stabilize the shape of the garment and conceal construction details.

ZIGZAG STITCH: A serrated line of machine stitching.

BASIC STITCHES

The diagrams below and opposite show how to make the elementary hand stitches referred to in this volume. Knitting and crocheting stitches are on the following pages.

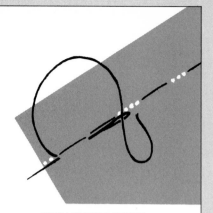

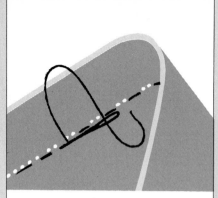

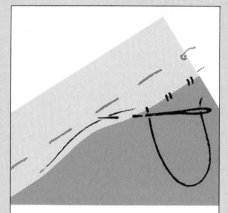

THE FASTENING STITCH

To end a row with a fastening stitch, insert the needle back 1/4 inch and bring it out at the point at which the thread last emerged. Make another stitch through these same points for extra firmness. To begin a row with a fastening stitch, leave a 4-inch loose end and make the initial stitch the same way as an ending stitch.

THE RUNNING STITCH

Insert the needle, with knotted thread, from the wrong side of the fabric and weave the needle in and out of the fabric several times, making 1/8-inch, evenly spaced stitches. Pull the thread through. Continue across, making several stitches at a time, and end with with a fastening stitch. When basting, make longer stitches, evenly spaced.

THE SLIP STITCH

Fold under the hem edge and anchor the first stitch with a knot inside the fold. Point the needle to the left. Pick up one or two threads of the garment fabric close to the hem edge, directly below the first stitch, and slide the needle horizontally through the folded edge of the hem 1/8 inch to the left of the previous stitch. Continue across in the same manner and end with a fastening stitch.

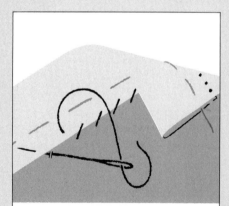

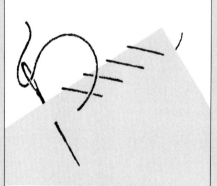

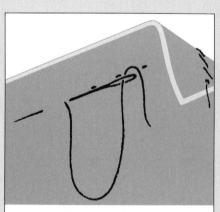

THE HEMMING STITCH

Anchor the first stitch with a knot inside the hem; then, pointing the needle up and to the left, pick up one or two threads of the garment fabric close to the hem. Push the needle up through the hem 1/8 inch above the edge; pull the thread through. Continue picking up one or two threads and making 1/8-inch stitches in the hem at intervals of 1/4 inch. End with a fastening stitch.

THE OVERCAST STITCH

Draw the needle, with knotted thread, through from the wrong side of the fabric 1/8 to 1/4 inch down from the top edge. With the thread to the right, insert the needle under the fabric from the wrong side 1/8 to 1/4 inch to the left of the first stitch. Continue to make evenly spaced stitches over the fabric edge and end with a fastening stitch.

THE PRICK STITCH

Using a knotted thread, draw the needle up from the bottom layer of fabric and pull it through. Insert the needle to the right three or four threads, and bring it out 1/4 to 3/8 inch to the left of where it last emerged. Continue the process, ending with a fastening stitch on the bottom layer of fabric.

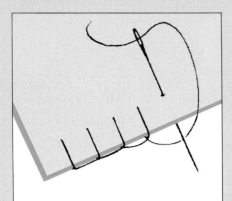

THE BLANKET STITCH

Using a knotted thread, bring the needle up from under the fabric 1/4 inch from the left edge. Pull it through. To make the first stitch, hold the thread down with your left thumb, and insert the needle just to the right of the point from which the thread emerged. Make sure the needle is at a right angle to the edge and goes over the thread before you draw the thread taut. Repeat, inserting the needle 1/4 inch to the right of each preceding stitch. End with a fastening stitch.

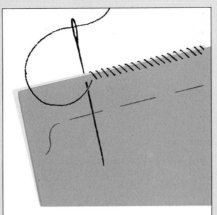

THE WHIPSTITCH

Using a knotted thread, draw the needle up from the bottom layer of fabric about 1/16 inch from the edge. Reinsert the needle, again from the bottom layer of fabric, about 1/16 inch to the left of the point from which the thread emerged, making sure the needle is at a right angle to the edge. Continue to make tiny, slanted, even stitches over the fabric edge. End with a fastening stitch.

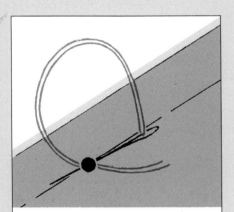

THE SINGLE TAILOR TACK

Using a double strand of unknotted thread, take a short stitch through the point to be marked, picking up the pattern piece and one or two layers of fabric, depending on whether or not the fabric is doubled. Leave 2-inch-long loose ends. Take another stitch through the same point, leaving a 2-inch loop on top of the pattern. End with at least 2 inches of loose thread.

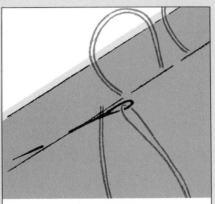

A ROW OF TAILOR TACKS

Using a double strand of unknotted thread, take a 1/2-inch-long stitch from right to left at the right-hand end of the pattern line to be marked. Leave 2-inch-long loose ends. Then make a line of 1-inch-long stitches, at least 1/2 inch apart, leaving a 2-inch loop on each stitch. Pick up the pattern piece and 1 or 2 layers or fabric, depending on whether or not the fabric is doubled. End with at least 2 inches of loose thread.

KNITTING

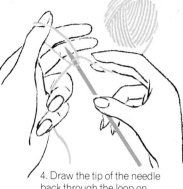

CASTING ON STITCHES
1. Form a slipknot in the yarn, leaving a free end long enough for the number of stitches to be cast on (allow about 1 inch per stitch).

2. Slide a needle through the slipknot and hold the needle in your right hand. Loop the yarn attached to the ball over your right index finger and loop the free end of the yarn around your left thumb.

3. Insert the tip of the needle through the loop on your left thumb and bring the yarn attached to the ball under and over the needle from left to right.

4. Draw the tip of the needle back through the loop on your thumb, then slip the loop off your thumb. Pull the short end of the yarn down to tighten the loop, which is now a stitch. Repeat Steps 2-4 for the required number of stitches.

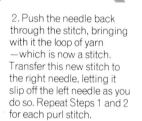

THE KNIT STITCH
1. Insert the right needle in the front of the stitch closest to the tip of the left needle, as shown. Bring the yarn under and over the right needle.

2. Pull the right needle back through the stitch, bringing with it the loop of yarn. Slide this loop—which is now a stitch—off the left needle and onto the right. Repeat Steps 1 and 2 for each knit stitch.

THE PURL STITCH
1. Insert the right needle into the stitch closest to the tip of the left needle, as shown. Bring the yarn around and under the right needle.

2. Push the needle back through the stitch, bringing with it the loop of yarn —which is now a stitch. Transfer this new stitch to the right needle, letting it slip off the left needle as you do so. Repeat Steps 1 and 2 for each purl stitch.

INCREASING STITCHES
1. On a knit row, insert the right needle through the back of a stitch. Knit the stitch, but do not drop it off the left needle.

2. Knit the same stitch in the ordinary way, and transfer the two stitches to the right needle.

DECREASING STITCHES
1. Insert the right needle into two stitches instead of one, either from front to back as shown, for a knit stitch, or from back to front as for a purl stitch. Proceed as though you were knitting or purling one stitch at a time.

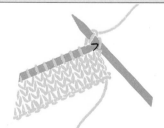

1. On a purl row, insert the right needle from right to left through the horizontal loop at the bottom of a stitch. Make a purl stitch but do not let it slide off the left needle.

2. Now insert the right needle into the vertical loop above the horizontal one. Purl the stitch in the ordinary way, and slide both loops onto the right needle.

BINDING OFF STITCHES
1. Knit (or purl) two stitches. Then insert the left needle through the front of the second stitch from the tip of the right needle.

2. With the left needle, lift the second stitch on the right needle over the first stitch and let it drop.

THE CHAIN STITCH

1. Form a loose slipknot around the crochet hook, about 1 inch from the end of the yarn. Grasp the yarn attached to the ball with the tip of the hook and pull the yarn through the slipknot with the tip of the hook, as shown.

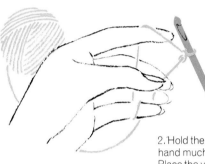

2. Hold the hook in your right hand much like a pencil. Place the yarn from the ball around the left little finger, then up and over the left index finger. Grasp the free end of the yarn between the thumb and middle finger of the left hand.

3. With your left index finger, bring the yarn from the back to the front of the hook and catch it under the tip of the hook.

4. Pull the tip of the hook through the loop in the hook, bringing the yarn with it to create the first chain stitch in the foundation chain. Repeat Steps 3 and 4 to form a chain of the desired length.

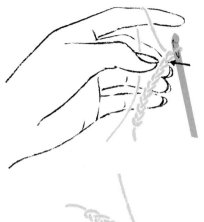

THE SINGLE CROCHET STITCH

1. To single crochet the first row after a foundation chain, insert the hook through the second chain stitch from the hook (arrow)—do not count the loop on the hook.

2. With two loops now on the hook, bring the yarn over the hook from back to front and catch it under the tip as shown. Then draw the yarn caught under the tip through the loop closest to the tip.

3. Bring the yarn over the hook again and draw it through both of the loops that were on the hook; there is now only a single loop on the hook. Insert the crochet hook into the next chain stitch and repeat Steps 1 and 2. At the end of each row, chain one stitch if the next row is to be worked in single crochet, two stitches for a double crochet pattern, and three stitches for a triple crochet pattern.

4. Turn the work to crochet back across the previous row. Insert the hook through both loops of the second stitch from the edge, as shown, and all subsequent stitches on this and all rows after the foundation chain.

THE DOUBLE CROCHET STITCH

1. To double crochet the first row of stitches after a foundation chain, chain 2 and count back to the third chain stitch from the hook *(arrow)*—do not count the loop on the hook. Swing the yarn over the hook from back to front, then insert the hook through this third chain stitch.

2. Bring the yarn over the hook again and draw it through the loop closest to the tip. Bring the yarn over the hook again and draw it through the two loops closest to the tip.

3. Bring the yarn over the tip again and draw it through the remaining two loops on the hook. At the end of each row, chain one stitch if the next row is to be worked in single crochet, two stitches for double crochet and three stitches for triple crochet.

4. Turn the work to crochet back across the previous row. Bring the yarn over the hook and insert the hook through both loops of the first stitch from the edge *(arrow)* on this and all rows after the first.

THE HALF DOUBLE CROCHET STITCH

1. To half double crochet the first row of stitches after a foundation chain, start by chaining 2. Then bring the yarn over the hook from back to front, and insert the hook through the second chain stitch from the hook *(arrow)*.

2. With 3 loops now on the hook, bring the yarn over the hook again.

3. Catch the yarn under the tip of the hook, and draw it through the loop closest to the tip.

4. Bring the yarn over the hook again, and draw it through all 3 loops remaining on the hook.

5. Repeat the stitch in each succeeding chain across the row. At the end of the row, chain 2, and turn.

6. To crochet the second row, bring the yarn over the hook, insert the hook into the first stitch and make a half double crochet stitch, following Steps 2-4. Then continue to make half double crochet stitches in each succeeding stitch across the row. At the end of the row, chain 2, and turn. Continue repeating row 2.

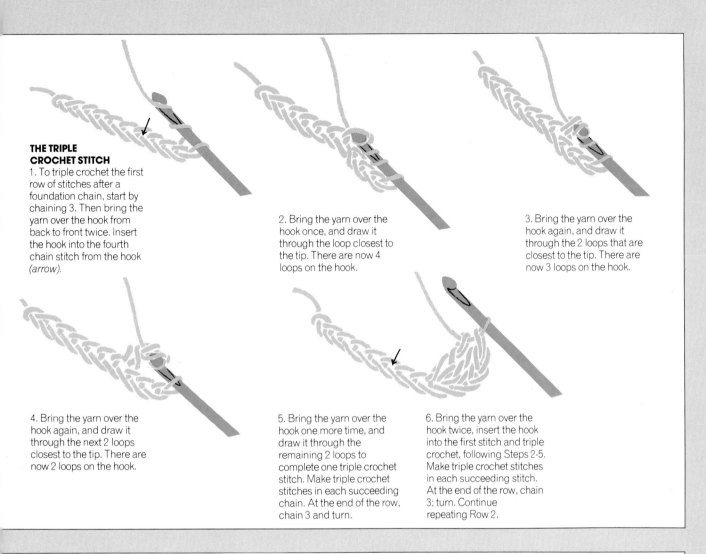

THE TRIPLE CROCHET STITCH

1. To triple crochet the first row of stitches after a foundation chain, start by chaining 3. Then bring the yarn over the hook from back to front twice. Insert the hook into the fourth chain stitch from the hook (arrow).

2. Bring the yarn over the hook once, and draw it through the loop closest to the tip. There are now 4 loops on the hook.

3. Bring the yarn over the hook again, and draw it through the 2 loops that are closest to the tip. There are now 3 loops on the hook.

4. Bring the yarn over the hook again, and draw it through the next 2 loops closest to the tip. There are now 2 loops on the hook.

5. Bring the yarn over the hook one more time, and draw it through the remaining 2 loops to complete one triple crochet stitch. Make triple crochet stitches in each succeeding chain. At the end of the row, chain 3 and turn.

6. Bring the yarn over the hook twice, insert the hook into the first stitch and triple crochet, following Steps 2-5. Make triple crochet stitches in each succeeding stitch. At the end of the row, chain 3; turn. Continue repeating Row 2.

DECREASING STITCHES, SINGLE CROCHET

1. To decrease in a row of single crochet stitches, insert the hook into both loops of a stitch. Bring the yarn over the hook and draw it through the two loops closest to the tip; this leaves two loops on the hook.

2. Insert the hook through both loops of the next stitch. Bring the yarn over the hook and draw it through the two loops closest to the tip. Bring the yarn over the hook again and draw it through the three remaining loops on the hook.

DECREASING STITCHES, DOUBLE CROCHET

1. To decrease in a row of double crochet stitches, bring the yarn over the hook and insert it through both loops of a stitch. Bring the yarn over the hook again, as shown, and draw it through the two loops closest to the tip. Then bring the yarn over the hook again and insert it through both loops of the next stitch.

2. Again bring the yarn over the hook and draw it through the two loops closest to the tip, as shown; there are now five loops on the hook. Bring the yarn over the hook again and draw it through the two loops now closest to the tip. Repeat the process until there are three loops remaining on the hook. Then pull the yarn through the three remaining loops.

THE SLIP STITCH FOR JOINING CROCHETED PIECES

1. Align the edges of the pieces to be joined. Insert the hook from front to back through both loops of the first stitch at the end of each piece. Then place a strand of yarn over the hook, and draw it through all 4 loops, leaving a loop on the hook.

2. Insert the hook through both loops of the next pair of stitches. Bring the yarn over the hook, and draw it —in one motion—through these stitches as well as through the loop on the hook. Repeat until the pieces are joined.

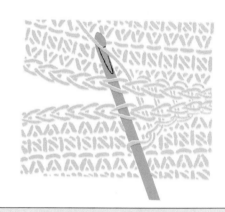

FASTENING OFF

Cut the yarn from the ball, leaving a 2-inch-long end. Pull this end through the loop on the hook to secure it and weave it through one or two nearby stitches.

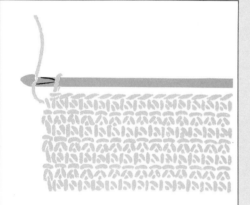

JOINING YARN

1. Join a new ball of yarn at the beginning of a row by drawing it through the first loop; leave a 1-inch-long end. Join a new color at the end of a row, working the last two loops on the hook with the new yarn.

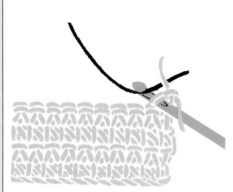

2. When you have crocheted two or three rows, weave the loose ends of the yarn through nearby stitches with the crochet hook.

INCREASING STITCHES

To increase stitches, work one stitch—either a single, double or triple crochet, as called for in the instructions —then insert the crochet hook back into the same loop or loops (arrow) and repeat the stitch.

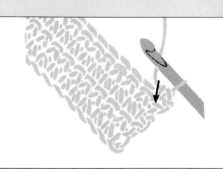

CREDITS

Sources for illustrations in this book are shown below. Credits from left to right are separated by semicolons, from top to bottom by dashes.

Cover fabric by Ernst Reiko. 6,7—Ann Spanos Kuhn. Dress by Stavropoulos. 11—Bud Lee. Dress from the collection of Union Française des Arts du Costume, Paris; dress from the collection of The Metropolitan Museum of Art, New York City; dress from the collection of Museum of the City of New York. 12 through 17—Photographs by Ann Spanos Kuhn. Set painted by Armand A. Catenaro. Hair styles by Bob Moore. 12,13—Dress by Fernando Sanchez for Ensuite Couture; pajamas by Halston; gown and robe by John Kloss for Cira. 14,15 —Dress by Albert Nipon; blouse by Giorgio di Sant'Angelo; blouse by Lux Sport. 16,17 —Dress and coat by Stavropoulos; overblouse by Oscar de la Renta; dress by Victoria Royal. 18 through 27—Photographs by Tasso Vendikos. 18 through 24 —Dresses by Stavropoulos. 25—Dress by Mary McFadden. 26,27—Dress by John Kloss for Cira; dress by Holly Harp. 28,29 —Drawings by Jane Poliotti except top right Raymond Skibinski. 30—Drawings by Jane Poliotti—drawings by Ted Kliros. 31 —Drawings by Ted Kliros. 32, 33—Tasso Vendikos. Dress by Stavropoulos; dress by Kasper for Joan Leslie. 34, 35—Drawings by Angela Alleyne. 36,37—Tasso Vendikos. Dresses by Stavropoulos. 38,39—Drawings by Raymond Skibinski. 42,43—Peter Levy.

46 through 49—Stephen Green-Armytage. 50—Ann Spanos Kuhn. Jacket by Halston, dress fabric by Ernst Reiko. 51,52,53 —Drawings by Raymond Skibinski. 54 —Ann Spanos Kuhn. Coat by Giorgio di Sant'Angelo. 55 through 59—Drawings by John Sagan. 60—Ann Spanos Kuhn. Dress by Stavropoulos. 61 through 65—Drawings by Carolyn Mazzello. 66—Ann Spanos Kuhn. Dress by Halston, fabric by Ernst Reiko. 67 through 71—Drawings by Raymond Skibinski. 72—Ann Spanos Kuhn. Dress by Jerry Silverman. 73 through 77 —Drawings by John Sagan. 78—Ann Spanos Kuhn. Dress by Concept VII. 79 through 87—Drawings by Raymond Skibinski. 88 —Ann Spanos Kuhn. Dress by Stavropoulos. 89 through 93—Drawings by John Sagan. 94—Ann Spanos Kuhn. 95 through 101—Drawings by John Sagan. 102,103 —Photograph by masca, color by Cardinal Studio. Outfit by Fernando Sanchez for Ensuite Couture. 106,107—U.S. Signal Corps (Brady Collection) National Archives; Radio Times Hulton Picture Library; Bettmann Archive (2)—undergarment insets, Bettmann Archive except for far right, drawing by John Sagan. 109—Culver; Nina Leen, from TIME-LIFE Picture Agency; Milton Greene (2); Howell Conant. 110 through 115 —Drawings by Raymond Skibinski. 116

—Photograph by masca, color by Cardinal Studio. 117 through 121—Drawings by Raymond Skibinski. 122—Photograph by masca, color by Cardinal Studio. Costume by Fernando Sanchez for Ensuite Couture. 123 through 127—Drawings by Raymond Skibinski. 128—Photograph by masca, color by Cardinal Studio. 129—Drawings by Carolyn Mazzello. 130 through 139—Drawings by John Sagan. 140,141—masca. Pillow sham by Lucy Ciancia. 142,143—Drawings by Nick Pliakis. 144,145—masca. Stole by Lucy Ciancia. 146,147—Drawings by Nick Pliakis. 148,149—masca. 151—Drawings by Penny Burnham. 152,153—Richard Jeffrey. Knit lace by Annette Feldman. 156 —Al Freni. Lace by Mrs. Dorothy Pardon. 157—Al Freni. Lace by Mrs. Gunvor Jorgensen. 158 through 161—Richard Jeffrey. Crochet and knit lace by Annette Feldman. 162 through 169—Drawings by Carolyn Mazzello. 170,171—Tasso Vendikos. Crochet overblouse by Annette Feldman. Dress by Korrigan-Lesur. 172,173—Drawings by John Sagan. 174,175—Tasso Vendikos. Crochet and knit shawls by Annette Feldman. Dress by Korrigan-Lesur. 176,177 —Drawings by Jill Losson. 178,179—Tasso Vendikos. Knit lace trim by Annette Feldman. 182 through 188—Drawings by John Sagan.

ACKNOWLEDGMENTS

For their help in the preparation of this book the editors thank the following individuals: *in Dublin:* Mary O'Donnell; *in New York:* Sirin Assanuvat; Scott Barrie; Kay Blockley, Stavropoulos, Inc.; James J. Coury, Alle Corp.; Brad Darrach; Solweig Hedin; Ruth Hellmann; Gertrude Hilpert; Gunvor Jorgensen; Richard Kassoway, Beaunit Corp.; Barbara Matera; Vincent Minetti, The Metropolitan Museum of Art Costume Institute; Robert David Morton; Dorothy Pardon; Penny Post; Jean-Pierre Radley, House of Trigère; Paula Saddler; Jo Springer; Gordon Stone, The Metropolitan Museum of Art Costume Library; *in Paris:* Jean-Guy Vermont.

The editors also thank the following: Bergdorf Goodman; Burlington Industries Inc.; Butterick Fashion Marketing Company; Celanese Fibers Marketing Company; Couleur International; Fabric Library, E. I. Dupont de Nemours & Company; Henri Bendel Inc.; Hoechst Fibers Inc.; Jax Manhattan, Inc.; The Metropolitan Museum of Art Costume Institute and the Textile Study Center; Roselon Industries Inc.; Staron-Lafitte; Weller Fabrics; Whelan Lace & Fabrics Corp.